Economic
Facts
and
Fallacies

ECONOMIC FACTS AND FALLACIES

Second Edition

THOMAS SOWELL

BASIC BOOKS
A Member of the Perseus Books Group
New York

First edition published in 2007 by Basic Books

Books published by Basic Books are available at special discounts
for bulk purchases in the United States by corporations, institutions,
and other organizations. For more information, please contact the
Special Markets Department at the Perseus Books Group,
2300 Chestnut Street, Suite 200, Philadelphia, PA 19103,
or call (800) 810-4145, ext. 5000,
or e-mail special.markets@perseusbooks.com.

A CIP catalog record for this book is available
from the Library of Congress.

LCCN 2011920911
ISBN: 978-0-465-02203-8
e-book ISBN: 978-0-465-02630-2
LSC-H
Printing 17, 2023

Facts are stubborn things; and whatever may be our wishes, our inclinations, or the dictates of our passions, they cannot alter the state of facts and evidence.

John Adams

CONTENTS

PREFACE

Some things are believed because they are demonstrably true. But many other things are believed simply because they have been asserted repeatedly— and repetition has been accepted as a substitute for evidence.

This new edition of *Economic Facts and Fallacies*, like the original edition, subjects many widely held beliefs to the test of hard facts— and finds that many beliefs cannot survive that test, including some that collapse like a house of cards and others where the truth turns out to be the direct opposite of what has been so often asserted.

The purpose of all this is not simply a debunking, in order to conduct a sort of demolition derby of ideas, but to reveal fallacies that have had harmful effects on the well-being of millions of people in countries around the world. Economic policies based on fallacies can be— and have been— devastating in their impacts. Seeing through those fallacies is more than an intellectual exercise because a clearer understanding of economics can open up many unsuspected opportunities for higher standards of living for whole nations.

This book, like others of mine, owes much to my two extraordinary research assistants, Na Liu and Elizabeth Costa. They not only found much material that I asked for, they often brought to my attention valuable material that I had not asked for. In addition, Ms. Costa did the copy editing and Ms. Liu created the computer files from which this book was printed.

Thomas Sowell
Hoover Institution
Stanford University

Chapter 1

THE POWER OF FALLACIES

Never underestimate the difficulty of
changing false beliefs by facts.

Henry Rosovsky[1]

Fallacies are not simply crazy ideas. They are usually both plausible and logical— but with something missing. Their plausibility gains them political support. Only after that political support is strong enough to cause fallacious ideas to become government policies and programs are the missing or ignored factors likely to lead to "unintended consequences," a phrase often heard in the wake of economic or social policy disasters. Another phrase often heard in the wake of these disasters is, "It seemed like a good idea at the time." That is why it pays to look deeper into things that look good on the surface at the moment.

Sometimes what is missing in a fallacy is simply a definition. Undefined words have a special power in politics, particularly when they invoke some principle that engages people's emotions. "Fair" is one of those undefined words which have attracted political support for policies ranging from Fair Trade laws to the Fair Labor Standards Act. While the fact that the word is undefined is an intellectual handicap, it is a huge political advantage. People with very different views on substantive issues can be unified and mobilized behind a word that papers over their differing, and sometimes even mutually contradictory, ideas. Who, after all, is in favor of unfairness? Similarly with "social justice," "equality," and other undefined terms that can mean wholly different things to different individuals and groups— all of whom can be mobilized in support of policies that use such appealing words.

Fallacies abound in economic policies affecting everything from housing to international trade. Where the unintended consequences of these policies take years to unfold, the effects may not be traced back to their causes by many people. Even when the bad consequences follow closely after a given policy, many people still may not connect the dots, and advocates of policies that backfire often attribute these bad consequences to something else. Sometimes they claim that the bad situation would have been even worse if it had not been for the wonderful policies they advocated.

There are many reasons why fallacies have staying power, even in the face of hard evidence against them. Elected officials, for example, cannot readily admit that some policy or program that they advocated, perhaps with great fanfare, has turned out badly, without risking their whole careers. Similarly for leaders of various causes and movements. Even intellectuals or academics with tenure stand to lose prestige and suffer embarrassment when their notions turn out to be counterproductive. Others who think of themselves as supporters of things that will help the less fortunate would find it painful to confront evidence that they have in fact made the less fortunate worse off than before. In other words, evidence is too dangerous— politically, financially and psychologically— for some people to allow it to become a threat to their interests or to their own sense of themselves.

No one likes to admit being wrong. However, in many kinds of endeavors, the costs of *not* admitting to being wrong are too high to ignore. These costs force people to face reality, however reluctantly and however painful that might be. A student who misunderstands mathematics has little choice but to correct that misunderstanding before the next examination, and someone in business cannot continue losing money indefinitely by persisting in mistaken beliefs about the market or about the way to run a business. In short, there are practical as well as intellectual imperatives to see through fallacies. The difference between sound and fallacious economic policies by a government can affect the standard of living of millions. That is what makes the study of economics important— and the exposure of fallacies more than an intellectual exercise.

There are far too many fallacies to list them all. However, we can sketch five widespread kinds of general economic fallacies here, and then investigate more specific fallacies in detail in the chapters that follow. These five widespread kinds of fallacies may be called the zero-sum fallacy, the fallacy of composition, the *post hoc* fallacy, the chess-pieces fallacy, and the open-ended fallacy.

THE ZERO-SUM FALLACY

Many individual fallacies in economics are founded on the larger, and usually implicit, fallacious assumption that economic transactions are a zero-sum process, in which what is gained by someone is lost by someone else. But voluntary economic transactions— whether between employer and employee, tenant and landlord, or international trade— would not continue to take place unless both parties were better off making these transactions than not making them. Obvious as this may seem, its implications are not always obvious to those who advocate policies to help one party to these transactions.

Let us start at square one. Why do economic transactions take place at all and what determines the terms of those transactions? The potential for mutual benefit is necessary but not sufficient, unless the transactions terms are in fact mutually acceptable. Each side may of course prefer terms that are especially favorable to themselves but they will accept other terms rather than lose the benefits of making the transaction altogether. There may be many terms acceptable to one side or the other but the only way transactions can take place is if these sets of terms acceptable to each side overlap.

Suppose that a government policy is imposed, in the interest of helping one side— say, employees or tenants. Such a policy means that there are now three different parties involved in these transactions and only those particular terms which are simultaneously acceptable to all three parties are legally permitted. In other words, these new terms preclude some terms that would otherwise be mutually acceptable to the parties themselves. With *fewer* terms now available for making transactions, fewer transactions are likely to be made. Since these transactions are mutually beneficial, this usually means that *both* parties are now worse off in some respect. This general principle has many concrete examples in the real world.

Rent control, for example, has been imposed in various cities around the world, with the intention of helping tenants. Almost invariably, landlords and builders of housing find the reduced range of terms less acceptable and therefore supply less housing. In Egypt, for example, rent control was imposed in 1960. An Egyptian woman who lived through that era and wrote about it in 2006 reported:

> The end result was that people stopped investing in apartment buildings, and a huge shortage in rentals and housing forced many Egyptians to live in horrible conditions with several families sharing one small apartment. The effects of the harsh rent control is still felt today in Egypt. Mistakes like that can last for generations.[2]

In other words, while landlords and builders simply lost an opportunity to make as much money as they could have otherwise, many tenants lost an opportunity to find a decent place to live. They all lost, though in different ways. Egypt was not unique. The imposition of rent control has been followed by housing shortages in New York, Hong Kong, Stockholm, Melbourne, Hanoi and innumerable other cities around the world.*

The immediate effect of rents set below where they would be set by supply and demand is that more people seek to rent apartments for themselves, now that apartments are cheaper. But, without any more apartments being built, this means that many other people cannot find vacant apartments. Moreover, long before existing buildings wear out, auxiliary services like maintenance and repair decline, since a housing shortage means that landlords are no longer under the same competitive pressures to spend money on such things in order to attract tenants, when there are more applicants than apartments during a housing shortage. Such neglect of maintenance and repair makes buildings wear out faster. Meanwhile, the lower rate of return on investments in new apartment buildings, because of rent control, causes fewer of them to be built. Where rent control laws are especially stringent, no new apartment buildings at all may be built to replace those that are wearing out. Not a single apartment building was built in Melbourne for years after World War II because of rent

---

* The concrete ways that these housing shortages develop are discussed in Chapter 3 of my *Basic Economics*.

control laws in Australia. In a number of Massachusetts communities, no rental housing was built for a quarter of a century, until the state banned local rent control laws, after which building resumed.

Some tenants undoubtedly benefit from rent control laws— those who already have an apartment when such laws are passed and who find the lower levels of repair, maintenance and other auxiliary services, such as heat and hot water, acceptable as a trade-off, in view of the money saved on the rent. As time goes on, however, with some deteriorating buildings eventually being boarded up, the circle of tenants who find the trade-off acceptable tends to decline, and places with especially stringent rent control laws tend to have especially bitter complaints about landlords' neglect in failing to supply adequate heat, hot water, maintenance and repair. In short, reducing the set of mutually acceptable terms tends to reduce the set of mutually acceptable results, with both tenants and landlords ending up worse off on the whole, though in different ways.

Another area where governments impose their own set of acceptable transactions terms are laws regulating the pay, benefits, and working conditions of employees. Improvements in all these areas make the worker better off and cost the employer money. Here again, this tends to lead to fewer transactions. Over the years, unemployment rates have tended to be chronically higher, and the periods of unemployment chronically longer, in European Union countries, where minimum wage laws and government policies requiring employers to provide various benefits to their employees have been more generous than in the United States— and the rate at which these countries create new jobs has tended to be far lower than the rate at which new jobs have been created in the American economy. Here again, the overlap between three sets of acceptable terms tends to be less than the overlap between the two sets of terms acceptable to the parties directly involved.

As in the case of tenants under rent control, those on the inside looking out benefit at the expense of those on the outside looking in. Those workers who keep their jobs are made better off by the various benefits that employers are required to provide by law but the higher unemployment rates and longer periods of unemployment deprive others of jobs that they could have had in the absence of laws which have the net effect of discouraging hiring and encouraging the substitution of capital for labor, as well as the outsourcing of jobs to other countries. The trite expression "There is no free lunch" has become trite precisely because it has turned out to be true for so long and in so many different contexts.

Perhaps the most detrimental consequences of the implicit assumption of zero-sum transactions have been in poor countries that have kept out foreign trade and foreign investments, in order to avoid being "exploited." Large disparities between the prosperity of the countries from which trade and investment come and the poverty in Third World countries receiving this trade and investment have led some to conclude that the rich have gotten rich by taking from the poor. Various versions of this zero-sum view— from Lenin's theory of imperialism to "dependency theory" in Latin America— achieved widespread acceptance in the twentieth century and proved to be very resistant to contrary evidence.

Eventually, however, the fact that many once-poor places like Hong Kong, South Korea, and Singapore achieved prosperity through freer international trade and investment became so blatant and so widely known that, by the end of the twentieth century, the governments of many other countries began abandoning their zero-sum view of economic transactions. China and India have been striking examples of poor countries whose abandonment of severe international trade and investment restrictions led to dramatic increases in their economic growth rates, which in turn led to tens of millions of their citizens rising out of poverty. Another way of looking at this is that the zero-sum fallacy had kept millions of very poor people needlessly mired in poverty for generations before such notions were abandoned. That is an enormously high price to pay for an unsubstantiated assumption. Fallacies can have huge impacts.

THE FALLACY OF COMPOSITION

What logicians call "the fallacy of composition" is the belief that what is true of a part is true of the whole. A baseball fan at a ballpark can see the game better by standing up but, if all the fans stand up, they will not all see better. Many economic policies involve the fallacy of composition, as politicians come to the aid of some particular group, industry, state or other special interest, representing the benefits to them as if they were net benefits to society, rather than essentially robbing Peter to pay Paul.

Many local governments, for example, follow policies designed to attract either new businesses or higher-income people, both of which are expected to provide more local tax revenues. Whole neighborhoods have been demolished and "redeveloped" with upscale housing and shopping malls as a means of "revitalizing" the community. Often the federal government subsidizes this operation, with no consideration that the businesses and higher-income people attracted there will simply be transferred from some other place, while the usually lower-income people displaced are also transferred to some other place, with no net benefit to the country as a whole. Yet governments from the local to the national level have set up innumerable programs to engage in what is usually at best a zero-sum operation, and is often a negative-sum operation, as millions of lives are disrupted across the country and billions of tax dollars are spent demolishing neighborhoods, accomplishing nothing on a national level other than a voluntary relocation of taxpayers to places where they can get property without having to bid it away from its current owners, and an involuntary relocation of the people displaced.

Since policies imposed by government are not voluntary transactions, like those of the marketplace, zero-sum and negative-sum operations can continue indefinitely.

Nevertheless, at any given location, there can be impressive drawings beforehand and impressive photographs afterwards to depict the scene "before" and "after" redevelopment and celebrate the visible improvement at a given location. For many years, photographers liked to take pictures of slums in Washington, with the capitol dome in the background. Eventually massive slum-clearance projects put an end to such embarrassing photos— but the people displaced went to live in other neighborhoods, turning many of these other neighborhoods into slums, even if these new slums were now located at a politically convenient distance from the capitol building.

Government spending is often said to be beneficial to the economy, as the money disbursed is spent and re-spent, creating jobs, raising incomes, and generating tax revenues in the process. But usually if that same government money had remained in the hands of the taxpayers from whom it came, they too would have spent it, and it would still have been re-spent, creating jobs, raising incomes, and generating tax revenues in the process. This again is usually at best a zero-sum process, in so far as the transfer of money is concerned, and a negative-sum process in so far as high tax rates to finance government spending reduce incentives to do all the things necessary to generate economic activity and the prosperity resulting from it.

Advocates of policies to preserve "open space" in order to prevent "overcrowding" ignore the fact that the size of the total population is unaffected by such policies, which means that the people who are prevented from living in a given area will make some other area more crowded than it would have been otherwise.

THE POST HOC FALLACY

One of the most common fallacies is so old that it has a Latin name from centuries ago: *Post Hoc, Ergo Propter Hoc*— in other words, "After this, therefore because of this." For example, one of the damning claims against the insecticide DDT, during the successful campaign to get it banned in many parts of the world, was that it caused cancer. In places where DDT had been widely used, cancer rates had in fact gone up. Many of these were countries subject to devastating ravages of malaria, which killed off vast numbers of people. In the wake of using DDT, which killed mosquitoes that transmitted malaria, that disease was drastically reduced, almost to the vanishing point in some places. Now millions of people, who would otherwise have died young, lived long enough to get cancer in their later years. But the DDT did not cause cancer, and its banning led to a resurgence of malaria that took millions of lives around the world.

When two things are both very striking, and one occurs right after the other, then the first is especially likely to be considered the cause of the second. After the record-breaking stock market crash of 1929 was followed by the record-breaking Great Depression of the 1930s, it has been widely believed, for generations, that the collapse of the stock market caused the collapse of the whole economy. However, a similar stock market crash in 1987 was followed by 20 years of economic growth, with low unemployment and low inflation rates.

As for the 1929 stock market crash, unemployment never reached double digits in any of the 12 months following that event. Unemployment peaked at 9 percent, two months after the stock market crashed, and began drifting generally downward until it reached 6.3 percent in June 1930. That was when the federal government made its first major intervention in the economy, with the Smoot-Hawley tariff. After that intervention, the downward movement in unemployment rates reversed and shot up far beyond the level it had reached in the wake of the stock market crash. Within six months of the first major federal intervention, unemployment reached double digits at 11.6 percent in November 1930. After a series of additional large federal interventions in the economy, unemployment stayed in double digits for the remainder of the decade. An economic analysis published in 2004 concluded that government interventions had prolonged the Great Depression by several years.[3]

The *post hoc* fallacy is more than an intellectual problem. In politics, the desire to take credit for beneficial changes and to blame others for detrimental changes has led to many *post hoc* fallacies. Presidents of the United States almost routinely claim credit for budget surpluses and are blamed by their critics for budget deficits. Yet all federal government spending bills originate in the House of Representatives, and only Congress can change tax rates. When the President and the Congress are of opposite parties, neither a deficit nor a surplus is likely to be due to decisions made in the White House.

THE CHESS-PIECES FALLACY

Back in the eighteenth century, Adam Smith wrote of the doctrinaire theorist who is "wise in his own conceit" and who "seems to imagine that he

10 Economic Facts and Fallacies

can arrange the different members of a great society with as much ease as the hand arranges the different pieces upon a chess-board."[4] Such theorists are at least as common today and have at least as much influence in shaping laws and policies.

Unlike chess pieces, human beings have their own individual preferences, values, plans and wills, all of which can conflict with and even thwart the goals of social experiments. Moreover, whatever the merits of particular social experiments, experimentation as such can have huge economic and social costs. Although some social experimenters may believe that, if one program or policy does not work, they can simply try another and another after that, until they find one that does work, the uncertainties generated by incessant experimentation can cause people to change their behavior in ways that adversely affect the economy.

Some economists, including John Maynard Keynes,[5] saw the uncertainties about the future generated by the experimental policies of the New Deal administration in the 1930s as tending to discourage investment that was much needed to get out of the Great Depression. Boris Yeltsin, the first non-Communist leader of Russia after the collapse of the Soviet Union, likewise spoke of "our country— so rich, so talented and so exhausted by incessant experiments."[6] Because people are not inanimate objects like chess pieces, the very attempt to use them as part of some grand design can turn out to be not merely unsuccessful but counterproductive— and the notion that "if at first you don't succeed, try, try again" can be a formula for disaster when consumers become reluctant to spend and investors become reluctant to invest when they have no reliable framework of expectations, since they have no way of knowing what will happen next in an atmosphere of unending experimentation.

THE OPEN-ENDED FALLACY

Many desirable things are advocated without regard to the most fundamental fact of economics, that resources are inherently limited and have alternative uses. Who could be against health, safety, or open space?

But each of these things is open-ended, while resources are not only limited but have alternative uses which are also valuable.

No matter how much is done to promote health, more could be done. No matter how safe things have been made, they could be made safer. And no matter how much open space there is, there could be still more. Obvious as this may seem, there are advocates, movements, laws, and policies promoting an open-ended commitment to more of each of these things, without any indication of a limit, or any principle by which a limit might be set, much less any consideration of alternative uses of the resources that some people want devoted to whatever desirable thing they are promoting.

Health is certainly something desirable and most people are happy to see billions of dollars devoted to cancer research. But would anyone want to devote half the national income to wiping out skin rashes? Crime control is certainly desirable but would anyone want to devote half the national income to wiping out the last vestige of shoplifting? While no one would advocate these particular trade-offs, what open-ended demands for open space, crime control, better health or cleaner air and water do advocate leaves out the very concept of trade-offs. That is what makes such demands open-ended, both as regards the amounts of money required and often also the amounts of restrictions on people's freedom required to enforce these demands. Open-ended demands are a mandate for ever-expanding government bureaucracies with ever-expanding budgets and powers.

Unlimited extrapolations constitute a special variation on the open-ended fallacy. Much bitter opposition to the building of homes, highways, or even water and sewage systems is based on the belief that these will just attract more people, more traffic and more urbanization, leading to the paving over of fast-vanishing greenery. But not only is there no unlimited supply of people, every person who moves from one place to another reduces the crowding in the place left while increasing crowding in the place that is the destination— with *no net change* in the amount of crowding in the society as a whole. As to the paving over of greenery, it takes quite an extrapolation to see that as a national problem in a country where more than nine-tenths of the land remains undeveloped.

Unlimited extrapolations are not confined to environmental issues. Courts' decisions in anti-trust cases have invoked a fear that a particular growing business is an "incipient" monopoly. In one landmark case before the U.S. Supreme Court, a merger between the Brown Shoe Company and Kinney shoe stores was broken up because Brown's acquisition of the Kinney chain— which sold one percent of the shoes in America— would "foreclose" that market to other shoe manufacturers, beginning the process of creating a monopoly which had to be stopped in its "incipiency." By such reasoning, the fact that the temperature has risen ten degrees since dawn means that we are all going to be burned to a crisp before the end of the month, if unlimited extrapolations are believed.

SUMMARY AND IMPLICATIONS

Many beliefs which collapse under scrutiny may nevertheless persist indefinitely when they are not scrutinized, and especially when skilled advocates are able to perpetuate those beliefs by forestalling scrutiny through appeals to emotions or interests. Some popular fallacies of today are centuries old and were refuted centuries ago, even if they are repackaged in up-to-date rhetoric to suit current times.

This brief sampling of general fallacies is just an introduction to many more specific fallacies that are examined in more detail, and tested against hard evidence, in the chapters that follow.

Chapter 2

URBAN FACTS AND FALLACIES

*In the Occident the city has been the greatest opportunity
and the worst influence; a place of creation and decay, of
freedom and subjection, of riches and poverty, of splendor
and misery, of communion and lonesomeness— an
optimal milieu for talent, character, vice and corruption.*

Eric Hoffer[1]

One of the first questions to ask about cities is: Why do they exist in the
first place? Looking back at history, what caused cities to be built at
all— and why in the particular kinds of places where they were built?
Looking at the present, what are the economic implications of urban life and
what causes cities to flourish or to flounder, deteriorate, and die? What
kinds of policies have what kinds of effects on such urban concerns as
housing, transportation, crime, and economic activity in general?

The facts are fairly straightforward but the challenge is to untangle the
fallacies.

TRANSPORTATION

Transportation costs have played a crucial role in the creation of cities
throughout history, and changing transportation costs in modern times have
had much to do with the ways in which cities have continued to change around
us. For most of the history of the human race, the transportation of people and

goods on land took place using human or animal power, and took place on water using currents, wind, or oars. Most cities were built before there were motorized vehicles on land or water, or of course in the air. The most fundamental fact is that land transport has always been far more costly than water transport, and especially so during the thousands of years before the invention of cars, trucks and trains. Even today, it is often cheaper to ship goods thousands of miles by water than to ship them hundreds of miles by land.

A city must continuously transport in vast amounts of food alone to feed its concentrated population, and it must also transport out the goods it produces to markets elsewhere in the country or around the world. Given these imperatives, it is hardly surprising that most cities throughout history have been built on navigable waterways— whether rivers, lakes, or the sea. These cities include river ports like Cairo on the Nile, Paris on the Seine, and New York on the Hudson; seaports on harbors like Singapore, Stockholm and Sydney; and ports on huge lakes or inland seas like Odessa and Chicago. The relatively few exceptions have been cities with other transportation advantages, such as Samarkand at the crossroads of routes through oases in the desert, Atlanta as a rail junction or Los Angeles, which became a major city only after the invention of automobiles and the building of a network of freeways.

Population Concentration and Dispersion

Internal as well as external transportation costs have shaped the history of cities. When most people traveled within a city on foot, ancient cities had to be much more compact and crowded than modern cities, which have buses, subways, and automobiles. Ancient Rome had a population similar in size to that of Dallas today— but living in an area only *two percent* of the size of Dallas.[2] In a sense, crowding is what cities are all about. That is, the concentration of many and varied activities— economic, social, cultural— within reach of large numbers of people is what attracts people, economic activities, and various institutions to cities. How reachable these attractions are depends on transportation costs in both money and time.

Before the building of subways in New York, it was not feasible for most people to live in the Bronx and work in downtown Manhattan. Indeed, what is today downtown Manhattan was the northern limit of urban settlement before horse-drawn rail carriages dramatically increased the area of the urban community, as it moved up from the original settlement at the southern tip of the island:

> Where woods, orchards, and cultivated fields had once stood, buildings suddenly appeared. Between 1832 and 1860 the northern boundary of the zone of concentrated settlement moved from Houston Street to Forty-second Street. This was astonishing: In that brief thirty-year period the urban frontier advanced twice as far as it had in the previous two hundred years.[3]

A few years later, the first elevated urban rail system appeared in Manhattan and, still later, at the beginning of the twentieth century, the city's first subway, which spread urban settlements to the northern end of the island and even across the Harlem River into the Bronx.

The spreading out of urban communities in general has been made possible by reductions in transportation costs. When trains first made their appearance in early nineteenth century England, this enabled many more people to live farther from their jobs, to spread out into the suburbs, leading the Duke of Wellington to blame the newly created railroads for encouraging "the common people to move about needlessly."[4] In the many years since then, there have been many other third party observers assuming that they know better than the people themselves where those people should be living.

The widespread availability and affordability of automobiles in the second half of the twentieth century has led to rapid suburbanization in affluent industrial societies, whether in the United States, Western Europe or elsewhere, with numerous economic and social consequences that remain controversial. While affordable transportation costs— including walking inside a tightly packed city— have been necessary for urban living, that has not been sufficient. There must be something inside the city worth walking to or riding to, otherwise people would remain scattered through the countrysides.

The tall and thick stone walls around many cities in Europe and elsewhere in centuries past indicate one of the things a city offered, protection against invaders or lawless marauders. In addition, many complementary activities can be carried on in proximity to one other in a city, and activities with large fixed costs, such as building a water supply system or a sewage disposal system, can be carried on economically when these huge costs can be spread over a large number of people crowded into a given area. Hospitals, theaters, and cathedrals are other structures with large fixed costs which are also more likely to be affordable when these costs can be spread over a large number of people concentrated in an urban community. These advantages of a city are what attract the people who produce the crowding.

One of many urban fallacies is that highly crowded cities are a sign of "overpopulation," when in fact it is common in some countries for more than half the nation's population to live in a handful of cities— sometimes in just one— while there are vast areas of open and largely vacant countrysides. Even in a modern urban and industrial society like the United States, less than five percent of the land area is developed, and forests alone cover six times as much land as all the cities and towns in the country put together.[5] Photographs of crowded slums in Third World countries may insinuate the conclusion that "overpopulation" is the cause of poverty, when in fact poverty is the reason for the crowding among people unable to afford the transportation costs of commuting or much urban living space, but who are yet unwilling to forego the benefits of urban living.

Many cities were more crowded in the past, when national and world populations were much smaller. The spread of faster and cheaper transportation, affordable to vastly larger numbers of people, has spread out the urban population into the surrounding countrysides as suburbs have developed. Due to faster transportation, these suburbanites now have proximity in *time* to the institutions and activities of a city from ever greater physical distances. Someone in Dallas, living miles away from a stadium, can get there in a car faster than someone in ancient Rome, living much closer to the Coliseum, could reach that stadium on foot.

Elites with their own horses and carriages have for centuries had greater proximity in time to urban attractions than the poorer masses have had, whether in Europe, Asia or the Western Hemisphere. Transportation costs have long tended to make suburbs the homes of more affluent people, who could afford such costs. As incomes have risen and transportation costs declined in modern times, ordinary people could now afford to move out to the suburbs in great numbers, while maintaining proximity to their jobs and urban amenities. This greater accessibility to urban institutions has been a result of the twentieth century revolutions in transportation brought about by the introduction and spread of subways, commuter trains, buses and automobiles. Ordinary people can in fact live much farther from an urban center today than the elite could in the past.

Before the transportation revolutions of the twentieth century, even New York City was quite different from what it has become since then. The home in which Theodore Roosevelt spent his late adolescence and early adulthood was a suburban mansion built in 1873 on "the outer fringes of New York City"[6]— West 57th Street! As late as 1881, "the streets were little more than numbers, and most of the land was vacant" in the west sixties and seventies.[7] People in Harlem were living out in the country and few, if any, were black. All that changed after the New York City subway system was built at the end of the nineteenth century, reducing transportation costs in both money and time as the twentieth century began.

The Automobile

A second transportation revolution profoundly affected the development of urban and suburban communities in the twentieth century, as well as many other aspects of life. This was the increased use of automobiles, as mass-production methods pioneered by Henry Ford drastically reduced the cost of cars, turning them from a luxury that only a few could afford into a means of transportation affordable by millions of people of moderate incomes. Between 1910 and 1916, for example, the cost of the standard Model T Ford was cut in half.[8] As of 2007, there were approximately 600 automobiles per thousand population of driving age in Western Europe and approximately 900 per thousand in the United States.[9]

Among the economic consequences of cars was that workers had access to a wider area in which to seek employment and employers had a wider area in which to seek workers. In Cincinnati, for example, a study found that most residents could reach 99 percent of the region's jobs within 20 minutes by car. But they could not reach even half that number of jobs by taking mass transit for twice as long, 40 minutes. A study in Portland, Oregon, found that people with no high school diploma were 80 percent more likely to have a job if they had a car, and they earned an additional one thousand dollars a month. That same study found that getting a car enabled such people to get a job more so than getting a high school equivalency diploma.[10]

The economic importance of the automobile is demonstrated graphically in places where automobiles are banned. One of the first automobile bans was instituted in 1959 in Kalamazoo, Michigan, where there was an attempt to "revitalize" its downtown areas by closing a street to automobile traffic, in order to create a pedestrian mall to compete with suburban malls. The idea spread to other cities in the decades ahead:

> Over the next 30 years, U.S. and Canadian cities created roughly 200 such pedestrian malls. Many won awards from planning groups.
> Yet far from revitalizing retail districts, most of the pedestrian malls killed them. Vacancy rates soared, and any pedestrians using the malls found themselves walking among boarded up shops or former department stores that had been downgraded to thrift stores or other low-rent operations. . . Despite these failures, cities continued to create pedestrian malls 25 years after Kalamazoo's initial experiment. In 1984, Buffalo closed 10 blocks of its Main Street to autos. In the following years, Main Street vacancy rates increased by 27 percent and property values declined by 48 percent. . . By 1990, many cities began restoring auto traffic to their pedestrian malls.[11]

That decades had to pass before a mistake with obvious negative consequences began to be corrected is one sign of the problems of decisions by third parties who pay no price for being wrong. The only test that the initial decision to ban automobiles, in order to create pedestrian malls, had to pass was that like-minded "experts" thought it was a good idea, as shown by the awards that such plans received. Once having committed themselves publicly to an idea, neither the city planners nor the politicians who employed them had any incentive to admit to being wrong and every incentive to ignore or verbally minimize the problems that arose, rather than jeopardize their careers by reversing decisions they had made, often with public fanfare and promises of great benefits to follow. Sometimes it is only a later generation of politicians or planners who can admit the mistakes of their predecessors with no jeopardy to their own careers. By contrast, people whose own money is at stake have to change course much more rapidly if they want to avoid bankruptcy.

While the advent of the automobile allowed people to live farther from where they worked, the need for large numbers of people to arrive at work at about the same time from widely varying distances and directions created a problem of rush-hour traffic congestion. In fact such congestion on highways and city streets during rush hours became a common problem in cities around the world.

Congestion has generally tended to grow worse over time. In 1983, there was only one urbanized area in the United States where the average driver spent more than 40 hours a year stuck in rush hour traffic congestion but, twenty years later, there were 25 such areas.[12] Such congestion has economic, environmental and even medical consequences. A study of traffic congestion in France, for example, found that the number of jobs reachable in a given amount of time, such as half an hour, affected not only workers' access to better paying jobs but also affected businesses' access to more customers, as well as access to more qualified employees, so that speedier traffic led to higher productivity. Similar results were found in studies of other urban areas around the world.[13] Traffic congestion also increases air pollution and, by delaying ambulances going to and from scenes of medical emergencies, affects death rates. For cardiac arrest, for example, medical people arriving on the scene a few minutes earlier or later can be the difference between life and death.

Communities around the world have tried to cope with traffic congestion in a variety of ways, with varying degrees of effectiveness. Julius Caesar banned carts during the day in ancient Rome and some modern cities have tried to reduce rush-hour congestion by either restricting or banning cars at certain times and places, or by charging fees for the use of streets in parts of London or toll roads in France and Australia, for example.[14] Washington, D.C., deals with rush-hour congestion by making some streets one-way in one direction during the morning commute and one-way in the opposite direction during the evening commute, a system that can create some dicey situations at the times when the direction of traffic reverses.

The fact that most city streets and most highways are free to the motorists— Los Angeles' freeways being classic examples— means that they tend to be used more extensively than they would be if motorists had to pay the costs that their travel imposed on others. These costs include not only the costs of building and maintaining these roadways but also, and perhaps even more costly, the impeding of other people's travel by rush-hour congestion. The annual costs in both wasted fuel and wasted time have been estimated at more than a thousand dollars per rush hour traveler in Washington, Dallas, Atlanta and San Francisco, and at more than $1,500 in Los Angeles, whose freeways are not in fact free to either the city or to individual motorists, when congestion costs are taken into account.[15]

Like most things that are available without an explicit charge, roads and highways tend to be used far beyond how much they would be used if the hidden costs had to be paid in cash whenever these things are used. Increasing numbers of cities around the world have begun to recognize that and to charge motorists accordingly. Singapore in the 1970s pioneered in charging motorists varying amounts according to the area and the time of day in which they drove. At first, these were manually collected tolls that to some extent impeded traffic but eventually this system was replaced by automatic methods of collecting tolls— either electronically or by billing motorists who were photographed in restricted areas or at restricted times. Even during the 1975-1998 era of manual toll collection, charging motorists according to the congestion involved sped up the movement of cars in Singapore. Prior to these tolls, the city's traffic moved at an average speed of 15 to 20 kilometers per hour during the working day. After the imposition of tolls, traffic moved at an average speed of from 26 to 32 kilometers per hour during the working day.

This happened despite the fact that the city was growing during these years and the number of cars in Singapore tripled. As in other times and places, incentives changed behavior. Some people changed the time of day when they drove, in order to avoid higher tolls and some whose journey began and ended outside the most congested areas with the highest tolls now drove around such areas, instead of through them, as they had before there were tolls collected. Others changed from driving to taking public transportation. Buses carried 46 percent of the commuters in Singapore before the toll system and 69 percent afterward.[16]

Stockholm in 2006 introduced an experimental program which charged only half as much for driving between 6:30 A.M. and 7:00 A.M. as was charged for driving an hour later, when the rush hour was in full swing. Given these costs, and especially the *differences* in costs at different times of day, not only did the total traffic passing through the controlled area decline by 22 percent, the ratio between the volume of rush-hour traffic and non-rush hour traffic changed from about three-to-one to about two-to-one,[17] as people either came to work earlier or stayed later to avoid the higher toll charges at the rush hour peaks. Put differently, the Stockholm experiment, like that in Singapore and elsewhere, showed that "free" roadways contribute to congestion, as most "free" things are used more extensively than when the costs of people's behavior are conveyed to them directly through prices.

While the prices charged or not charged for the use of streets and highways can affect the demands made on these traffic arteries, the supply is also important. One of the persistent fallacies about urban transportation is that it is futile to build more roads because that will only encourage more drivers to add to the traffic, restoring the previous congestion. When the *Miami Herald* said, "The region can't pave its way out of traffic gridlock,"[18] it was expressing a very widespread view— but one which will not stand up under scrutiny. When Houston, for example, added a hundred miles a year to its road network from 1986 to 1992, average delay per traveler at the rush hour peaks *declined* 21 percent. But, when Houston drastically cut back on road building between 1993 and 2000, while its population was still growing, travel delays nearly doubled.[19] Similarly, between 1989 and 1997, despite the fact that the San Jose region added 100,000 new jobs, the average commuting time during the rush hour declined by 50 percent because its roadway system was growing.[20]

In other words, building more roadways to keep pace with the growth of traffic only works when you do it. So do most things. Following the kind of reasoning used by those who say that it is futile to build more roads to cope with traffic congestion, it would be possible to say that it is "futile" to deal with hunger by eating because people just get hungry again later on.

One of the reasons so many are committed to the idea of the futility of building more streets and highways to cope with traffic congestion is that they prefer to rely on mass transit as part of a more sweeping program of centrally planned development or redevelopment. City planners, consultants and "experts" all have a vested interest in the idea that people cannot be left to live their lives as they see fit but must have their transportation and their housing patterns, among other things, controlled by city planners, consultants and "experts." One of the reasons for a failure to ease traffic congestion is that many see this congestion as a way to "get people out of their cars" and into mass transit. Urban politicians have an additional reason to be against highways and automobiles: Both facilitate the movement of taxpayers out into the suburbs, beyond the tax-collecting jurisdiction of city officials.

The fixation on mass transit, as a substitute for high levels of automobile usage, cannot be justified by the actual track record of mass transit or by its underlying economics. While mass transit played a major role in the development of New York City, that is today the exception, rather than the rule. Nearly forty percent of all American mass transit commuters are in fact in New York. Even so, only about one-fourth of New Yorkers get to work on mass transit. Chicago is the next highest, with 11 percent. Nationwide, mass transit ridership was two million people fewer in 2000 than in 1960, even though there were more than 60 million more workers in 2000. Europe has had similar trends, with mass transit accounting for a declining share of travel in London, Paris, Stockholm, and Frankfurt, for example, and its share of European travel as a whole declined from 25 percent in 1970 to 16 percent in 2000.[21]

There are economic reasons for this. With rising levels of prosperity, more automobile ownership and increasing suburbanization, there are fewer places with the high population densities needed to make mass transit a predominant means of transportation:

> The typical suburban community houses about 2,500 or 3,000 people per square mile, but transit's share of commute trips is insignificant for tracts with fewer than 4,000 people per square mile. . . . Generally speaking,

transit's market share doesn't exceed 20 percent on average until densities reach five and six times the density of a typical suburban community.[22]

In short, most places are not like Manhattan— and are becoming more and more *unlike* Manhattan as time goes on. Making mass transit a substitute for the automobile is a daunting task, when so many people prefer the automobile. For one thing, automobiles can deliver people directly from home to work, avoiding trips to and from the points where mass transit can be boarded, as well as transfers that are often necessary. Moreover, just over half of all Americans do *not* make a beeline between home and work in their cars but make other stops[23]— for shopping or picking up their children, for example— and for this mass transit is no substitute for an automobile.

Nevertheless, government subsidies have been poured into mass transit. In 1964, Congress passed the Urban Mass Transportation Act, under which the federal government would provide grants to cities that operated their own transit systems. Even though the number of people riding on these systems was declining and most of these transit systems were privately owned in 1964, over the next eight years cities purchased these systems from their private owners. But the number of riders declined an additional 21 percent.[24] Clearly, what politicians and planners wanted was not what the riders themselves wanted. Still, third parties who pay no price for being wrong continue to favor mass transit and the larger role it provides for themselves in shaping society to reflect their vision.

Where these third parties are in government, they are in a position to implement their vision, even in spite of, and counter to, the expressed views of the public. One way has been to divert money earmarked for highways into mass transit instead. Thus, in California, where the voters of Santa Clara County in 1990 approved a sales tax increase to build new highways, the Santa Clara Valley Transportation Authority diverted those tax revenues to mass transit. Among the results:

> Now the San Jose region is poised to spend more than 80 percent of its transportation funds on the 1 percent of travel in the region that goes by transit.[25]

Many who condemn the automobile for pollution seem to imagine a pre-automobile society very different from the way the pre-automobile world was in fact. The streets of New York City in the nineteenth century were an example:

> Much of the muck followed from the still-unavoidable reliance on horses— forty thousand of them, who each working day generated some four hundred tons of manure, twenty thousand gallons of urine, and almost two hundred carcasses. . . [26]

A 1972 study showed that the amount of pollution per mile traveled by horse was a hundred times the amount of pollution per mile traveled by automobile.[27] Since the cars produced in later years have had reduced pollution levels, the disparity today would be even greater. It should also be noted that the replacement of horses by automobiles made it possible to "restore more than 80 million acres of forestlands that had once been cleared for horse pasture."[28]

Social Pathology

Important as urban transportation has been, there are limits to what it can explain, as with any other factor— and some people have exceeded those limits when seeking to explain some social phenomena by transportation costs. For example, the movement of inner city jobs to the suburbs, especially after the 1960s, has been regarded by some as the reason for the dramatic rise in rates of unemployment in inner city ghettoes, and that in turn has been seen as a reason for the sharp increase in such other social pathologies as rising crime rates and disintegrating families in these neighborhoods.[29] But the fact that these striking trends have been correlated does not tell us which one caused the others, or whether they were all caused by something else. However, the movement of jobs has been undeniable and of a major magnitude, as in the case of a Chicago neighborhood:

> Two large factories anchored the economy of this West Side neighborhood in its good old days— the Hawthorne plant of Western Electric, which employed over 43,000 workers; and an International

Harvester plant with 14,000 workers. The world headquarters for Sears, Roebuck and Company was located there, providing another 10,000 jobs. . .But conditions rapidly changed. Harvester closed its doors in the late 1960s. Sears moved most of its offices to the Loop in downtown Chicago in 1973. . .The Hawthorne plant gradually phased out its operations and finally shut down in 1984.[30]

From this, some have concluded that the movement of jobs to the suburbs created such high transportation costs, in both time and money, that these jobs were now beyond the range of most inner city residents. The resulting economic breakdown in these communities is then blamed for such social breakdowns as a welfare culture with fatherless children and skyrocketing rates of crime and violence. However, businesses and jobs did not leave this neighborhood for no reason. It costs considerable money to relocate operations that employ thousands of people. Moreover, in Chicago as in other cities, massive movements of businesses out of the inner city followed the urban riots which swept across the country in the 1960s. The Chicago community mentioned above lost an estimated three-quarters of its businesses during the decade of the 1960s.

In short, the riots represented a social breakdown that occurred *before* the movement of businesses out of inner city ghettoes. Moreover, in Indianapolis, where the employers did not move as far away as in some other cities, there was the same inner city social pathology of a rapidly increasing welfare culture, with accompanying increases in crime and violence, as that found in Chicago and other cities where these phenomena were attributed to transportation costs.[31] Put differently, inner city ghettoes had lower rates of crime and violence, as well as lower unemployment rates, and most black children grew up in two-parent households, in an earlier era that was by no means free of racial discrimination. The reasons for the changes for the worse in inner city neighborhoods from the 1960s on must be sought elsewhere because the movement of businesses out of these neighborhoods came after these social breakdowns. Getting the sequence wrong is one of many urban fallacies.

Meanwhile, it has become a common sight in many American cities to see immigrants from Latin America gathered at particular places where employers drive by and hire them, taking them to whatever factory, construction site, private home, or other place of employment has a demand for them. In other words, these workers provide no transportation of their own but still get employed. Usually, these are unskilled laborers with low incomes and the jobs may be temporary for varying amounts of time, but somehow employer and employee manage to get together. Nor is this a unique situation.

In earlier times, when black workers were poorer than today and most lived in rural areas where public transportation was seldom available, black labor force participation rates were at least as high as the labor force participation rates of whites from the late nineteenth century on into the early decades of the twentieth century. The change to today's situation, in which blacks have lower labor force participation rates than whites, cannot be explained by changing costs of transportation to work, in either time or money, for employers can and do arrange for vans to pick up workers, not only in the case of casual labor hired off the street for a day or for the duration of a given project, but also workers hired as on-going employees for businesses located some distance away from the source of the labor they are seeking. In earlier times, the Ford Motor Company sent buses into Detroit's black neighborhoods to recruit workers.[32]

What is crucial is that employers have a demand for such labor at a price at which such labor is available. Many things reduce the demand for inner city workers today, including wage rates set higher than their productivity and things which reduce that productivity, such as deficiencies in education and attitudes.

HOUSING

The biggest economic fallacy about housing is that "affordable housing" requires government intervention in the housing market, perhaps with subsidies, rent control, or other devices to allow people with moderate or low incomes to be able to have a decent place to live, without paying ruinous prices for homes or apartments. Ruinous prices for housing are certainly a fact of life in some places, leaving people of moderate or low incomes with inadequate amounts of money for other things. The question is whether government programs offer a way out of such situations for most people.

The idea that government intervention improves the situation is a notion which has been repeated innumerable times in many ways, but endless repetition is not a coherent argument, much less proof. When we turn from political rhetoric to hard facts, we find that those facts tell a story directly opposite to what is being said in politics and in much of the media. It is precisely government intervention in housing markets which has made previously affordable housing unaffordable. Both the history and the economics of housing show this.

History

If we go back to the beginning of the twentieth century, before government intervention became pervasive in housing markets, we find people paying a *smaller* percentage of their expenditures for housing than at the end of that century. Even though real incomes at the beginning of the twentieth century were only a fraction of what they were at the end, a smaller percentage of the expenditures out of those smaller incomes was sufficient to cover housing costs. Back then, the rule of thumb was that housing costs— whether rents or mortgage payments— should not take more than one-fourth of a person's income. In 1901, housing costs took 23 percent of the average American family's spending. By 2003, it took 33 percent of a far larger amount of spending.[33] In California, where government interventions in housing markets have been especially pervasive, the proportion of income required for housing has increased even more steeply, in an even shorter span of time:

> Most people know that the San Francisco Bay Area has one of the most expensive housing markets in the nation. However, not everyone realizes that, as recently as 1970, Bay Area housing was as affordable as housing in many other parts of the country.
> Data from the 1970 census shows that a median-income Bay Area family could dedicate a quarter of their income to housing and pay off their mortgage on a median-priced home in just 13 years. By 1980, a family had to spend 40 percent of their income to pay off a home mortgage in 30 years; today, it requires 50 percent.[34]

In Salinas, California, about a hundred miles south of San Francisco, the median price of a home required 60 percent of the median family income in 2006. A real estate agent in that area reported selling a 1,013-square-foot house, more than fifty years old, to an immigrant farm worker for $490,000, with a monthly mortgage payment that took 70 percent of his pay. Nevertheless, the buyer, whose family had lived for years in a rented room, "was so thrilled that he cried when he signed the loan." Three-quarters of the land in the county is legally blocked from development.[35] With such a severe restriction on supply, high land prices were virtually guaranteed—and therefore also high prices for the housing built on that land. It is not uncommon in California for the land to cost far more than the housing that is built on it.

History can be looked at another way, in terms of when pervasive government regulation of housing markets began and when housing prices skyrocketed. Since these were mostly state and local regulations, the beginnings of stringent housing regulations have varied somewhat from community to community. By and large, however, the decade of the 1970s marked the beginning of severe government restrictions on the building of houses and apartments. That same decade marked the meteoric rise of housing prices in those places where the restrictions were particularly severe, such as coastal California. While many cities and counties in California, Oregon, Hawaii, and Vermont created restrictive housing laws and policies during the 1970s, many other places did not or did so at different times. Housing price rises reflected those differences. An economic study of housing prices concluded:

> In most cases, the decade in which housing markets became unaffordable closely followed the approval of state growth-management laws or restrictive local plans.[36]

The same high correlation between government intervention and sharply rising housing costs can be found in other countries as well, where housing restrictions are particularly severe, under a variety of politically attractive names such as "open space" laws or "smart-growth" policies. An international study of 26 urban areas with "severely unaffordable" housing found 23 of those 26 to have strong "smart-growth" policies.[37] The results belie the phrase.

Restrictions on the building of homes and apartment buildings take many forms. "Smart-growth" laws restrict the expansion of home-building in suburban areas. There are also "open space" laws which simply forbid the building of anything on land set aside in various areas— 40 percent of the land in Montgomery County, Maryland, for example, more than two-thirds of the land in San Mateo County, California and, as already noted, three-quarters of the land in Monterey County, California. Although a typical middle class single-family home is usually built on a quarter-acre lot, minimum lot-size laws forbid the building of homes on less than an acre of land in some places or several acres of land in others. Such laws alone are enough to cause housing prices to skyrocket beyond the reach of millions of people. Then there are zoning laws, environmental laws, historic preservation laws, and others, including arbitrary limits on the number of building permits issued and/or requirements that builders conform to whatever arbitrary preferences and preconditions members of planning commissions choose to impose before issuing permits.

Contrasts in housing prices are sharp between places that have numerous or severe restrictions and places that do not. Houston, Texas, for example, does not even have zoning laws, much less the array of severe housing restrictions found in some other cities. A nationwide real estate firm estimated that a typical middle-class home on a quarter-acre lot that costs $152,000 in Houston would cost more than $300,000 in Portland, Oregon, $900,000 in Long Beach, California, and more than a million dollars in San Francisco.[38] At the beginning of the twenty-first century, home prices in Tampa and Tallahassee, Florida, were not very different from prices in Houston but, after restrictive home building laws passed in the late twentieth century began to take effect, "housing prices in most Florida markets have at least doubled relative to Houston," according to a study just a few years later.[39]

Even in California, with its housing prices three times the national average, the situation was radically different before the crucial decade of the 1970s, when building restrictions proliferated. In the same San Mateo County where home prices averaged more than a million dollars in 2007,[40] a vast privately built middle-class development called Foster City was built in the 1960s with home prices starting as low as $22,000, and with even waterfront homes on its lagoons being available for under $50,000.[41]

Even allowing for inflation during the intervening years does not account for the later escalation in home prices in Foster City. The consumer price index showed approximately a five-fold increase in the general price level between the time when Foster City was built and the early twenty-first century. But the average home price in Foster City exceeded a million dollars in 2005— which is to say, the *average* price of a home in Foster City was now more than twenty times the price of an *upscale* home in the same community in the 1960s. In other words, even allowing for inflation, the real price of homes in Foster City had more than quadrupled.

While it is hard to imagine that these historical patterns are just coincidences, correlation is not causation, so we need to consider the economics of the situation as well as the history— and to scrutinize alternative explanations of these patterns.

Economics

Many things can cause housing prices to rise, including anything that affects either supply or demand. Rising incomes and growing population obviously affect the demand for housing. Supply is affected to the extent that the land area is so built up that little land remains to build on in a given area. The innumerable legal restrictions and bans on building also affect the supply of land available for housing, as does the ease of delaying construction with environmental, aesthetic or other objections raised by officials, non-governmental organizations, or individual citizens. Even when these objections are found to be groundless or are otherwise over-ruled, delay in itself can cost millions of dollars when vast sums of borrowed money are financing a project and interest has to be paid on that money, regardless of whether the building is proceeding on schedule or is stalled by claims that take time to investigate or adjudicate.

How do we know which of these factors is responsible in any given case? Only by examining each of these possibilities in each specific case.

If population is growing rapidly in a given area, it might seem that this would tend to cause more demand for housing and therefore rising housing prices in that area. But neither supply nor demand *by itself* can explain prices, which are determined by the combined effects of the two. As one economic study pointed out: "The population of Las Vegas almost tripled between 1980 and 2000, but the real median housing price did not change."[42] However, the average price of houses in Palo Alto, California, nearly quadrupled in one decade without any increase in population at all.[43] The difference is that severe building restrictions began in Palo Alto during that decade— the 1970s— but not in Las Vegas, where builders could simply construct new homes as the demand for housing increased. But not one new home was built in Palo Alto during the decade when its housing prices nearly quadrupled.

A similar pattern showing housing prices affected more by building restrictions than by increased demand for housing was found in New York City, where "tens of thousands of new units were built in Manhattan during the 1950s, while prices remained flat."[44] In later years, especially after severe building restrictions began in the 1970s, that all changed: "In spite of skyrocketing prices, the housing stock has grown by less than 10 percent since 1980" in Manhattan, according to an article in an economic journal 25 years later.[45] Moreover, the proportion of new housing units in buildings 20 stories tall and higher, which had been increasing in Manhattan from the beginning of the twentieth century until 1970, suddenly reversed and began a decades-long decline.[46]

Height restrictions are among the many building restrictions which can be imposed, either directly or by allowing complaints by neighbors to initiate costly construction delays while these complaints are adjudicated before various authorities. Those who make such complaints pay little or no costs, even when their complaints turn out to be completely unfounded and cost millions of dollars in construction delays to builders— and ultimately to those who buy or rent the housing that is being built.

Height restrictions have both economic and social consequences. Since the cost of housing includes both construction costs and the cost of the land on which the housing is built, the taller an apartment building on a given plot of

land the lower the land cost per apartment. In places where the cost of the
land exceeds the cost of constructing housing, height restrictions can mean
that much higher rents or condominium prices must be charged. If economic
considerations would lead to the building of a 20-story apartment building
but local laws restrict the height of buildings to 10 stories, then twice as much
land will be required to house the same number of people. Moreover, if a
growing community cannot expand upward, then it must expand outward,
leading to longer commutes to work, more highway congestion and, almost
inevitably, more highway fatalities. All that is in addition to higher rents.

Income is another factor in housing prices. With or without population
growth, rising incomes can lead to a rising demand for houses by people
who would otherwise be living in apartments and a rising demand for bigger
or better houses by people otherwise living in more modest homes. To what
extent does income growth explain housing prices in those places where
these prices have skyrocketed?

Prior to 1970, housing prices in California were much like housing prices
in the rest of the country, even though California housing prices later rose
to become three or more times housing prices in the country at large. Since
this meteoric rise in California housing prices began in the 1970s, how did
California income increases compare to national income increases during
that decade? Income rose *less* sharply in California during that decade than
in the country as a whole.[47] Meanwhile, in Houston during the late 1970s,
"average incomes surged well ahead of the rest of the US," but nevertheless
Houston remained "one of the fifteen least-expensive housing markets of
the 319 US regions examined by Coldwell Banker." As already noted,
Houston does not even have zoning laws, much less the large array of
housing restrictions found elsewhere. The city grew rapidly but housing
prices rose less than in the country as a whole. Adjusting for inflation, real
housing prices in Houston in the early twenty-first century were found to
be "15 percent below the 1980 peak."[48]

Unlike Houston, Dallas does have zoning laws but their effect is more
limited than in other communities where zoning is an instrument of severe
building restrictions. Over all, Dallas, like Houston, "has had little in the
way of growth management." The result:

Dallas has consistently maintained family incomes about 10 percent above the US average, while its housing prices are generally lower than the US average.[49]

One of the obvious factors in the price of housing is the cost of constructing homes and apartment buildings. These construction costs can vary from place to place and from one time period to another, especially as people begin buying bigger and higher quality housing with more associated amenities, such as garages and air conditioning. The question here is: How far does this factor go toward explaining housing prices in those communities where housing prices are some multiple of what they are in other communities?

As already noted, in Palo Alto, California, where home prices nearly quadrupled during the decade of the 1970s, there was not a single new home built during that decade, so this was simply a question of the same existing homes selling for far more than before, and obviously had nothing to do with construction costs, since there was no new construction. Many other communities with strikingly higher housing prices than the national average, and sharply rising housing prices as well— Boston, Boulder, San Diego and San Francisco, for example— have likewise had severe limits on new construction, so that construction costs there cannot explain skyrocketing housing prices in these communities either, since so little new construction was permitted.

An economic study of 21 housing markets around the country found that, in 12 of these markets, the cost of housing exceeded the combined costs of construction and the land by no more than 10 percent. It was precisely in *other* communities with extremely high housing prices that these prices exceeded construction and land costs by more than 10 percent— as high as 33 percent to 50 percent in Los Angeles, San Francisco, Oakland, and San Jose. In midtown Manhattan, the prices charged for condominiums have been double their construction and land costs.[50] A *New York Times* story provided a glimpse of the market for condominiums in Manhattan:

> Katalin Shavely, a 30-year-old bedding designer in Manhattan, devotes her weekends to scanning the classifieds and attending open houses, searching for just the right one-bedroom apartment for less than $750,000. She can't find it.[51]

Even after the housing market collapsed, and prices fell drastically, an apartment in Manhattan barely met the $750,000 limit. In 2010, a 950-square-foot apartment near New York University was advertised for $749,000. That same day, a 3,200-square-foot home in Ann Arbor, near the University of Michigan, was advertised for $720,000.[52]

Where builders are allowed to construct homes and apartments without severe government restrictions, even growing populations and rising incomes do not cause housing prices to shoot up, because the supply of newly constructed housing keeps up with the growing demand, as in Houston. High profit margins, over and above the costs of construction and land, attract more builders who wish to share in these lucrative returns on investments in home building. This increased supply of new housing then drives prices back down or else prevents them from rising in the first place. There is little opportunity for housing prices to continue to greatly exceed construction and land costs in communities without severe legal restrictions on building or a monopolistic collusion among builders.

Far from being a monopolistic industry that can maintain high profit margins by keeping out competing newcomers, the construction industry has more than 7,500 firms constructing multi-family homes and more than 138,000 firms constructing single-family homes. More than 100 firms constructing multi-family homes are headquartered in Manhattan alone.[53] High profit margins in communities with high housing prices cannot be explained by monopoly in the private market but by government-imposed restrictions on home building.

Ironically, having created artificially high housing prices, government then often supplies token amounts of "affordable housing" to selected individuals or groups. Such selective generosity may be subsidized by taxpayers or by making it mandatory that private builders sell a certain percentage of their housing at prices "below market," as a precondition for receiving building permits. These "below market" prices may nevertheless be higher than housing prices would be in the absence of building restrictions. Moreover, where these prices represent losses to the builders, these losses are made up by raising the prices of their other housing even higher. But such well-publicized programs perpetuate the belief that government intervention is the key to creating "affordable housing," when in fact such intervention has often been a key factor in making housing unaffordable.

Politics

How did the kind of building restrictions that send housing prices sky-high get started in the first place and then acquire such political momentum? Part of the answer is the heady but misleading concept of "planning." What is called "planning" in political rhetoric is the government's suppression of other people's plans by superimposing on them a collective plan, created by third parties, armed with the power of government and exempted from paying the costs that these collective plans impose on others.

The desire to control what other people do— whether in housing or in other things— existed long before the sharp rise in housing prices which began in some communities during the decade of the 1970s. What held in check the ability of government officials to micro-manage housing markets were property rights recognized by state constitutions restricting state and local governments and by the Constitution of the United States restricting what the federal government could do. However, court decisions over the years eroded property rights, which were increasingly regarded as simply private privileges of people who happened to be fortunate enough to own substantial property— these private privileges then being seen as expendable for the greater "public good" represented by the plans of political authorities. The landmark court decision in the *Petaluma* case[54] in 1975 opened the flood gates to a vast expansion of housing restrictions in communities where "planning" was in vogue.

One of the ironic consequences of regarding property rights as simply benefits enjoyed by more fortunate people— rather than as fundamental checks on government power— was that affluent and wealthy communities could now restrict the ability of moderate-income and low-income people to move into their communities. In the normal course of events, a growing demand for housing leads not only to new housing being built on unoccupied land but also to old communities being transformed as existing housing is torn down to make way for new homes and apartment buildings.

Sometimes the housing torn down is replaced by larger or more upscale housing— "gentrification"— but often what happens is that luxurious homes or mansions on large lots or estates are bought up by developers and then torn down to be replaced by more numerous and less expensive homes or apartment buildings on smaller lots, for sale or rent to more numerous people of more modest incomes.

The overriding of property rights by judicial and political authorities means that such changes in affluent or wealthy communities have been resisted or forbidden by a wide range of housing restrictions such as minimum lot-size laws, historic preservation laws, "open space" laws, "smart-growth" policies, and by the creation of planning commissions and environmental agencies armed with arbitrary powers to approve or disapprove applications to build, or the power to impose arbitrary and costly preconditions on the issuance of permits. In short, the erosion of property rights has allowed affluent and wealthy communities to keep out people of moderate or low incomes and prevent the building of housing for ordinary people that would change the character of existing upscale communities.

The high housing prices created by these restrictions do not have to be paid by home-owners already living in these communities, who either own their own homes outright or whose mortgages date from earlier times before the sharp rise in housing prices that these restrictions create. Therefore newcomers would have to be at least as affluent as existing residents in order to afford the higher housing prices. Far from losing anything by housing restrictions, existing home-owners see the value of their property shoot up— and it is existing residents who vote on local housing restrictions that raise housing prices for newcomers. Among those residents, only renters are likely to be made worse off, as the inability of newcomers to afford artificially higher home prices may encourage some to compete for existing rental units.

This asymmetrical process is made possible by judicial erosions of property rights. Where property rights prevail in a free market, housing circulates regularly among different classes of people. Harlem, for example, was a middle class white community in the early twentieth century but in just one decade it became a working class black community. Although the affluent and the rich, by definition, have more income and wealth per person than the average member of society, often the total purchasing power of a far larger number of people is enough to bid away luxury homes and estates, replacing them with middle-class or even working class homes and apartment buildings, changing the composition of a whole community.

Where an existing community consists of people in upscale homes on large estates, and there is a growing demand for housing in their area, some of the existing residents may find the offers made by developers to buy up their property too tempting to resist. Once that happens on a large scale, the remaining residents can find the community changing around them, not only as regards the kind of housing being built but also as regards the kind of people who move in.

Respect for property rights means that existing residents and potential newcomers compete for the same space on an equal basis in the marketplace, rather than in a political process in which only the existing residents can vote. While the existing residents may choose to believe that they have a right to "protect" their community against outsiders by using the power of government, the Constitution of the United States requires "equal protection of the laws" to everyone, regardless of where they happen to live or how long they have lived there. Moreover, what existing residents choose to call "our community" is in fact *not* their community. Each resident owns only the private property which that particular resident has paid for. Those existing residents who choose to sell to developers have just as much right to do so under the Constitution as those who prefer to keep the community as it is.

Another crucial insulation from free market forces has been having the government take over vastly more surrounding land than any or all of the existing homeowners paid for, in the name of "open space." Where thousands of acres of land are taken off the market around an upscale community, that can mean millions— or even billions— of dollars' worth of land being made unavailable to others, for the benefit of the existing residents of that community. Local residents do not need to pay for that land nor need the governmental unit that takes the land off the market. Merely by forbidding or restricting what can be built on that land, the government automatically lowers its market value, often drastically. At these artificially lower prices, various entities— private or governmental— can then take over the land as "open space" at a fraction of what other people would be willing to pay for it as a place for building housing. In other words, the real value of the land, as a resource which has alternative uses, can be some multiple of the money that changes hands when governmental or private non-profit organizations acquire it as "open space."

The city of Salinas, in Monterey County, California, had the least affordable housing in the nation in 2005, as measured by the percentage of the median family income required to make mortgage payments on the median-priced home. Existing residents were able to keep three-quarters of the land in the county off-limits to development. In other words, the land that all the residents put together paid for as their private property was less than one-third of the land that they controlled politically and barred other people from acquiring as private property. One of these residents quoted by the *Wall Street Journal* expressed an attitude common in such situations, whether in Monterey County or elsewhere:

> "Nobody wants to give up this way of life," says Carol Harrington, who has lived in the Salinas area since her youth. Wild turkeys, wild pigs and deer roam on her 16 acres.[55]

Land-use restrictions protecting "this way of life" have a cost paid by others, not only in housing prices in the county that take 60 percent of the median family income for mortgage payments, but also in the fact that 39 percent of the homes in the Salinas area had more people per room than 99 percent of all homes in the United States.[56] In other words, the "open space" of some has entailed the overcrowding of others, as less affluent families have had to double up in a home or apartment built for one family, or else a whole family may have to live in one rented room, in order to cope with artificially high housing prices.

Often the character of a community includes a bucolic setting or expansive views of the surrounding area which those who live there cherish. But they did not buy those settings or those views or pay to have them guaranteed to remain the same in perpetuity. Other people with other preferences have had the same rights under the Constitution, at least until courts began to erode both property rights and the "equal protection of the laws" prescribed by the

Fourteenth Amendment. Political authorities in various jurisdictions began to take advantage of that erosion of property rights to pass restrictive housing laws under a variety of politically attractive names such as "open space," "smart-growth," and the like. Such restrictions have been especially prevalent in overwhelmingly upscale liberal communities such as those in coastal California, where concerns are often expressed for the poor, for minorities, and for children— all of whom are among those most often forced out of such communities by high housing prices.

In San Francisco, for example, the exodus of people of modest to middle-class incomes was shown in census data which revealed that, between 2002 and 2006, the number of households with incomes below $150,000 a year declined by more than 16,000, while the number of households with incomes of $150,000 and up increased by more than 17,000.[57] Like low-income minorities, families with children have also been disproportionately forced out of such communities by sharply rising housing prices. Sharply declining school enrollments— from 15,000 to 9,000— caused several schools in Palo Alto to be closed within a few years, beginning during the decade of the 1970s, when that community's housing prices nearly quadrupled.[58] Declining populations of children have likewise led to many school closings in San Francisco and San Mateo counties during the same decade and in later decades, even though the total population in these counties increased.

Despite the negative effects of land use restrictions on families with children, these children can still be invoked politically to justify such restrictions. Not only are children invoked generally as "posterity," for whom various things such as "open space" are to be "preserved," they have been invoked more specifically as supposed current beneficiaries of current land use restrictions. Thus when surplus land owned by the Veteran's Administration in upscale West Los Angeles, adjacent to affluent Bel Air and Beverly Hills, was being scheduled to be sold, the *Los Angeles Times* argued against its being sold in the market because so few children in Los Angeles live within "walking distance of a public place to play," which was the use preferred to what the paper called "thoughtless" development.[59] While this argument might be plausible in some circumstances, its application is much more dubious for land adjacent to Beverly Hills and Bel Air, where homes have their own swimming pools and often tennis courts, not to mention other recreational facilities on their own grounds and in their mansions.

Nor are poor children likely to live within walking distance of Beverly Hills and Bel Air. As for the argument about "preserving" things for "posterity," that boils down to allowing the posterity of existing residents to keep out the posterity of other people.

Blacks are another group adversely affected by the high housing prices created by severe building restrictions. The black population of San Francisco was reduced by more than half from 1970 to 2005, from 96,000 people to an estimated 47,000.[60] The number of deaths exceeds the number of births in San Francisco's black population,[61] suggesting that here, as in the white population, people with young children are disproportionately forced out by high housing costs. Similar patterns of black population declines have been found in other California communities at or near the coast, such as Los Angeles, Marin County, Monterey County, Alameda County, and San Mateo County— each of which had a declining black population. All of these have long been overwhelmingly upscale liberal communities with overwhelming government restrictions on the building of housing. "San Francisco's black population has dropped faster than that of any other large U.S. city's," according to the *San Francisco Chronicle*.[62]

URBAN ECONOMIC ACTIVITIES

Cities are not only places where people consume various benefits, they are places where many of these benefits are produced, not only for their own inhabitants but also for people in the hinterlands and around the world. These goods and services are distributed both through markets and through political processes, the two processes operating under very different incentives and very different constraints.

Cities reduce the costs of some things and increase the costs of others. The high fixed costs of building reservoirs, hospitals, or electric power lines can be spread over vast numbers of people living in a limited urban area, reducing the cost per person, compared to what it would cost per person to supply the same things to a population more thinly spread over vast countrysides. There are other ways in which a city reduces production costs. The many varieties of economic activities taking place within city limits mean that complementary resources are more readily available nearby— which is to say, at lower transportation costs in both time and money. A manufacturer with a complicated machine that breaks down is more likely to quickly find someone qualified to repair it in a big city, thereby reducing the time during which that machine is unable to operate.

Other kinds of costs are greater, rather than less, in a city. The disposal of sewage, for example, seldom requires as high a cost per person in a thinly populated countryside as in a city. In the country, human wastes, as well as discarded food, can be left to be absorbed by the land as these wastes decompose. Rivers and streams can also safely absorb limited amounts of sewage and discarded food from a small population spread over a wide area. The human race could not have survived for thousands of years if every trace of impurities was fatal. But the human wastes and discarded food from a million people living in a 50-square-mile area cannot be absorbed by the land or water as fast as it is created. Without building costly water supply systems and costly sewage systems, the water will quickly become too dangerous to drink and perhaps even too dangerous to wash with. Much of the urban land, being paved over, has even less capacity to absorb the wastes, so that discarded garbage alone is a deadly menace to public health unless there are costly systems in place to keep collecting and disposing of it outside the city.

Crime control can also be more costly per person in a city, where the anonymity of vast numbers of people can enable criminals to more readily escape detection than in a small community where most people know one another and a stranger stands out like a sore thumb. In such small communities, personal ties make witnesses more likely to come forward after a crime or even to intervene while crimes are being committed.

In short, the crime control exercised by both citizens and police in a small community— the former free of charge to the taxpayers— is more likely to be left more heavily in the hands of the police in an urban community, where people are much less likely to intervene or even to come forward as witnesses. Particular close-knit urban neighborhoods, where many people are relatives or long-time friends, may have some of the low crime control costs of a small community. Moreover, even strangers living in such communities or neighborhoods benefit from the fact that criminals know that such places are not promising places for committing crimes.* But seldom will a whole city enjoy such an advantage. Urban residents must therefore pay more for police protection because deterrence or intervention by ordinary citizens is less available.

Urban residents in low-income neighborhoods often also pay more for ordinary grocery items or other common purchases from drugstores, hardware stores, and other merchants. One reason is that it is often not economically realistic to locate large supermarkets or "big box" retail stores with economies of scale in such neighborhoods. What this means is that the stores that do locate in low-income neighborhoods have higher operating costs that will be reflected in higher prices. It is cheaper to deliver a huge amount of merchandise to one gigantic Wal-Mart store than to deliver the same amount of merchandise to a dozen or so smaller stores scattered around town. While it is economically feasible to locate a gigantic Wal-Mart store in Page, Arizona— a community of about 7,000 people— it would not be feasible to locate a Wal-Mart in a low-income urban neighborhood of 7,000 people.

What makes the Wal-Mart in Page, Arizona, economically viable is that it is located on a highway from which customers arrive from places far beyond the small town of Page, and that there is a vast parking lot on which customers can park in a place where building such parking lots is feasible because land prices are nowhere near what they would be in a city. Not only are people in low-income urban neighborhoods less likely to have cars, the stores there are unlikely to be able to afford the land prices required to build huge parking lots for cars if they did have them. Moreover, if this low-

---

* As a personal note, I once lived in a neighborhood where some well-known mafia leaders also lived. Few criminals were willing to risk trying to mug someone in that neighborhood, where a weak old lady might be some mafia leader's mother or a young woman might be his wife or daughter. Some nights, while I was asleep, my wife would go out at midnight to buy a morning newspaper at a news stand a few blocks away. The very fact that the news stand was open at midnight meant not only that the owner of the news stand had little fear of crime but also that there were enough other people in the neighborhood with a similar lack of fear of crime to provide him with a profitable business.

income neighborhood is also a high-crime neighborhood, people from outside the neighborhood are less likely to shop there, as people from far beyond Page, Arizona, drive to its Wal-Mart.

Crime and violence affect the local economy more directly when riots destroy many or most of the businesses there and new businesses are afterwards reluctant to move in to replace them. As already noted, in just one decade— the 1960s— riots in Chicago's west side destroyed or forced the abandonment of an estimated three-quarters of that neighborhood's businesses.[63] Thus inhabitants of low-income neighborhoods— most of whom are neither criminals nor rioters— end up paying higher prices because of those among them who are.

There is no need to attempt to determine the net effect of cities on costs in general. First of all, there is no such thing as costs in general. There are particular costs that matter differently to particular individuals and enterprises, and those individuals and enterprises can weigh for themselves the various costs and benefits that affect them. The assumption that third-party observers can make better decisions than the people directly involved has produced many urban fallacies and many economic and social disasters. The belief that third parties with no stake in the outcome are empowered, morally as well as politically, to override the decisions of those who do have a stake in the outcome has been institutionalized in "city planning" studies at universities, in "smart-growth" laws and policies, and in various crusading movements to stop "urban sprawl" or to cure neighborhood "blight"— as third parties choose to define these terms.

Slums and Crime

One of the oldest urban fallacies was at one time summarized in the phrase, "slums are nurseries of crime." Physically run-down neighborhoods have often had much higher crime rates than neighborhoods where more affluent people have had newer and more upscale housing. However, as statisticians have long pointed out, correlation is not causation. Moreover, even where causation is involved, that does not determine the *direction* of causation. Do bad physical surroundings promote bad behavior or does bad behavior cause physical surroundings to deteriorate and prevent people from earning higher incomes that would enable them to live in better surroundings?

For well over a century, the prevailing view behind much government policy has been that bad physical surroundings promote crime and other activities detrimental to society and to the individuals who engage in these activities. From this belief have followed massive and costly government programs to demolish slums or "blighted" areas and to relocate individuals from those areas into either newly built government housing projects or to scatter individuals and families from bad neighborhoods into good neighborhoods.

Whatever the merits of the belief in the causal role of physical surroundings as a hypothesis to be tested empirically, its role in the real world has not been that of a hypothesis, but rather of a belief seldom tested against facts and even resistant to facts. In Jane Jacobs' classic book on urban life, *The Death and Life of Great American Cities*, she recalled visiting a Boston working class neighborhood called the North End and then discussing it with a city planner she knew. The North End had been settled by poor Italian immigrants and, like many neighborhoods inhabited by people struggling to get started, it was initially very crowded and rundown. Over time, however, as these Italian Americans and their offspring began to find their way in the American economy and society, the neighborhood changed for the better, as many people were able to afford to move out, relieving the crowding, and those who remained behind began to upgrade their homes by remodeling and adding new amenities. Third party observers, however, could not see those improvements that took place behind the walls of these people's homes, much less the improvements in the people themselves as they adjusted to American life and norms.

When Jane Jacobs phoned a city planner friend and told him of her excursion into the North End, he asked: "Why in the world are you down in the North End?" He declared: "That's a slum!" Then followed this exchange between them:

> "It doesn't seem like a slum to me, " I said.
> "Why, that's the worst slum in the city. It has two hundred and seventy-five dwelling units to the net acre! I hate to admit we have anything like that in Boston, but it's a fact."

"Do you have any other figures on it?" I asked.

"Yes, funny thing. It has among the lowest delinquency, disease and infant mortality rates in the city. It also has the lowest ratio of rent to income in the city. Boy, are those people getting bargains. Let's see. . .the child population is just about average for the city, on the nose. The death rate is low, 8.8 per thousand, against the average city rate of 11.2. The TB death rate is very low, less than 1 per ten thousand, can't understand it, it's lower even than Brookline's. In the old days the North End used to be the city's worst spot for tuberculosis, but all that has changed. Well, they must be strong people. Of course it's a terrible slum."

"You should have more slums like this," I said.[64]

In short, the hard facts contradicted the assumptions of this city planner and of city planners in general. Yet his only response was to regard these facts as isolated anomalies, something "funny," something he "can't understand," as compared to housing statistics that he used to define a slum. Like many other educated professionals, he was unlikely to consider the possibility that these less educated, working class people had achieved something that was both worthwhile and a contradiction of the prevailing doctrines among city planners and other professionals. To the powers that be, the North End was simply a slum and one that needed to be demolished.

Boston is not the only place where physical appearances can be very misleading as to the human reality. The same has been true in San Francisco:

> During the 1960s, one neighborhood in San Francisco had the lowest income, the highest unemployment rate, the highest proportion of families with incomes under $4,000 per year, the least educational attainment, the highest tuberculosis rate, and the highest proportion of substandard housing of any area of the city. That neighborhood was called Chinatown. Yet in 1965, there were only five persons of Chinese ancestry committed to prison in the entire state of California.[65]

Nevertheless, the idea that housing conditions cause social pathology has survived for generations. It appeared on the national level as far back as the administration of Herbert Hoover and was developed further during the subsequent New Deal administration of Franklin D. Roosevelt, as Jane Jacobs pointed out:

> Herbert Hoover had opened the first White House Conference on Housing with a polemic against the moral inferiority of cities and a panegyric on the moral virtues of simple cottages, small towns and grass.

At an opposite political pole, Rexford G. Tugwell, the federal administrator responsible for the New Deal's Green Belt demonstration suburbs, explained, "My idea is to go just outside centers of population, pick up cheap land, build a whole community and entice people into it. Then go back into the cities and tear down whole slums and make parks of them."[66]

The demolition of any neighborhood will of course destroy not only the physical structures of that neighborhood but also the human relationships that make it a viable community, as its inhabitants are scattered to the winds.

The idea that third-party observers have both the right and the duty to arrange other people's living conditions differently from the way that those people have arranged these conditions themselves was not even peculiar to the United States. Various European countries have carried this belief even farther. What made such massive government rearrangements of people's homes and lives possible in the United States, despite the Constitution's protection of private property, was the power of eminent domain, granted by the Constitution to allow private property to be taken for "public use" by the government, presumably for such things as building reservoirs, bridges, or highways. Even so, the government was supposed to pay "just compensation" for the property seized. However, expansive judicial interpretations of such Constitutional provisions in more recent times have given increasing leeway to government officials to seize private property for an ever wider range of reasons, including "urban redevelopment."

Requirements for "just compensation" to property owners when their property is seized by government are by no means always honored. Appraisers hired by government officials obviously have a conflict of interest when they know that making high or low appraisals can affect whether they will be hired again in the future.* Even with honest and objective appraisals, the very fact that the government has threatened to use its power of eminent domain to destroy and "redevelop" a given area means that the market value

---

* The same is true of firms hired to assess the existence and extent of "blight" in an area to be redeveloped. Columbia University, for example, paid more than $180,000 for a study of an area it planned to take over for "redevelopment." In this case, later research by others uncovered the fact that almost all of the properties designated as "blighted" were owned by Columbia University itself. See Jonathan V. Last, "Columbia University, Slumlord," *The Weekly Standard*, December 8, 2008, pp. 18–26.

of properties in that area is likely to fall, perhaps drastically. Prospective home buyers are less willing to buy in neighborhoods that are scheduled to be torn down. Banks become less willing to lend to homeowners or businesses in that area, so even if the area was not blighted before, the unavailability of loans to maintain or upgrade local homes and businesses means that these homes and businesses can be expected to deteriorate faster than usual during the years that can pass between the time when "redevelopment" plans are announced and the time when the threat of demolition through eminent domain hanging over them is eventually carried out.

More fundamentally, however, what the government compensates for is the value of what they take, not the value of what the property owner has lost. When the owners of small businesses like restaurants, barbershops, or hardware stores own a building where these businesses are carried on, they have typically invested not only in acquiring a building but also have invested years of effort in developing reputations and contacts that continue to build their clientele. Moreover, their clientele may over the years become far more valuable than their building. Yet when the government decides to level that part of town and replace existing homes and businesses with some new redevelopment, it compensates the owners of these businesses only for the value of the physical structure, not for the often much larger value of the loss of their clientele, who are now scattered to the winds by mass evictions.

Property owners are not the only people who lose when forcibly displaced to make room for redevelopment, and financial losses are not the only losses. For example, a study of people who had been displaced from a close-knit community in Boston found about half of them disturbed or depressed.[67] While many of them found better housing elsewhere, 86 percent of them paid higher rents than before they had been forced out of their former neighborhood.[68] These particular displaced people were white. Other studies show even higher proportions of displaced blacks suffering the same emotional reactions and even higher proportions of their incomes now being required to pay rent in their new homes. For displaced people in general, one study concluded that the "the average uncompensated loss which each is compelled to suffer amounts to the confiscation of from 20 to 30 per cent of one year's income."[69]

The rationale for transferring people and resources is that what ends up being built is more valuable than what was torn down. If this is true, then it should be possible to completely compensate the losers for their losses and yet have enough left over for the new users to be better off as well. But, if the compensation paid to the losers covers only a part of their losses, then government redevelopment plans which create more losses than benefits are still viable, both economically and politically, because they are heavily subsidized by the unwilling victims of eminent domain. Put differently, those who plan and carry out such redirection of resources and people have incentives to exercise their authority far beyond the point where there is any net benefit to society.

Many of the costs of these disruptions of communities would be difficult to tabulate for compensation, even if the authorities wished to do so, since it is difficult to put a price tag on disrupted human relations, which can include an increased susceptibility of crime when informal community constraints are lost as the people are scattered. Perhaps the clearest indication of these costs are the prices that would have to be paid to get people to voluntarily relinquish their homes and businesses, instead of having them seized by government through the power of eminent domain.

Behind much of this governmental activity to redirect people and resources is the implicit assumption that social problems in general and crime in particular will be reduced by removing people from bad physical surroundings to the kind of physical surroundings that third parties consider better. That assumption need not be tested by planners, politicians, bureaucrats, or judges, because seldom will any of these have to pay any price for being wrong. Nor are they likely to have the kind of intimate knowledge of the lives, values and behavior patterns of the very different people whom they are moving about like pieces on a chess board to carry out some grand design. Given the incentives and constraints at work, it can hardly be surprising that attempts at reducing crime by destroying slums have so often proved not only futile but even counterproductive.

Time and again, moving slum dwellers into brand new public housing projects has only created new centers of crime in those projects, with the new buildings rapidly deteriorating into new slums. Widely praised designs for projects, like the Pruitt-Igoe projects in St. Louis, have ended up such abject failures in practice that they have had to be dynamited. By 2002, Philadelphia had blown up twenty high-rise public housing projects. Chicago blew up twenty-eight 16-story buildings, containing more than 4,000 apartments.[70] But, while such projects have been demolished, the assumptions behind those projects have not been demolished. They continue on in still more schemes based on similar assumptions, such as housing vouchers to enable slum dwellers to go live in middle class communities— in utter disregard of the years of sacrifice that the people in those middle class communities may have made, precisely in order to be able to afford to go live away from the hoodlums and criminals now being placed in their midst by government programs. The Chicago area has been typical:

> In south suburban Chicago, with one of the highest concentrations of voucher holders in the country, middle-class African-American residents complain that they thought they'd left the ghetto behind— only to find that the federal government is subsidizing it to follow them.[71]

Among the consequences have been "the small signs of disorder that have come with voucher tenants," such as lawns that don't get mowed, "shopping carts left in the street," unsupervised children, and boom boxes playing late at night. None of this is peculiar to the Chicago area. Similar complaints about voucher tenants have inundated local officials in cities across the country, from Philadelphia and in suburban communities in Prince George's County, Maryland and Riverdale, Illinois, to the city of Antioch, California. Voucher tenants often "do not pay their utility bills or their required 30 percent share of the rent" in Prince George's County. In Riverdale, a school "once boasting a top academic reputation" has seen its achievement levels drop, refuting "the idea that shipping poor families to good schools in the suburbs will cause an education ethic to rub off."[72] Residents of Antioch "complained of constant problems with gang members' blaring car stereos and under-age drinking on the street."[73]

Similar results followed an unplanned experiment that took place after Hurricane Katrina struck New Orleans in 2005. The city of Houston took in more than 100,000 people who had fled New Orleans in the wake of that hurricane. These were people whose household incomes averaged only about half of the incomes of existing Houston residents, people whose children did less well than other children in Houston's schools, and people from a city whose murder rate was almost four times that in Houston. Their transfer to Houston was followed by a sharp increase in Houston's crime rate, especially murder.[74]

Whether moving people into government housing projects, giving them vouchers to subsidize their living in middle-class neighborhoods, or moving large numbers of them from one city to another, the evidence is clear that changing people's location does not change their behavior. Yet the implicit assumption that it does continues to dominate social thought and government policy, both shaped by people who seldom live in the places to which problem people are moved and who pay no price for being wrong. On the contrary, what would cost them dearly, in both personal and career terms, would be admitting that they were wrong, that they had disrupted thousands of lives and wasted billions of taxpayer dollars.

"Urban Sprawl"

From the second half of the twentieth century onward, a variety of programs created by planners and social reformers has sought to limit the housing choices of people across a broad socioeconomic spectrum. While many of these programs have artificially limited the housing choices of low-income people through building restrictions that raise housing costs, other programs have targeted more prosperous people who have moved out of the cities and into the suburbs, creating what has been called "urban sprawl." The definition of this term has been elusive but the fervor of the attack on it has been unmistakable. Sometimes these attacks have been aesthetic, sometimes economic, and sometimes social.

One of the leading critics of urban sprawl, Lewis Mumford, said:

> Circle over London, Berlin, New York, or Chicago in an airplane, or view the cities schematically by means of an urban map and block plan. What is the shape of the city and how does it define itself?[75]

Like many other critics, he deplored the "sprawl and shapelessness" of cities *as seen from overhead.* In other words, the aesthetic criticism of much suburban development has been that it does not look attractive to third parties flying over it. But obviously such development would not have taken place and grown if it were not attractive to those on the ground who moved into such places. The underlying basis for the criticisms rests on a presumption of better aesthetic taste on the part of third party observers, as compared to the taste of ground-level inhabitants. This presumption is often explicit and has been part of the criticism of urban expansion into the surrounding countrysides for more than a century.

Modern critics blame the automobile for suburbanization or "sprawl," just as in the nineteenth century the Duke of Wellington blamed the newly created railroads for encouraging "the common people to move about needlessly." Obviously the "common people" themselves would not have moved if they had considered it needless. But implicit in the duke's criticism is that third-party elites know better than those making their own decisions at their own expense. "Taste is utterly debased," according to another British critic who deplored those who were said to be "destroying" the countryside in 1932.[76] A similar aesthetic theme was sounded later in the twentieth century by American folk singer Pete Seeger, who sang of suburban development houses, such as those in Daly City, California, as "ticky tacky" boxes, "little boxes all the same."[77]

Obviously such developments would not exist if those who bought these homes did not find the lower prices made possible by mass production of identical houses more important than the lack of differentiation. People with different tastes and priorities remained free to live elsewhere in more distinctive and more expensive housing. Moreover, the much disdained "ticky tacky" boxes may well have been a step upward for many of those who moved into them from crowded urban apartment buildings. It is doubtful whether many people moved to Daly City from Beverly Hills or to Levittown from Park Avenue. The aesthetic criticism of suburban "sprawl" has been only one of many criticisms but it has remained central and enduring and, since it is subjective, it cannot be refuted by any objective facts, as other claims against "urban sprawl" can be.

It is not only the quality of particular housing in itself but also the apparently chaotic expansion of urban communities as a whole which has been criticized. However, the fact that observers with an overhead view of a community do not see a pattern does not mean that there is no pattern relevant to the desires of the people living in those suburban communities— suburbanites who are, after all, not living their lives for the purpose of presenting a tableau pleasing to third parties.

"Planned" communities— whether planned by governments or by private builders under the direction or constraints of government planning commissions— may better meet the preconceptions of observers without necessarily serving the functional purposes desired by most people. One of the internationally renowned planned communities— Vällingby in Sweden— remains the exception, rather than the rule, even in Sweden, where most people choose to live in communities very much like "unplanned" communities deplored by critics in the United States and in other countries. As one study notes: "With its freeways, shopping centers, and big-box Ikea stores, much of suburban Stockholm looks more like suburban America than like Vällingby."[78]

What is called "smart-growth" in some places is government imposition of the preferences of observers, critics, activists, or "experts" to over-ride the desires of the people themselves, as expressed in what they are willing to spend their own money to buy or rent. Although the term "smart-growth" is new, the concept itself is not. The first Queen Elizabeth issued an edict in the sixteenth century forbidding building around the city of London. Centuries later, an elaborate Greater London Plan of 1944 and other plans to control growth likewise imposed radical changes in land use law but in the end still failed to stop urban sprawl around London.

It is as misleading to speak of "planned" and "unplanned" communities as it is to speak of planned versus unplanned economies. In both cases, individuals and enterprises making decisions independently of government officials do not behave randomly or chaotically but plan just as much as any planning commission. What government planning means in practice is the suppression of individual plans and the imposition of a politically or bureaucratically determined collective plan instead. The history of centrally planned economies, most of which were increasingly superseded by more market-oriented economies by the late twentieth century— even in countries controlled by socialists and communists— suggests that what seems more plausible to observers does not necessarily produce end results desired by most people. "Unplanned" communities, like "unplanned" economies, must be guided by the desires of people at large, in order to earn their money, whether or not those desires are understood or approved by third party observers.

Specific factual claims by critics of "urban sprawl," as distinguished from their aesthetic or other presumptions, can be subjected to the test of evidence. Among these claims is that laws limiting growth are necessary in order to preserve fast-disappearing open space from being paved over. But, as noted earlier, only about 5 percent of the land in the United States has been developed. In other words, if every city and town in America doubled in size— which could take generations— that would still leave 90 percent of the land undeveloped. Some of the most alarming claims and urgent demands for more "open space" preservation laws and policies have been made in places where much, if not most, of the land is already open space on which nothing is allowed to be built.

In 2006, for example, various conservation groups in the San Francisco Bay Area advocated setting aside an additional one million acres as open space on which building would be forbidden by law— even though, as the *San Francisco Chronicle* reported, "the Bay Area enjoys what is likely the most open space of any metropolitan area in the world."[79] Of the 4.5 million acres in the San Francisco Bay Area, only 720,000 acres were developed— which is to say, five-sixths of the land remained undeveloped, despite rhetoric which might suggest that open-space advocates were trying to save the last few patches of greenery from being paved over. More than a million acres were already legally off-limits to building anything.

Nevertheless, despite a growing population and some of the highest housing prices in the nation, a coalition of conservation groups advocated putting another million acres of land off-limits to building, which would virtually guarantee a further escalation of housing prices in an area where it was not uncommon for half of the average new home buyer's income to be going for housing.

The question here is not whether open space is desirable but whether an open-ended commitment to ever more open space— or anything else— is desirable. It is especially important to weigh costs against benefits when there is crusading zeal and heady rhetoric in favor of something that virtually everyone regards as desirable, because crusaders seldom pause to do cost-benefit analysis.

A related claim, made not only in the United States but in other countries, is that agricultural land must be preserved. Such claims are common even in countries where agricultural surpluses have been chronic and costly problems for generations, such as the United States and countries of the European Union. The American government in fact pays farmers billions of dollars to take farm land out of production, in order to try to keep agricultural surpluses from being even larger and more costly than they are.

The fact that so many farmers are abandoning farming, and that so much agricultural land is available for building residential communities, ought to be decisive evidence against those who raise alarms about the dangers of "losing" farmland. Indeed, the very need to pass laws to prevent this land conversion from taking place contradicts the rationale used to justify such laws. But, here again, what seems plausible to third-party observers whose views are promoted among the intelligentsia and echoed in the media can be politically decisive, despite the desires of far more numerous other people directly involved, whose desires as tenants or home owners can be thwarted by laws based on beliefs in more elite circles and whose economic consequences are not widely understood.

Claims of environmental pollution created by the spread of suburbanization are also among the claims that can be scrutinized in the light of empirical evidence. It is certainly true that places where there are people tend to generate more air pollution from burning fuels, as well as pollution from sewage and other waste products, as compared to the pollution generated in open, uninhabited countrysides. But it is people— not their location— which both generate pollution and use up natural resources.

When half the people in a city relocate to the countryside, half the pollution may go with them but, if so, that can mean that there is only half as much pollution back where they left. The case that there is a *net* increase in either the total pollution or the total use of natural resources from a relocation of people is one that would have to be made explicitly and supported empirically, not insinuated by showing that pollution and resource use are greater in occupied places than in unoccupied places. Moreover, the farmland that many are anxious to preserve generates pollution of ground water from the run-off of chemicals used in growing crops and pollution of the air from the use of insecticides and fertilizers.

It is often assumed that suburbanization means an increased use of automobiles and therefore an increased use of fuels, resulting in an increased pollution of the air. That would be virtually axiomatic if suburbanites all commuted to jobs in the central cities. But "urban sprawl" includes the movement of jobs as well as people out of the central cities. Moreover, this is not a new pattern but one seen generations ago. At the beginning of the twentieth century, one-third of all manufacturing jobs in the United States were located outside the central cities and, by mid-century, half of these jobs were located outside the central cities. Similarly, as the population of London spread out into the suburbs back in the 1920s, commuting to work from one part of the suburbs to another became as common as commuting from the suburbs into London. In 2008, *The Economist* reported a Brookings Institution study which "calculates that 45% of the jobs in America's 100 biggest metropolitan areas are found more than ten miles from the downtown core."[80]

Similar patterns have been found in Hamburg and other northern European cities, to a greater extent than in southern European cities. Many American cities showed a pattern similar to that of London:

> In North American urban areas the movement outward in the 1920s was even more of a mass movement than in Europe. The expansion and intensification of retail and office uses in the old downtowns led to a sharp decrease in the number of people who lived at the center of cities. In this trend, American cities followed the process long visible in the city of London in which the downtowns came to be intensely crowded during the workday and relatively deserted at night and weekends...

Unprecedented levels of affluence, excellent public transportation, and rising automobile ownership allowed a large portion of the American urban population, including even a substantial percentage of blue-collar families, to have the option of living in single-family detached houses in the suburbs. Much of this housing was developed in small subdivisions by thousands of small-scale real estate developers. In the 1920s, hundreds of square miles of houses sprang up seemingly overnight. . . Although few middle-class American suburban parents today would consider a 1,000-square foot bungalow an ideal place to raise a large family, for many families at that time a small single-family house where they could live under their own roof and enjoy their own yard represented a real revolution in expectations.[81]

In general, whether or not suburbanization today leads to more commuting to work by car or not is an empirical question, not a foregone conclusion, and the answer can vary from one place to another. The fact that air quality has been improving in many places during the era of suburbanization suggests that there is no iron law that "urban sprawl" means more pollution. Nor does preserving open space necessarily reduce pollution.

When preserving open space drives up housing prices, that can increase the amount of driving (and the resulting air pollution) by people who work in communities where they cannot afford to live. While some jobs can move out of the city with the people, some other jobs cannot. Firemen must be in the city to put out fires in the city, as policemen must be in the city to deal with urban crime,* teachers to teach urban children, and nurses to tend to people sick or injured in the city. Most people in these particular occupations cannot afford to live in those cities where housing prices have been driven up to extremely high levels by land-use restrictions designed to prevent "urban sprawl," and so must commute from whatever distance is required for them to find housing that they can afford. In short, it cannot be

---

* The sheriff's department in Redwood City, California, has leased a house, so that its deputies will have a place to sleep after they have worked long hours of overtime. That is because these deputies typically live so far from Redwood City that it would be dangerous for them to drive home tired at night after having worked overtime on some local law enforcement problem. Various schemes for providing "affordable housing" for teachers have surfaced in a number of communities on the San Francisco peninsula, though these schemes seldom go beyond token numbers of housing units, for the same reasons that "affordable housing" through subsidies are seldom adequate for dealing with the housing problems of other groups.

assumed that such land-use restrictions, on net balance, reduce either highway congestion or air pollution.

SUMMARY AND IMPLICATIONS

Over thousands of years and in countries around the world, cities have been concentrations not only of people but also of industrial, commercial, cultural and artistic enterprises. Indeed, it is these enterprises that have drawn people to the cities. Moreover, cities have been in the vanguard of many different civilizations, the places where new ways of doing things are developed and spread out into the provinces and the countrysides. Because so many cities are ports, whether on rivers or harbors, they import not only goods but also new ideas and new technologies, which they can then diffuse into the hinterlands. Like everything human, cities are imperfect and their benefits have costs— something accepted matter of factly by most people but, among some, a reason for laments, crusades and, sometimes worst of all, "solutions."

The title of Edward Banfield's classic, *The Unheavenly City*, reminded us that cities have never been perfect. The book itself showed that many current urban issues are not new, nor are the new proposals for government interventions likely to make things better, rather than worse. There are many complex empirical questions revolving around urban communities and the dispersal of urban populations, and there have been many studies analyzing these questions, with some of these studies contradicting others. But much of what is said about such things as "urban sprawl" is based not on empirical evidence but on echoes of the Duke of Wellington's view that there is a "needless" movement of "common people" to places where more upscale people want them kept out.

It is very doubtful if the effort to keep them out could succeed politically if presented openly in terms of what is actually being done, rather than enveloped in a fog of lofty and idealistic-sounding rhetoric. Few votes would be likely to be won by saying that the government should devote billions of dollars' worth of land to providing a vast buffer zone around a community of affluent and wealthy individuals, in order to keep out ordinary people and preserve the vistas of a relative handful of upscale people at other people's expense. Instead, political rhetoric focusses on celebrating a particular way of life in that community or "saving" greenery or animal habitat, as if both were in grave danger of disappearing in a country where more than nine-tenths of the land is undeveloped. The benefits of a particular way of living are not at issue. The only issue is who should pay for those benefits. If those enjoying such benefits are unwilling to pay for them, why should the taxpayers or people seeking an affordable place to live be forced to subsidize those who are economically better off than themselves?

Politically, few people today can speak as plainly as the Duke of Wellington did in the nineteenth century. More modern objections to suburbanization include the view that the results don't look neat from airplanes. Those whose sensibilities are offended by what they see out of airplane windows can of course close the shades. But some prefer instead to disrupt the lives of millions of people on the ground.

Chapter 3

MALE-FEMALE FACTS
AND FALLACIES

In most societies, for most of history, women have earned lower incomes than men. That fact is not in dispute. What is open to question— and what has generated many fallacies— have been various attempts to explain this fact.

Plausible possibilities are many: Employers might discriminate against women, parents might raise girls and boys differently, women and men might have different skills or make different choices in education or careers. These and other possibilities are often collapsed into one prevailing conclusion: When and where there are significant differences between women and men in their employment, pay, or promotion, discrimination can be inferred and, where there has been a lessening of such disparities over time, it has been due to a lessening of discrimination under the pressures of government, the feminist movement or a general increase in enlightenment.

Such reasoning has been common from the media to the political arena to courts of law. But this explanation cannot withstand a scrutiny of history or of economics. It is one of the central fallacies of our time.

HISTORY

There is no question that the sexes have often been treated differently from childhood on. In some societies, girls have not been educated as often or to the same extent as boys, so that in such societies women on average are less qualified to hold jobs requiring education. Such societies in effect throw away much of the economic and other potential of half their population.

59

Such discrimination on the part of those controlling the education of children obviously produces income differences between adult females and adult males— even if employers do not discriminate among comparable workers— because women and men end up with different levels and kinds of knowledge, skills and work experience.

Few societies today have such severe restrictions on the education of girls, at least not in the Western world. But whether, or to what degree, employer discrimination exists or can explain much of the male-female income differences is a question rather than a foregone conclusion because, for whatever reasons, differences in job qualifications between women and men have often been demonstrable and substantial. Moreover, these differences have changed over time, so that a lessening of income disparities between the sexes cannot be automatically attributed to a lessening of employer discrimination when it may also be due to a lessening of differences in education, job experience, or availability to work outside the home. These are all questions that require empirical evidence rather than blanket assumptions.

Even in the twenty-first century, "two-thirds of the world's illiterate adults are women," according to *The Economist* magazine. However, at the other end of the educational spectrum, women in the most industrially advanced countries are going on to higher education in numbers comparable to men— and, in some countries, more often than men. In Japan there are 90 women enrolled in higher education for every 100 men, in the United States 140 women for every 100 men and, in Sweden, 150 women for every 100 men.[1] Nor is such predominance of women purely quantitative. In 2006, the *New York Times* reported, "at elite institutions like Harvard, small liberal arts colleges like Dickinson, huge public universities like the University of Wisconsin and U.C.L.A. and smaller ones like Florida Atlantic University, women are walking off with a disproportionate share of the honors degrees."[2] But these are developments in relatively recent times.

Among the other factors in differences between male and female incomes have been differences between women and men in physical strength, a factor once very important during the long eras of history when most people in most countries worked in agriculture or in other occupations requiring much physical strength, such as mining, shipping or metallurgy. The replacement of human muscle by machine power in our own times has so reduced the importance of physical strength that it may be difficult today to imagine how important that factor was in centuries past. For example, at one time desperately poor people in China, living on the edge of starvation, often killed newborn baby girls because only boys were likely to grow strong enough, soon enough, to produce enough food to sustain themselves, and the poorest families had little or no surplus food with which to supplement what a girl could produce with primitive implements on small farms. For such desperately poor people, baby girls were often seen as a threat to the physical survival of the family. Higher levels of economic development in other countries, and in China in later times, made such anguished and brutal acts no longer necessary.

The replacement of human muscle by machine power, and the growing importance of industries and occupations not dependent on either, have made sex differences and age differences no longer as significant as they had once been. The economic consequences could be seen in the rising age at which people reached their peak earnings, now that experience and skill were more important than physical strength. Other economic consequences included reductions in male-female pay differentials, even before laws were passed mandating equal pay for equal work.

Another physical difference between women and men, child-bearing, has continued to have major economic consequences. Mothers as a group tend to fall furthest behind men in income, as competing domestic responsibilities reduce the ability of women with babies and small children to be able to maintain continuous, full-time employment in the workforce. This factor is especially important when it comes to high levels of achievement in the most demanding professions:

> In the arts and sciences, forty is the mean age at which peak accomplishment occurs, preceded by years of intense effort mastering the discipline in question. These are precisely the years during which most women must bear children if they are to bear them at all.[3]

While the relative weights of these and other factors in male-female economic differences cannot be pin-pointed, nevertheless there is empirical data that are suggestive, even if not definitive.

History is important in testing prevailing beliefs about male-female occupational and income differences in another way. It is widely believed that the rise of American women, for example, in professional and other high-level occupations since the 1960s has been due to anti-discrimination laws and policies imposed by government, and that these in turn have been due to more enlightened views of women by society at large promoted by the feminist movement and others. Plausible as this might seem, whenever a causal relationship is asserted between any variables, it should be possible to test whether these things in fact vary with one another with any consistency or whether they vary with other factors that have been left out of the equation.

Declines in Higher Education and Professional Occupations

History shows that the career paths of women over the course of the twentieth century bore little resemblance to a scenario in which variations in employer discrimination explain variations in women's career progress.

In reality, the proportion of women in the professions and other high-level positions was greater during the first decades of the twentieth century than in the middle of the twentieth century— and all of this was before either anti-discrimination laws or the rise of the feminist movement. For example, the proportion of women among the people listed in *Who's Who in America* in 1902 was more than double the proportion in 1958.[4] A study published in 1964 concluded: "The period of the first two decades of the twentieth century was the heyday of academic women." The trend of women as a percentage of academics was "up from 1910 to about 1930 and down thereafter, with a possible upward trend in recent years," according to the same 1964 study.[5]

Hard data substantiate this pattern. In 1921 and again in 1932, the proportion of women among people receiving doctoral degrees was about 17 percent but this was down to 10 percent by the late 1950s and early 1960s. This general pattern was common across a number of fields. In the biological sciences, women received from about one-fifth to one-fourth of the doctorates in the 1930s but only one-eighth by the late 1950s. In economics, women's share of doctorates declined from 10 percent to 2 percent. There were similar declines in women's shares of the doctoral degrees awarded in the humanities, chemistry, and law.[6] A 1961 study of women's share of college faculty positions found that to be lower than it was in 1930.[7]

Declines in the representation of women among academic faculty during this era occurred even at women's colleges, run by women, such as Smith, Wellesley, Vassar, and Bryn Mawr,[8] so this trend could hardly be attributed to increased male employer discrimination against women. But even if we were to assume for the sake of argument that employer discrimination against women was the crucial factor, such widespread negative trends for women in higher occupational levels over a period of decades are hardly consistent with the idea that employer discrimination against women declines over time with enlightenment. A closer scrutiny of facts suggests that what changed over these decades was not employer discrimination but women's marriage and child-bearing patterns. This in turn raises questions as to whether later positive trends in the occupational advancement of women reflected changes in employer discrimination or changes in marriage and child-bearing patterns. History strongly suggests the latter.

During the early decades of the twentieth century, when women's representation in higher level occupations and in the postgraduate education required for such occupations was higher than in the 1950s, the median age at which women first married was also higher than at mid-century.[9] Most of the women who staffed women's colleges during this earlier era were not married at all.[10] Neither were most women who taught in elementary and secondary schools, until the late 1940s.[11] As the median age of marriage began to decline, the representation of women in high-level occupations and among recipients of postgraduate degrees also declined.

Rises in Higher Education and Professional Occupations

The decline in women's median age of first marriage ended in 1956 and began to rise thereafter. The birth rate also began to decline, from 1957 on, and by 1966 the birth rate was again as low as it had been back in 1933.[12] Women's share of postgraduate degrees closely followed these reversals of trends in age of marriage and birthrate.

The 1970s saw women's share of doctoral degrees rise. By 1972 that share was again as high as it had been back in 1932. It was much the same story with Master's degrees, where it was 1972 before women's share of these degrees reached the level of 1930, except for the World War II years when millions of young men were away in the military. With both Master's degrees and doctorates, women's share declined precipitously after the war to levels below those of the 1930s.[13] These were of course the years of the "baby boom," indicating again the role of child-bearing in limiting women's educational and career prospects.

Women's rise in higher-level occupations in the second half of the twentieth century continued to follow the rise in their age of marriage, which rose sharply and finished the century significantly higher than it was at the beginning,[14] while the birth rate fell sharply and was much lower at the end of the century than it was at the beginning.[15] As the age of first marriage climbed to record high levels, women rose to record high levels in higher education and higher occupations. Women's percentage of postgraduate professional degrees in general, master's degrees in business in particular, law degrees, medical degrees, and Ph.D.s all skyrocketed from the 1970s on.[16]

It was not just in higher-level occupations that women's changing marriage and child-bearing patterns were reflected in their work patterns. The gap between men's and women's participation in the labor force in general narrowed dramatically. In 1950, 94 percent of men but only 33 percent of women were in the labor force. This gap of 61 percentage points narrowed to 45 percentage points by 1970. At the end of the century, the gap was only 12 percentage points, as 86 percent of men and 74 percent of women were in the labor force.[17] In addition to entering the labor force in general, more women also entered occupations where men were previously predominant, especially those occupations requiring a college degree.[18] The continuity of women's employment also increased after 1970, though the gap between the continuity of men's and women's employment did not disappear and women continued to work part-time more so than men.[19]

These positive changes in the second half of the twentieth century, as well as the negative changes during the earlier decades of that century, all follow remarkably closely changes in women's age of marriage and child-bearing.

Male-female differences in income did not disappear completely, however. How much of those remaining differences can be attributed to employer discrimination, rather than to different career choices or differences in choices as to whether to work full-time, is another empirical question, one involving economics as well as history.

ECONOMICS

Ideally, we would like to be able to compare those women and men who are truly comparable in education, skills, experience, continuity of employment, and full-time or part-time work, among other variables, and then determine whether employers hire, pay, and promote women the same as they do comparable men. At the very least, we might then see in whatever differences in hiring, pay and promotions might exist a measure of how much employer discrimination exists. Given the absence or imperfections of data on some of these variables, the most that we can reasonably expect is some measure of whatever residual economic differences between women and men remain after taking into account those variables which can be measured with some degree of accuracy and reliability. That residual would then give us the upper limit of the combined effect of employer discrimination plus whatever unspecified or unmeasured variables might also exist. However, even if we were to find zero economic differences between those women and men who were truly comparable, that would not mean that women and men as a whole had the same income or the same likelihood of being hired or promoted, if the sexes as a whole were distributed differently between full-time and part-time employment or in different fields or levels of education or in other ways that affect people's economic prospects. In short, even an absence of discrimination would not mean an absence of male-female economic differences.

Occupational Differences

Even when women and men earn the same incomes in the same occupations, differences in the distribution of the sexes among different occupations lead to differences in their average incomes. The distribution of women and men in various occupations has long differed, partly due to restrictions placed on women and partly due to choices made by women themselves.

In times and places where women have been restricted from working outside the home, this limitation on the range of occupations open to women has in effect also been a limitation on their earnings prospects— again, even without whatever employer discrimination might or might not exist. Put differently, how much of male-female differences in income has been due to employer discrimination and how much to other differences arising from social restrictions or other factors is a question rather than a foregone conclusion. Many social restrictions, especially in the past, have been based on attempts to forestall problems growing out of the attraction of the sexes for one another.

In times, places, and social classes where a young woman's chastity was a prerequisite for favorable marriage prospects, her parents were often very concerned that she be kept from work environments or other environments where she would have unsupervised contact with young men, in order to avoid even the appearance of an unchaste life, much less the temptations that could result in an unwed pregnancy that could ruin her life and disgrace the family.

Work restrictions based on such concerns are inherently asymmetrical, since whatever troubles young men might encounter or create while working outside the home, these did not include anything so visible or with so much social and economic impact as becoming pregnant. In times and places when the cost of supporting an unwed daughter's child fell solely on her own family, the family sought to reduce the risk of this happening by much more severe restrictions on young women's freedom and much more monitoring of whom she associated with and under what conditions. However, during the era when agriculture was the predominant occupation of most people, working at home was less of a restriction than in later times, when more and more jobs were outside the home in industry and commerce.

As more societies became more industrial and commercial, the asymmetrical opportunities of young women and young men to work outside the home meant different income prospects. Even before then, families were more likely to allow young men to go off to work beyond parental supervision as apprentices, sailors, or soldiers.

Women, even when they did non-agricultural work, were more likely to do such work in the home, such as spinning cloth. The word "spinster" for unmarried women survives in the language today from that era. Brewing beer was another job that could be performed in a family enterprise and women who did this work were known as "brewsters," while men were called "brewers," both of these words eventually becoming family names, much as other occupations such as carpenter, weaver, cook, and shepherd also gave rise to family names.

While families had incentives to curtail women's work outside the home, employers had countervailing incentives to try to tap this large potential source of workers. Early New England mill owners, for example, tried to reassure parents of the safety and propriety of letting their daughters work in their businesses by having all-female workforces, often overseen by older women who in effect were chaperons, especially when the young women lived away from home. Even before the industrial era, highly respected and affluent families were likewise able to attract live-in maids, either because the supervision or reputation of these particular families were considered to be some assurance of lower risks of sexual misconduct or because the poorest families needed the daughter's earnings so much as to have little choice but to take chances that other families would not. The sexual molestation of servant girls by their employers, their employers' sons, or male servants, was among these dangers, as was the succumbing to temptation by the girls themselves.

Employers had very different reasons for segregating women from men at work, typically assigning them to different jobs. If an occupation was one that attracted predominantly males, the distraction of a female worker in their midst could adversely affect productivity, even if the woman herself was just as productive as the men. This was analogous to what also happened in times and places where ethnic or other differences among the workers adversely affected productivity on the job, though the distraction in this latter case was often due to animosities between Irish and Italian workers, for example, which interfered with their getting the work done, just as mutual attractions between women and men did.

Thus whole occupations could be off-limits to women simply because it was mostly men who worked in those occupations and the few women who might want to work in such occupations were not considered by employers to be worth the adverse effect which their presence could have on the productivity of the men. Where there were large numbers of women seeking work in these occupations, then the employer had the option of hiring both women and men, and segregating the sexes on the job, though maintaining such separation was not easy.* What was easier was to have either all-male or all-female workforces.

Although physical strength is no longer as major a factor as it once was in the days when agriculture was the largest economic endeavor in most countries, or during the times when heavy industry or mining dominated various countries' economies, there are still particular industries today where considerable physical strength remains a requirement. Women are obviously not as likely to work in such fields as men are— and some of these are fields with jobs that pay more than the national average. While women have been 74 percent of what the U.S. Census Bureau classifies as "clerical and kindred workers," they have been less than 5 percent of "transport equipment operatives." In other words, women are far more likely to be sitting behind a desk than to be sitting behind the steering wheel of an eighteen-wheel truck. Women are also less than 4 percent of the workers in "construction, extraction, and maintenance." They are less than 3 percent of construction

---

* One of the few modern employers who was able to do this successfully was the American Telephone & Telegraph Company, when I worked in their New York headquarters in the 1960s. Even though there were women and men working in the same groups, somehow company policy became known without explicit public pronouncements and they avoided social contacts. How far this went was dramatized for me one day when my wife came over from our nearby apartment and joined me for lunch in a company cafeteria. After looking around this large facility, my wife said: "Do you realize that we are the only man and woman having lunch together in this whole place?" By the time I got back to work that afternoon, word had spread all over the office that I had been seen having lunch with a woman in the company cafeteria!

workers or loggers, less than 2 percent of roofers or masons, and less than one percent of the mechanics and technicians who service heavy vehicles and mobile equipment.[20]

Such occupational distributions have obvious economic implications, since miners earn nearly double the income of office clerks when both work full-time and year-round.[21] There is still a premium paid for workers doing heavy physical work, as well as for hazardous work, which often overlaps work requiring physical strength. While men are 54 percent of the labor force, they are 92 percent of the job-related deaths.[22]

Continuity of Employment

Within the external limitations placed on the range of occupations open to women have been further limitations due to occupational choices made by women themselves. In addition to avoiding occupations requiring more physical strength than most women possess, women have tended to make career choices influenced by the likelihood that they would at some point or other become mothers. Since motherhood has usually entailed a period of withdrawal from full-time work outside the home, the cost of such withdrawal becomes a factor in occupational choices.

Where an occupation is unionized and withdrawal from the workforce means a loss of seniority, reducing the prospects of being promoted or of being retained during lay-offs, such an occupation in effect imposes costs on women that are likely to be greater than the costs imposed on men, as well as greater than in occupations where seniority is not such a factor or is no factor at all. However, even some non-unionized companies may have seniority systems which have the same economic effect, reducing women's earnings prospects more than those of men. Seniority is often also a factor in civil service jobs, likewise reducing women's earnings prospects more than those of men.

Quite aside from formal seniority rules, interruptions of labor force participation, in order to take care of small children until they are old enough to be placed in day care facilities while the mother returns to work outside the home, mean that a woman may have fewer years of job experience than a man of the same age, since such interruptions are less common among men. How much difference that makes in productivity on the job depends on the kind of work being done, so the difference it makes can range from considerable to trivial or non-existent, depending on the particular occupation. Where promotions over time are a normal part of a given career, not only are promotions less likely to come to a woman of a given age who does not have as much job experience as a man of the same age, the prospects of even a woman who has never had any interruption in her career are reduced to the extent that the likelihood of future interruptions because of her prospective role as mother can make placing her in a senior position more of a risk than placing a man of similar ability in that same position.

Interruptions in labor force participation have other costs which fall disproportionately on women. The occupational skills required change over time and at varying rates for different occupations. Rapidly changing computer technology, for example, means that computer engineers and programmers must be constantly upgrading their skills to keep up with advances in their field. Similarly, tax accountants must keep up with changing tax laws, and attorneys must keep up with changes in laws in general, in order to effectively serve their clientele— and therefore continue to have a clientele to serve. To drop out of such fields and then return in a few years after children have gotten old enough to be put into day care facilities can mean having fallen significantly behind developments in these occupations, and therefore having lower earning capacity, whether as an independent practitioner or as an employee of a firm.

Careers involving military combat in a high-tech age are likewise careers that are hard to leave and resume a few years later because weapons technology changes rapidly and continuously, so that a combat pilot or a nuclear submarine officer who returns to active duty after a few years away would find it hard to catch up on technological changes made while he or she was away, while at the same time trying to keep abreast of the continuing changes taking place after returning to active duty.

From the standpoint of a young woman looking ahead when making career choices, the relative rates of obsolescence of given knowledge and skills in a given field become a serious consideration in choosing a field in which to specialize. It has been estimated that a physicist loses half the value of his or her knowledge in four years, while a professor of English would take more than a quarter of a century to lose half the value of the knowledge with which he or she began that career.[23]

Given the asymmetrical effects of career obsolescence on woman and men, it is hardly surprising that women tend to work in fields with lower rates of obsolescence— as teachers and librarians, for example, rather than as computer engineers or tax accountants. Even as the proportion of women receiving Ph.D.s rose dramatically from the 1970s on, male-female differences in the fields of specialization remained large. As of 2005, for example, women received more than 60 percent of the doctorates in education but less than 20 percent of the doctorates in engineering.[24]

Regular and Irregular Work

While many jobs have regular nine-to-five hours, many others require putting in whatever hours happen to be required, whenever and wherever they happen to be required. When a multimillion-dollar lawsuit is in progress or a death penalty case is being appealed, the attorneys involved cannot simply quit work at five o'clock and go home. If the case requires working nights and weekends, then the attorneys have to work nights and weekends, in order to build the strongest case they can before they are scheduled to appear in court.

In principle, it does not matter whether the attorney is male or female but, in practice, with women more often than men carrying the burden of domestic responsibilities for children and the care of the home, careers that involve much unpredictable night and weekend work are less attractive to women. *Having it all*— a career and a family and an upscale lifestyle— is fine but *doing it all* is often harder for a woman, given the usual division of domestic responsibilities between the sexes and the inevitable differences in childbearing. Those young women who think ahead may take this into account in choosing a career, while older professional women have often decided that "having it all" is not worth the toll it exacts.

This may not put a whole profession off-limits but it can restrict the range of work situations within a given profession. Thus women who want to be attorneys may tend to find being a civil service attorney with regular hours to be more attractive than working in a leading high-pressure law firm, where the work week not only averages 60 or 70 hours, but where those hours may have to be worked at whatever unpredictable times the client's case requires. Large law firms with offices in several cities or countries may require an attorney to fly off to some distant place on short notice and stay there for whatever period of time it takes to settle some legal matters at that location.

In principle, this is the same problem for men and women. In practice, however, a mother is more likely to stay home with the children while the father is tied up at the office, or has to fly off someplace to deal with legal emergencies, than a father is to stay home while the mother does the same. Moreover, since men are never pregnant, women are disadvantaged in such work by the physical limitations of pregnancy, which can be work limitations as well in jobs that require long, irregular and unpredictable hours, and sudden trips to distant places, as well as the heightened stress of high-stakes legal cases. A *Harvard Business Review* survey among people whose earnings were in the top 6 percent showed that 62 percent worked more than 50 hours a week and 35 percent worked more than 60 hours a week. Among those who held "extreme" jobs— extreme in both hours and stress— less than one-fifth were women. Moreover, even among those people who held such high-pressure jobs, women were only half as likely as men to say that they wanted to still be working like this five years afterwards.[25]

Such pressures are not confined to business and the law. A noted professor of biology pointed this out in advice to his students:

> I have been presumptuous enough to counsel new Ph.D.'s in biology as follows: If you choose an academic career you will need forty hours a week to perform teaching and administrative duties, another twenty hours on top of that to conduct respectable research, and still another twenty hours to accomplish really important research.[26]

A number of studies have shown that women are far less likely than men to choose occupations that require very long hours.[27] A follow-up study of mathematically gifted youngsters now in their thirties found a higher proportion of women than men working less than 40 hours a week and a higher proportion of men than women working 50 or more hours a week.[28]

In general, men and women alike tend to prefer regular hours and less stressful work, so that jobs with these characteristics can attract both sexes more readily and, because of supply and demand, pay less than similar jobs in more taxing situations. However, to the extent that the less taxing jobs fit in with domestic responsibilities that fall disproportionately on women and so attract women especially, male-female income differences can be considerable even if men and women are paid the same in both the taxing and the non-taxing work environments, if women and men are distributed differently between the different environments within the same profession, as well as being distributed differently among different occupations. *The Economist* magazine observed:

> The main reason why women still get paid less on average than men is not that they are paid less for the same jobs but that they tend not to climb so far up the career ladder, or they choose lower-paid occupations, such as nursing and teaching.[29]

That is confirmed by other studies. Among the jobs where women with college degrees earn at least as much as men are computer engineer, petroleum engineer, and a variety of other engineering occupations, as well as journalist, portfolio manager and medical technologist.[30] But in most of these jobs, especially most engineering jobs, there are fewer women than men. The most important reason why women earn less than men is not that they are paid less for doing the very same work but that they are distributed differently among jobs and have fewer hours and less continuity in the labor force. Among college-educated, never-married individuals with no children who worked full-time and were from 40 to 64 years old— that is, beyond the child-bearing years— men averaged $40,000 a year in income, while women averaged $47,000.[31] But, despite the fact that women in this category earned more than men in the same category, gross income differences in favor of men continue to reflect differences in work patterns between the sexes, so that women and men are not in the same categories to the same extent.

Even women who have graduated from top-level universities like Harvard and Yale have not worked full-time, or worked at all, to the same extent that male graduates of these same institutions have. Among Yale alumni in their forties, "only 56 percent of the women still worked, compared with 90 percent of the men," according to the *New York Times*.[32] It was much the same story at Harvard:

> A 2001 survey of Harvard Business School graduates found that 31 percent of the women from the classes of 1981, 1985 and 1991 who answered the survey worked only part time or on contract, and another 31 percent did not work at all, levels strikingly similar to the percentages of the Yale students interviewed who predicted they would stay at home or work part time in their 30's and 40's.[33]

Those who reach the highest echelons in many industries and professions have typically worked not only long hours but continuously throughout a long career. Even the most highly educated women have often chosen not to do that, with obvious implications for their incomes. While those women are the best judges of what suits their own individual circumstances, priorities, and sense of well-being, third parties looking at statistical data see only the artifacts of disparities based on paychecks. Such income disparities between women and men are equaled or exceeded by disparities among women, between those who work full-time and those who work part-time. The hourly pay of women who work part-time has been found to be 20 percent lower than the hourly pay of women who work full-time, even when comparing women with the same levels of education and the same family circumstances such as being married, divorced, or with dependents.[34]

Even this disparity understates the rate at which part-time and full-time workers are compensated, since part-time workers— whether women or men— are far less often included in employers' health insurance or pension plans. Working part-time also restricts the range of industries and occupations available, since not all work can be done as readily on a part-time basis. Half of all women who work part-time do so in only ten industries out of 236 industries surveyed.[35]

Domestic Responsibilities

In principle, family responsibilities can be divided equally between husband and wife, father and mother. In practice, however, that has not been the norm in most places and in most periods of history. Since economic consequences follow from practices, rather than principles, the asymmetrical division of domestic responsibilities produces male-female differences in incomes in many ways besides those already mentioned. Moreover, statistical records of money payments can be misleading as to economic realities. Family income is pooled income, and how it is spent, for whose benefit, does not depend on whose name is on the paycheck or paychecks, or whether one paycheck is larger than the other. In some families, for example, the largest share of the family income is spent on people who earn no income at all, the children, especially when they are attending expensive colleges.

Who decides how much of family income is spent, where, for what, or for whom, cannot be determined by income statistics based on whose name is on paychecks. According to *The Economist* magazine, "Surveys suggest that women make perhaps 80% of consumers' buying decisions— from health care and homes to furniture and food."[36] A government study in early twenty-first century America showed that the average American family spent 70 percent more on clothing for women and girls than on clothing for men and boys.[37] In some of the most traditional cultures, where male dominance has been most visible, it has not been uncommon for the man to be the sole income-earner and to turn over the bulk of that income to his wife to budget and spend at her discretion. Such practices have been common in Southern Italy in the past and in Japan today, as well as among many traditional working-class American families in times past, even— if not especially— in what have been described as "male-dominated societies."

The earning of that income can also be a joint enterprise, regardless of whose name appears on the paycheck. Time that a bachelor spends shopping, preparing meals or going out to restaurants, taking his clothes to the laundry or dry-cleaners, entertaining guests or arranging dates, is available to many married men to put into advancing their careers instead, because their wives relieve them of such concerns. Given these and other ways in which traditional wives have freed up the time of their husbands, it is hardly surprising that married men have usually earned higher incomes than single men of the same age and education.

Given the incentives created by having children to support, it is likewise not surprising that married men with children have usually earned the highest incomes of all, since higher earnings are more imperative for fathers, whether these additional earnings are obtained by working overtime or by choosing more taxing jobs that pay more. Because the situations of husbands and wives have not been symmetrical in traditional families, it is likewise not surprising that marriage has had *opposite* effects on the incomes of women and men. Women who have never married have higher average incomes than women who have, and women with no children have higher average incomes than women with children.

Another way of looking at this is that the traditional division of family responsibilities has meant that wives have sacrificed their own income-earning potential possibilities and enhanced that of their husbands, with the resulting family income then being jointly spent. In so far as this situation is mutually agreeable and on-going, statistical data based on whose name is on what paycheck are largely irrelevant. However, rising rates of divorce make such data very relevant and such traditional arrangements more problematical.

In effect, the traditional wife has been investing in her husband's career, and a divorce means that the value of that investment— made for years or even decades— can be lost to her. Alimony and child-support payments made after a divorce may or may not recoup the value of that investment. Quite aside from the sacrifice of earnings potential by the wife during the marriage, she has also lost the economic value of work experience, continuity, skills upgrading, and seniority, so that her earning capacity upon re-entering the labor force after a divorce is lower than if she had remained single, while the earning capacity of her former husband is higher than if he had remained single, as a result of her sacrifices.

Those who think in terms of principles, rather than practices, see no reason why ex-husbands are not as much entitled to alimony as ex-wives, at least in cases where the woman has a higher income, a higher earning potential, or a higher level of wealth. However, in terms of practices, what is the ex-husband being compensated for?

EMPLOYER DISCRIMINATION

Equally as important as determining how much discrimination exists is determining where it occurs— and what the economic incentives and constraints are. People who discriminate against girls when it comes to education pay no price for that but employers who discriminate against women workers do. If employers pay a woman only three-quarters as much as they would pay a man for doing the same work with the same skill, this means that those employers who hire an all-female workforce can get four workers for what other employers are paying for three. Smaller production cost differences than that can mean that some companies prosper while some other competing companies go out of business because their high production costs prevent them from selling profitably at competitive prices. Even if discriminatory employers do not think things through this way, the competition of the marketplace will tend to force the higher-cost producers out of business, whether they understand why or not.

Much discussion of employer discrimination against women has focused on employer beliefs or attitudes which could lead to such discrimination. However, as in the case of racial and ethnic minorities, the employer's beliefs or attitudes are not the only factor, nor necessarily the most important factor, in determining what actually happens. The more highly competitive the market for labor and for the employer's products, the higher the cost paid for discrimination and consequently the less leeway the employer has for indulging his prejudices without risking his own profits and ultimately the financial survival of the business. On the other hand, enterprises not subject to the full stress of a competitive market— monopolies, non-profit enterprises, government agencies— have greater leeway. The empirical question of how much employer discrimination there is and how much of the male-female income gap it explains requires comparing comparable people and comparable situations. Simple as that might seem, it is seldom simple in practice.

Where a particular job involves contact with the customers or clientele of an employer, the prejudices or biases of these people outside the firm itself can become incentives for the employer to discriminate, which must then be weighed against the costs of discrimination. In times past, some people had less confidence in the professional ability of a female attorney or doctor, or else just felt more comfortable dealing with men in roles where they were accustomed to dealing with men. In any event, the question before the employer was not whether these feelings were justified but how widespread they were and therefore whether adding a woman would help or hurt a private medical practice or a given law firm, even if the woman were fully as qualified as the men currently employed.

In short, there are economic incentives both for and against discrimination, and the net balance of their effects is an empirical question. So are the effects of other factors. Alternative explanations of male-female differences can be tested against empirical evidence not only for the present but also for the past, especially when considering changing male-female income ratios over time and the changing representation of women in various professions.

Comparability

In order to determine the existence or magnitude of sex discrimination by employers, as distinguished from other sex discrimination which may have occurred in education, or domestic differences between the sexes which affect job choices, we must compare women and men who have similar education, skills, job experience and other relevant characteristics.

Many statistics on male-female income differences do not do this but simply make gross comparisons of women and men in general as groups, either without regard to comparability or with very limited attempts to hold the differing variables constant. Thus a study in Britain found that women as a group earned 17 percent less per hour than men when both worked full-time. However, this same study found that the pay differential was not due to women and men being paid different wages or salaries for doing the same job, but that women took lower-paying jobs more often than men, especially after returning to the labor force after having children. As young beginning workers, British women's incomes were 91 percent of that of British men but, as mothers, their incomes were just 67 percent of that of men who were fathers. Mothers' incomes declined as a percentage of male incomes more or less steadily until about a dozen years after giving birth, when it began to rise again, though never getting back to where it was before a child was born, perhaps indicating the permanent income loss due to interrupted careers.[38] In the United States, a study of graduates of the University of Michigan Law School found a similar pattern:

> The gap in pay between women and men was relatively small at the outset of their careers, but 15 years later, women graduates earned only 60 percent as much as men. Some of this difference reflected choices which workers had made, including the propensity of women lawyers to work shorter hours.[39]

Attempting to control simultaneously for part-time versus full-time employment and for the effect of children and domestic responsibilities, another study found "that the gender pay gap is 5 percent for part-time workers age 21–35 without children, under 3 percent for full-time workers age 21–35 without children, and that *there is no pay gap* for full-time workers age 21–35 living alone."[40] All these gaps represent the upper limit of the effect of employer discrimination *plus* whatever other factors might favor men, such as differences in education and in occupations involving physical strength or dangers. That the income gaps between women and men are so small without even taking these other factors into account suggests that employer discrimination by itself has far less influence on the gross income gaps between the sexes than gross statistics might suggest.

While comparing truly comparable individuals is something that must also be done when trying to determine the existence or effect of discrimination against ethnic or racial groups, achieving similar comparability between women and men is more challenging. That is because, while such factors as education and experience affect different racial or ethnic groups the same way— that is, blacks with more education earn more than blacks with less education, just as among whites, even if not to the same extent— the same factors can have *opposite* effects on women and men: As we have already noted, marriage and parenthood tend to lead to increased incomes for men and reduced incomes for women.

Nor are single women and single men comparable, when "single" people include people who have been married for years, and have then been divorced. That is because the long-term negative economic effects of marriage on women, such as the interruption or even cessation of full-time employment, do not disappear with a change in marital status and re-entering the labor force with less experience than a man of the same age. By the same token, the beneficial economic effects of marriage for men do not disappear completely after a divorce, since past seniority and increased job skills continue to make the man a higher earner than a man who was never married or a woman who was never married.

To get comparability among people of both sexes who have not had their incomes affected by marriage means comparing women and men who were "never married" rather than simply "single." For purposes of separating out the effects of marriage, and the asymmetrical domestic arrangements which marriage often creates, from the effects of employer discrimination, the most comparable women and men are those who were never married. If male-female income gaps remain large among women and men who were never married, then obviously the economic effects of marriage do not explain sex differences in income. But if that differential changes substantially according to marital status and parenthood, then the employer is correspondingly less of a factor in income differences between women and men.

What are the facts?

As already noted, comparing never-married women and men who are past the child-bearing years and who both work full-time in the twenty-first century shows women of this description earning *more* than men of the same description. As far back as 1969, academic women who had never married earned more than academic men who had never married, while married academic women without children earned less and married academic women with children earned still less.[41] For women in general— that is, not just academic women— those single women who had worked continuously since high school were in 1971 earning slightly *more* than men of the same description.[42] All this was *before* affirmative action was defined as "under-representation" in a 1971 Executive Order which went into effect in 1972, and so represents what was happening under competitive labor market pressures before any major government intervention to advance women. Later data for law school graduates in 1994 showed that men's beginning salaries averaged $48,000 and women's beginning salaries averaged $50,000.[43]

Both trends over time and studies of women at given times show the same pattern of a negative correlation between marital responsibilities (including children) and women's educational levels and career advancement. Whether in the earlier or the later era, women who were married and had children lagged furthest behind men in income, career advancement, or even working at all. A study published in 1956 showed that most women with Ph.D.s from Radcliffe were not working full-time and those who were averaged fewer children than those who worked part-time, intermittently, or not at all.[44]

In gross terms— that is, ignoring differences between the sexes in continuous versus discontinuous employment, career choices, or full-time versus part-time employment, etc.— the ratio of female-to-male incomes in the general population remained relatively unchanged at about 60 percent during the decades of the 1960s and 1970s, and then began to rise significantly from the early 1980s, reaching 70 percent in 1990 and 77 percent in 2004.[45] Finer breakdowns of the data to compare women and men of comparable ages, education, and employment histories showed the sexes much closer in earnings. Merely comparing full-time, year-round workers showed women's pay to be 81 percent of men's pay in 2005.[46] Part-time workers not only earn less total pay, they are also paid less per hour and are less likely to be promoted.[47] There have been, and continue to be, more women than men who are part-time workers.[48]

Very substantial income differences between women and men in a particular field can co-exist with little or no income differences between women and men who are comparable within that field. For example, a study published in *The New England Journal of Medicine* found:

> In 1990, young male physicians earned 41 percent more per year than young female physicians. . . . However, after adjusting for differences in specialty, practice setting, and other characteristics, no earnings difference was evident.[49]

The young male physicians in this study worked over 500 hours a year more than the young female physicians.[50]

In general, it makes a difference whether the male-female income gap is compiled on an annual basis, a monthly basis or as per-hour earnings. Since women tend to work fewer hours than men, the largest gap tends to be in annual income and the smallest in per hour pay. For example, the U.S. Department of Labor has reported weekly male-female earnings differences, showing women's earnings to be 76.5 percent of that of men in 1999, for example, but women's hourly earnings were 83.8 percent of that of men that same year. Comparing women and men who were comparable in occupation, industry and other variables, the per-hour difference shrank to 6.2 cents.[51]

While there are factors tending to reduce the male-female income gap over time, there are other factors tending to widen it. For example, as job experience becomes more important in the economy and more highly rewarded, this tends to widen the gap between men's incomes and women's incomes, since women of a given age tend to have less job experience than men of the same age. Shifts in demand from one industry to another and from one occupation to another also affect male-female income gaps, since women and men continue to form different proportions of the workforce in different industries and occupations.[52] Moreover, these proportions have changed over time: Nearly half of female college graduates in 1960 became teachers, while less than 10 percent did so by 1990.[53] The net effect of conflicting trends on male-female earnings differentials makes explanations of their income differences far from easy.

Although the male-female income gap has generally been declining over time since the 1960s, within a given lifetime that gap tends to widen. That is, young women tend to have earnings closer to the earnings of young men than older women's earnings compared to older men. What happens in between is that women's labor force participation rates are affected by domestic, and especially child-rearing, responsibilities. A study in the *American Economic Review* showed:

> In March 2001, at ages 25–44, the prime period for career development, 34 percent of women with children under the age of six were out of the labor force, compared to 16 percent of women without children. Thirty

percent of employed mothers worked part-time, compared to 11 percent of women with no children. Among men, however, the presence of children is associated with an increase in work involvement. Only 4 percent of men with children under the age of six are out of the labor force, and among employed fathers only 2 percent work part-time.[54]

In short, having children has major effects on labor force participation rates— and *opposite* effects on women and men. Although younger women are of course more likely to have children, it is older women whose job qualifications have been most affected by the accumulated differences in job experience from that of men of similar ages. This difference is reflected in the wider male-female earnings gap in the older years. All this is particularly relevant to the notion of a "glass ceiling" restricting how high women are allowed to rise, especially in top management positions. These are positions usually reached after many years of experience. Empirically, the gaps between women and men are huge in both representation among high-level executives and in incomes at the executive levels, but shrink dramatically when comparing women and men of comparable experience, including continuous experience with a given company.

For example, only about 2.4 percent of top-level management positions were filled by women, according to a study in the *Industrial and Labor Relations Review*, and "the gender gap in compensation among top executives was at least 45%." Part of the reason for the compensation gap was that women were more likely to be executives in smaller corporations, whose executives tend to be paid less than executives in the largest corporations— and part of the reason for women being executives in smaller corporations is that this reflects their lesser experience. Taking these and other differences into account shrinks the male-female compensation gap considerably:

> Women in the sample were much younger, and had much less seniority in their company, than men. Part of the effect of age and seniority on the gender gap seems to be reflected in the size of companies women managed. All in all, we find that the unexplained gender compensation gap for top executives was less than 5% after one accounts for all observable differences between men and women.[55]

Despite the complexities revealed by a closer examination of statistical data, lawsuits continue to be filed, claiming discrimination, based on purely numerical differences in the economic situations of women and men. As the *New York Times* reported in 2007:

> In the lawsuit, the lead plaintiff— a former assistant store manager who was upset about not being made a store manager— asserts that Costco discriminated against women in promotions because 13 percent of the company's store managers were women, while nearly half of its employees were women.[56]

This lawsuit was by no means unique. A similar claim was made against Wal-Mart in 2004, likewise based on statistical disparities. Back in 1973, the Equal Employment Opportunity Commission filed a sex discrimination lawsuit against Sears, based solely on statistical disparities, rather than on any woman who claimed that a man of lower qualifications than her own was hired or promoted when she was not. Yet this case went on for years, until it was finally decided in 1988 by the Seventh Circuit Court of Appeals, which pointed out that the EEOC had failed to come up with even "anecdotal evidence of discriminatory employment practices" or any "flesh and blood victims of discrimination." The court pointed out that the EEOC "did not present in evidence even one specific instance of discrimination"[57] in a company with hundreds of stores from coast to coast.

Sears won that case but its legal victory obviously did not stop sex discrimination lawsuits against other companies based on statistical disparities. Employers who were not as large as Sears were in no financial position to fight a federal lawsuit for 15 years, and spend the $20 million that Sears spent defending this case, might well be forced to agree to a consent decree that would brand them in the public mind as guilty of sex discrimination.[58] Moreover, the spread of cases like that, settled by employers not able to afford the cost of fighting through the courts for years, would be enough to convince many observers that sex discrimination was widespread and was the primary source of male-female economic differences.

The Minority Analogy

Many have analogized the situation of women to that of low-income minorities, explaining income disparities in both cases by employer discrimination and attempting through anti-discrimination laws and affirmative action policies to advance both groups economically. But there are fundamental differences between the circumstances of women and those of minorities which affect both analysis and policy.

In analyzing the economic situation of minorities, it is possible to get some idea of how much of the income disparities between minorities and the general population is explained by various factors besides employer discrimination by comparing individuals who are comparable in age, education, and other relevant factors. But while more education, for example, raises the incomes of both blacks and whites, even if not to the same degree, one of the biggest factors in income differences between women and men— parenthood— has *opposite* effects on their incomes. Comparing married women with married men does not mean comparing individuals who are comparably affected. Only the never-married women and men are in comparable circumstances, and here women have had comparable or higher incomes than men, years before there were laws or government policies against sex discrimination.

Women and minorities are different in a more fundamental historical sense. Low-income minorities are usually descendants of poorer and less educated people, so that they inherit both a cultural and an economic background that is less helpful to them in trying to rise economically and socially than are the backgrounds of other members of society. Women, however, are not descended just from women. Whatever educational or economic advantages men had in the past, those men were their fathers and grandfathers just as much as the women were their mothers and grandmothers. Today's generation of women inherit whatever advantages their male forebears had as much as they inherit whatever disadvantages their female forebears had— and so do the brothers of today's women. Obvious as this may seem, it is often ignored by those making analogies between women and minorities. One sign of the difference is that female Ph.D.s have long come from higher socioeconomic backgrounds than male Ph.D.s and have had higher test scores,[59] just the opposite of the situation among blacks and other low-income minorities.

In the academic world, the history and present circumstances of women and minorities are especially different. First of all, female academics have been common far longer than black academics, reaching a peak proportion of all academics back in 1879 that was not equaled again in the next ninety years.[60] Black professors and administrators were rare in the nineteenth century, even in colleges for black students.[61] Although an early set of federal guidelines on affirmative action asserted that "women and minorities are often not in word-of-mouth channels of recruitment" for academic positions,[62] that is certainly not true of women. Women with doctorates have for years received those degrees from prestigious institutions about as often as men have,[63] so that they have long been in the so-called "old boy network" of academic recruitment just like male Ph.D.s.

SUMMARY AND IMPLICATIONS

Among the many factors which influence male-female economic differences, the most elusive is employer discrimination. Since no one is likely to admit to discriminating against women, which is both illegal and socially stigmatized, in principle discrimination can only be inferred indirectly from the disparities between women and men that remain after all the other factors have been taken into account. In practice, however, there is no way to take all other factors into account, since no one knows what they all are and statistics are not always available for all the factors we do know about. What we are left with, after taking into account all the factors that we are aware of and for which statistics are available, are residual differences which measure the upper limit of the *combined* effect of employer discrimination *plus* whatever other factors have been overlooked or not specified precisely. That residual is often much smaller than the gross income differences between women and men, sometimes is zero, and in a few instances women earn more than men whose measured characteristics are similar.

The empirical fact that most male-female economic differences are accounted for by factors other than employer discrimination does not mean that there have been no instances of discrimination, including egregious instances. But anecdotes about those egregious instances cannot explain the general pattern of male-female economic differences and their changes over time. Those changes are continuing. While in the period from 2000 to 2005 most women were still holding jobs making less than the weekly median wages, women were also 1.7 million out of 1.9 million new workers earning *above* the median wages.[64]

While hard data are preferable to anecdotes, even hard data have their limitations. Statistics may not be available on all the factors that determine hiring, pay, or promotions. Nor can the direction of causation always be determined when the data are available. For example, the effect of marriage on women's economic opportunities and rewards may be estimated by comparing women who seem to be comparable in things that can be measured, but what if women who are more driven to pursue a career are less likely to marry early or perhaps at all? That is not measurable, which is not to say that it is not important. Income differences between less driven and more driven women may be falsely attributed to marriage, when in these cases differences in marriage patterns may be an effect rather than a cause. In other words, it need not be marriage, as such, which accounts for income differences between married and unmarried women.

It can sometimes be difficult to distinguish income differences between the sexes caused by external barriers confronting women and differences caused by choices made by the women themselves. In addition to choices of educational specialties, occupations, and continuous or discontinuous employment, many married women have chosen to allow their husbands' best job opportunities to determine where the couple will live, with the wife then taking whatever her best option might be at that location, even if there would be better options for her somewhere else. Such wives' reduced occupational opportunities in such cases are in effect an investment in their husbands' enhanced occupational opportunities.

This is a special handicap for women in the academic world, where the wife of a man who teaches at Cornell University, for example, will not have a comparable academic institution in which she can pursue her own career within a hundred miles. It would be quite a coincidence if there was an opening in her field at Cornell at the same time when there was an opening there for her husband in his field. In some places, anti-nepotism policies would preclude her being hired, even if there were such an opening. While some professors have sufficient clout to make the hiring of a spouse a precondition for accepting an academic appointment at a given institution, such a precondition can reduce the number and quality of the institutions that will make an appointment to either husband or wife.

A more general indicator of wives' investments in their husbands' earning capacity is the changing ratio of husbands' earnings to their wives' earnings over time. As far back as 1981, one-third of all wives in the 25 to 34 year-old bracket had higher earnings than their husbands— but that percentage declined successively in older age brackets, so that fewer than 10 percent of wives who were age 65 or older had higher earnings than their husbands.[65] In other words, the passage of time increased husbands' earnings more than the wives' earnings, another indication suggesting wives' investments in their husbands' earning capacity.

Given the numerous factors that impact the incomes and employment of women differently from the way they impact the incomes and employment of men, it can hardly be surprising that there have been substantial income differences between the sexes. Nor can all these differences be assumed to be negative on net balance for women— that is, taking other factors into account besides income. For example, the wives of affluent and wealthy men tend to work less and therefore to earn less. But the wife of a rich man is not poor, no matter how low her income might be. In homes where the income of the husband exceeds the income of the wife, the actual spending of that income cannot be determined by whose name is on what paycheck, and research indicates that the wife usually makes more of the decisions about how the pooled family income is spent than the husband does.[66] Such ultimate realities are beyond the reach of most statistics— but whatever arrangements wives and husbands agree to between themselves are certainly no less important than what third party observers might prefer to see.

While fallacious inferences can be based on gross income data, the fallacy is not in the undisputed fact of male-female income differences but in the explanation of that fact. Much also depends on whether the social goal is equal opportunity or equal incomes. As Professor Claudia Goldin, an economist at Harvard, put it:

> Is equality of income what we really want? Do we want everyone to have an equal chance to work 80 hours in their prime reproductive years? Yes, but we don't expect them to take that chance equally often.[67]

Research by another female economist lends empirical support to that conclusion. Sylvia Ann Hewlett surveyed more than 2,000 women and more than 600 men. Her conclusions:

> About 37% of women take an off-ramp at some point in their career, meaning they quit their jobs— but just for an average 2.2 years. Another substantial number take scenic routes for a while— intentionally not ratcheting up their assignments. For instance, 36% of highly qualified women have sought part-time jobs for some period, while others have declined promotions or deliberately chosen jobs with fewer responsibilities. . . The data show that highly qualified women aren't afraid of hard work and responsibility. But it's hard to sustain a 73-hour workweek if you have serious responsibilities in other parts of your life.[68]

Chapter 4

ACADEMIC FACTS AND FALLACIES

As the price of college continues to outpace both inflation and the growth of average family incomes, students, parents, and policy makers are demanding to know just what families are getting for their money.
The short, unsettling answer: No one really knows.

The Chronicle of Higher Education[1]

Colleges and universities operate under different incentives and different constraints from those of businesses which must earn enough from the sale of their goods and services to sustain themselves and provide a return on the investments made by those whose money created them and enables them to continue functioning.

Only a fraction of the income that sustains academic institutions comes from the tuition that they charge students. Less than one-third of the revenues received by private, non-profit four-year degree-granting American institutions came from students' tuition in 2003–04. Of approximately $134 billion in revenues, approximately $38 billion came from students' tuition. Among state and federal degree-granting institutions, student tuition supplied just 16 percent of their revenues.[2] Since even private colleges and universities receive money from the federal government, and state colleges and universities often get most of their money from sources other than the state government,* the distinction between private academic institutions and state institutions is not as sharp as it once was. Institutions of higher education supporting themselves primarily from the tuition of their students, such as the University of Phoenix, are a recent and very exceptional profit-based phenomenon in a field where most colleges and universities are non-profit enterprises. *The Chronicle of Higher Education* reported that 77 percent of the revenues received by the five largest companies based on profit-making colleges come from student financial aid provided by government.[3]

American universities are usually ranked among the best in the world, based primarily on having some of the best scholars in the world on their faculties— even if many of these top scholars are from other countries. "The US has 11 of the top 20 universities in the world," according to the British publication *The Times Higher Education Supplement*.[4] Another British publication, *The Economist*, said, "many American universities have big endowments" which "allow them to lure the world's best academics." While Oxford and Cambridge are Britain's best endowed universities, their endowments are exceeded by six American institutions, with Yale having more than twice as large an endowment as Oxford or Cambridge, and Harvard having more than three times as large an endowment. The net result: "Leading British academics earn around half of what their counterparts in America get. Their teaching loads are heavier and their administrative tasks more arduous."[5]

Differences in the way that institutions function and differences in the conditions for their financial survival create differences in the incentives that influence their behavior. Many people think of non-profit organizations as being free of selfish motives and therefore dedicated to the well-being of others, including society at large. However, that assumption is seldom subjected to empirical tests. Nor does it survive such tests very well when it

---

* In academic year 2007–2008, state governments supplied only 30 percent of the revenues received by the University of California at Berkeley, 17 percent of the revenues received by the University of Texas at Austin and 12 percent of the revenues received by the University of Michigan at Ann Arbor. Paul Fain, "Cuts Intensify Identity Crisis for Washington's Flagship Campus," *Chronicle of Higher Education*, September 3, 2010, p. A28.

is. Back in the eighteenth century, Adam Smith— himself a professor—
pointed out how the faculty of endowed academic institutions are enabled
to indulge themselves[6] in ways that they would not be able to in an
enterprise dependent on its performance for its economic survival. Having
an endowment means that an institution does not have to earn its way by
the sale of goods or services to a satisfied clientele at cost-covering prices.

The special economic factors in academic institutions affect not only the
faculty but also the way that colleges and universities as institutions handle
their costs and the education of their students.

ACADEMIC GOVERNANCE

Legally, the ultimate authority at a college or university rests with the board
of trustees. However, these are usually people with full-time careers in other
fields, who meet only periodically to oversee campus operations and vote on
major decisions, including the hiring and firing of university presidents. A
survey by *The Chronicle of Higher Education* found that 42 percent of trustees
spend five hours or less per month on their duties on the board of trustees and
only 23 percent spend 16 hours or more per month. About half are from the
world of business and less than one-fifth work in education.[7]

A former dean of Harvard College observed that governing boards in
general "do not know what is going on" on college campuses and that
members of Harvard's Board of Overseers "learn of important changes at
Harvard by reading about them in the papers."[8] Nor is this a new
phenomenon or one confined to large universities. A long-time president of
Lawrence College during the first half of the twentieth century likewise
observed, "most trustees had only the vaguest knowledge of the business of
the college."[9] In short, most trustees have neither the time nor the personal
experience to either monitor or evaluate campus activities closely. Because of
tenure, trustees cannot hire and fire the faculty but must deal with them as
a fact of life. Given these circumstances, it is not surprising that, over the
years, boards of trustees have usually been increasingly guided by what the

faculty want. It is the path of least resistance and there are few countervailing incentives to do otherwise.

College and university faculty are both labor and management. They both work for the academic institution and determine most of its policies regarding curriculum, hiring, and campus rules. When General Dwight D. Eisenhower became president of Columbia University after World War II, he once referred to the faculty as "employees" of the university— whereupon a professor rose to inform Eisenhower: "We *are* Columbia University."[10] Few academic presidents can survive in office if most of the faculty are opposed to him or her.

The high levels of expertise required in many academic fields mean that the only people competent to make fundamental decisions in those fields are the professors of those subjects. No university president or dean could possibly be competent to decide what courses or course contents should be taught in chemistry, mathematics, economics, physics, and many other fields. Nor could any given academic administrator know how to evaluate the knowledge of people being considered to be hired to teach in each of the wide range of disciplines at even a small college, much less at a large university.

The principle of faculty self-governance is therefore central to the operation of an academic institution. Moreover, that principle has been extended over the years to apply to many things outside the areas in which professors can claim special expertise, so that faculty opinion influences or controls institutional policies on things ranging from whether or not students will be allowed to enroll in R.O.T.C. to who can be invited to give commencement addresses. In these areas outside their expertise, including areas in which there is no such thing as expertise, professors can simply indulge their personal notions at no cost to themselves.

Thus the provost of Stanford University reported faculty members urging the university to refuse to accept donations from oil companies or other businesses or government agencies that particular professors dislike.[11] Moreover, the Stanford medical school— like medical schools at Yale and the University of Pennsylvania— has forbidden its professors from accepting free samples of medications from pharmaceutical companies,[12] which are unpopular like oil companies, even though these free medications would be passed along to patients, who would save money while finding out if a new pharmaceutical drug could help them. This ban is one of a number of symbolic decisions made at no cost by academics with no stake in the consequences. In a similar vein, the Harvard Law School decided to waive the third-year tuition for those of its students who go to work after graduation in government agencies or non-profit organizations— subsidizing the professors' predilections at the cost of several million dollars a year to the law school but at no cost to the professors. In 2009, however, Harvard's own financial difficulties led to the suspension of this program, though the subsidizing of summer jobs in organizations that law professors defined as "public interest" continued.

THE FACULTY

Academic faculty are unique not only in having managerial authority, as well as individual autonomy in their own work, but also in the nature of the arrangements for their careers. Such arrangements as lifetime tenure are made possible by the fact that most colleges and universities are non-profit organizations. Not only is tenure virtually unknown in commerce and industry, profit-making colleges and universities such as the University of Phoenix or Strayer University seldom offer tenure. This makes most academic institutions rare, if not unique, examples of organizations whose key decision-makers cannot be fired for bad decisions. Voting at faculty meetings for policies that turn out to have a detrimental impact on the institution's finances or academic quality are not among the very few things for which a tenured professor can be fired.

The rationale for tenure is that it provides security of employment for the faculty and therefore enables them to have academic freedom in teaching and research, without fear of retaliation for their views or approaches. However, what the actual effect of tenure is depends on the incentives and constraints it creates for the institution and for the individual faculty members.

Teaching

The unique position of college and university faculty members as both labor and management offers many different kinds of opportunities to serve their own interests, rather than the interests of the students or of the academic institution. This can range from apparently small things like the scheduling of classes to the selection of the curriculum.

When professors arrange their class schedules to suit their own convenience— for example, being able to drive to campus after the morning rush hour and leave before the afternoon rush hour— this means that many classes meet at the same times, creating time conflicts for students that can make it difficult or impossible for many students to schedule the required classes they take in a way that will allow them to graduate in four years. Thus students may have to spend an extra year or more to graduate, and their parents have to pay tuition and living expenses for another year or more, in order that professors can avoid traffic or get in their tennis or swimming before dinner time.

The concentration of classes within a narrow band of hours also means that the college must build and maintain more classrooms than if the classes were spread out from early morning through the end of the day. All this adds to the cost of education. Stanford University's provost, for example, complained of "wastes of space" and "unused classrooms," and said: "Walk around and see all the empty classrooms that you'll find at most hours. But the way we currently schedule classes makes it very difficult to fit all of the classes into the classrooms that we have." Constructing classroom buildings is expensive, and building classrooms that will be empty most of the time adds to the cost of education.

Such needless costs could be fatal to an ordinary business operating in a competitive market because competing businesses could avoid such costs and sell the same product or service cheaper, taking away customers. But colleges and universities are insulated from such consequences in a number of ways. Private academic institutions have endowments, whose dividends and interest can subsidize inefficiency, and state colleges and universities have the taxpayers to do the same. In either case, those whose money provides the subsidy are seldom in any position to monitor the efficiency with which that money is used. Moreover, such organizations as the American Association of University Professors and accrediting agencies protect existing practices from competition by condemning less expensive alternatives as educational quality deterioration.

The particular courses offered in colleges and universities often also reflect the professors' convenience more so than the students' educational needs. For example, a history department may offer a course on the history of motion pictures or the history of wine-making, while not offering a course on the history of the Roman Empire or the history of medieval Europe, even though these broader courses would offer much more insight into the way Western civilization has developed and the way our world today has evolved. More narrowly focused courses are a consequence of the fact that professors must do research in order to advance their careers, beginning with their doctoral dissertations. Therefore they must narrow their focus to something that has not been written about in great depth before.

Having done original research or made original analyses on such subjects as the history of motion pictures or the history of wine-making, a professor would then find it much easier to teach a course on such a narrow subject than to do the vast amount of research required to teach a course on a subject as broad as the history of the Roman Empire or of medieval Europe— research unlikely to have any publication pay-off, since both subjects have already been widely researched and written about by others for generations.

On many campuses, including some of the most prestigious, the disappearance of a meaningful curriculum, geared to the educational development of students, rather than to the convenience or career-advancement of professors, is in part a consequence of a proliferation of courses in narrow subjects. There may be a curriculum listed in the college catalogue but that can mean little if there are many disparate options for meeting a particular curriculum requirement— if, for example, a course on the history of motion pictures can be used to satisfy a social science requirement instead of a course on leading nations or empires of the world. Thus a student may graduate from some of the most prestigious colleges fundamentally ignorant of history and of all the insights and implications of history.

Because similar factors are at work in other departments, whether in the humanities, sciences, or social sciences, the knowledge that a diploma is supposed to represent may in fact be only isolated fragments of knowledge on whatever narrow subjects the student's particular professors happened to write about in their doctoral dissertations, books, or academic journal articles, instead of an education featuring a broad and coordinated knowledge and understanding of a number of intellectual disciplines. However desirable broader courses might be from the standpoint of the students' education, former Harvard president Derek Bok has pointed out "the difficulty of finding enough professors willing and able to teach such courses."[13]

For Harvard to insist that its professors teach such courses would be to risk an exodus of its top faculty to Yale, Stanford, and other leading universities that would be happy to welcome these professors and the millions of dollars in research grants they would bring. "They could all get jobs elsewhere at the drop of a hat," as a former Harvard dean put it. He also summed up the net result: "The old ideal of a liberal education lives on in name only."[14]

Harvard's high ranking as a research university is often confused with a high ranking as a place for a college education, such confusion being promoted by the ranking system used, for example, by *U.S. News & World Report* magazine in its annual publication, *America's Best Colleges*. Moreover, research remains as much of a faculty priority on flagship state university campuses, such as those at Berkeley or Ann Arbor, as at Ivy League institutions.

Finally, there are many public and private colleges and universities— perhaps most— whose quantity and quality of research may not be sufficient to justify neglect of undergraduate education or the high costs of the kinds of light teaching loads common at leading research universities. Such considerations led the president of Fort Hays University in Kansas to increase the teaching loads of its professors, enabling the institution to have a tuition level moderate enough to attract more students, though angering the faculty. However, as a study pointed out, "serious cutting-edge research has never been present to a high degree at schools like Fort Hays, and arguably all that Dr. Hammond has done is sharply reduce the school year leisure time of the instructional staff."[15]

Grade inflation is another practice that serves the convenience of the professors rather than the interests of the students. While those students who do not wish to study hard may enjoy grade inflation, it has been found that students who take lower-level courses from professors who give easy grades do not do as well in upper-level courses as students who took their preparatory courses from professors with stricter grading standards.[16] In short, the long-run interests of students as a whole are sacrificed by grade inflation. However, grade inflation makes life easier for professors who need not face time-consuming complaints from students about low or failing grades nor put up with the unpleasantness that can accompany such complaints. Moreover, the unpopularity of professors who give low grades can also be reflected in negative student evaluations at the end of a course, which in turn can negatively affect career advancement, especially for young faculty who have not yet achieved tenure.

Educational Quality

In ordinary commercial transactions, for the seller's interests to completely over-ride the buyer's interests would be to risk losing customers to someone else. But, in academia, almost by definition, the student does not fully understand the nature of the product being sold. If a student already understood the content of a course, there would be no point taking that course. What a student can judge is how well the professor conveyed the information in the course— how clearly the material was presented and how interesting it seemed— but what the student is *not* equipped to judge is what contrary information and conflicting analysis was left out or how well the same subject was taught somewhere else. Depending on the subject, misconceptions or even errors may be wonderfully taught to students who are in no position to detect either at the time, even if they discover in later life the falsity of what they were taught.

While consumers of commercial products may often be similarly unable to determine directly and immediately the quality of the merchandise they buy, most of the things they buy are bought more than once and experience can guide future purchases. But most people go through college only once and seldom take the same course more than once. Moreover, there are innumerable organizations capable of testing commercial products and reporting on them to the public. These include not only organizations which test and publicize their findings on a wide range of products, such as *Consumer Reports* and *Good Housekeeping* magazines, but also specialized organizations and publications that evaluate stereo equipment, automobiles, cameras, hotels, cruise ships, and innumerable other products and services.

The closest analogues for evaluating the quality of academic education are the annual rankings of colleges and universities by *U.S. News & World Report* but these rankings have not only been widely and severely criticized, growing numbers of colleges are refusing to supply the data used in such rankings, which itself undermines the validity of the rankings, regardless of the merits of the criticisms.[17]

Moreover, while most rankings of goods and services are based on assessments of the end products, rankings of academic institutions are almost invariably rankings of the inputs used, rather than rankings of the educational output. As *The Economist* magazine reported:

> At the moment, just two institutions make annual attempts to compare universities round the world. Shanghai's Jiao Tong University has been doing it since 2003, and the *Times Higher Education Supplement*, a British weekly, started a similar exercise in 2004. But both these indices, which are closely watched by participants in a fickle and fast-expanding global education market. . . reflect "inputs" such as the number and quality of staff, as well as how many prizes they win and how many articles they publish.[18]

The intellectual achievements of professors in the United States or dons in Britain do not automatically translate into better education for students. As *The Economist* also notes, "dons may be so busy writing and researching that they spend little or no time teaching— a big weakness at America's famous universities." Moreover, the rankings of academic institutions depend crucially upon what weights are arbitrarily assigned to the various factors that produce these rankings, so that "changes in methodology can bring startling shifts":

The high-flying London School of Economics, for example, tumbled
from 17th to 59th in the British rankings published last week, primarily
because it got less credit than in previous years for the impressive number
of foreign students it had managed to attract.[19]

One of the few attempts to measure educational outputs, rather than
inputs, by a think tank in Washington, brought similarly large changes in
rankings from those of *U.S. News & World Report*. When the Center for
College Affordability and Productivity ranked academic institutions by their
students' achievements in later life and by those students' own ratings of
their professors, Whitman College rose from 37th to 9th among liberal arts
colleges, Wabash from 52nd to 10th and Barnard from 30th to 8th.[20]

A more official evaluation, with consequences that include eligibility or
ineligibility for receipt of government money in the United States, is
provided by the various accrediting agencies that approve or disapprove the
colleges and universities they visit across the country. However, these
agencies too measure inputs rather than outputs, since they have neither the
time nor the resources to do in-depth studies of what happens in the
classrooms of thousands of academic institutions or what kinds of
educational outcomes they produce. Yet few institutions could afford to
engage in the kind of open criticism of these accrediting agencies, or a flat
refusal to cooperate with their endeavors, as growing numbers do with the
U.S. News & World Report rankings.

Accrediting agencies must rely on broad-brush indicators of campus
resources, such as the number of books in campus libraries and student:faculty
ratios— in short, the same kinds of *input* criteria, rather than measures of
educational output, for which *U.S. News & World Report* has been criticized.
Far from providing reliable indicators of educational quality or efficiency, the
use of such indicators can become a barrier against newer and lower-cost ways
of educating students that could be reflected in lower tuitions.

For example, reading materials available on-line or on DVDs can replace
books and bound volumes of academic journals and other periodicals that
would be far more costly for a college or university to buy, and which would
require more expensive storage space on library shelves. But if the accrediting
agency uses the number of books in a college or university library as a criterion
for accreditation, then it negates the cost advantages of lower-cost newcomers

who could otherwise compete more effectively against existing traditional colleges by offering students and their families more affordable tuition.

There are also ways of economizing on the number of faculty members but, here too, accrediting criteria can protect existing high-cost institutions from the competition of lower-cost newcomers. If student:faculty ratios are among the criteria for accreditation, then a university with many professors engaging primarily in research, with these professors' graduate students doing most of the teaching of introductory courses, has a better chance of getting accredited than a new institution set up specifically for teaching, whose professors have heavier teaching loads and are not expected to spend much time doing research. Thus an institution where the crucial introductory courses are taught by professors, rather than by graduate students, will look worse in terms of student:faculty ratios, since their professors have heavier teaching loads, even if class sizes are no larger than at institutions with lower student:faculty ratios.

The correlation between student:faculty ratios and class size is very tenuous. Texas A & M University, for example, has a lower student:faculty ratio (20:1) than Miami Dade College (26:1) but 32 percent of the classes at Miami Dade have fewer than 20 students, while only 21 percent of the classes at Texas A & M are that small. At the other end of the scale, only one percent of the classes at Miami Dade have 50 or more students, while 24 percent of the classes at Texas A & M are that large.[21] Class sizes could be inferred from student:faculty ratios only if all the faculty were present and were teaching. But the proportion of professors who are present and teaching can vary considerably between a teaching-oriented college and a research-oriented university. Not only are professors at research universities more likely to take time off from teaching to do research on campus, they are also more likely to go on leave to do research or other things elsewhere.*

---

* As a personal note, although I was officially on the faculty of UCLA for 12 years, I actually taught there only 5 years, spending other years doing research in Washington and Palo Alto, as well as teaching as a visiting professor at Amherst. But I may well have been counted in compiling student:faculty ratios when I was nowhere within a hundred miles of UCLA.

There are various innovative ways of economizing on the use of faculty which can lower costs but which also can lower the prospects of an institution's being accredited. Some law schools, for example, hire many practicing attorneys and judges to teach part-time in their respective specialties, such as estate law or anti-trust law, while having a relatively small number of full-time, tenured professors who teach such broader and more fundamental courses as Constitutional law. Some judges and lawyers are willing to teach an evening course in their particular specialties for modest pay, and may be quite knowledgeable and up to date within those specialties, without being the kind of academic scholars who publish in law journals and become professors at prestigious law schools. Inexpensive faculty and modest campus physical facilities enable some law schools to charge far lower tuition than more traditional law schools charge.

The American Bar Association, however, has refused to accredit a number of law schools run this way, even when most of these law schools' graduates are able to pass the bar examination on the first try. The existing accreditation of the University of Colorado's law school was threatened, despite the fact that 92 percent of its graduates passed the bar exam on the first try— which is not only higher than the national average, but higher than the percentage of graduates from prestigious law schools at Harvard and Yale who pass on the first try.[22] According to the *Denver Post*:

> An accrediting association for law schools has renewed its concerns over the University of Colorado's inability to construct a new law building in the absence of state funding.
> The Chicago-based American Bar Association is requiring CU president Betsy Hoffman and incoming law dean David Getches to appear before its accreditation committee in January to show why the law school shouldn't be placed on probation or removed from the list of approved law schools. . .
> The ABA also is asking CU to explain a lack of minority and female faculty, and says it is concerned about the number of courses taught by adjunct professors (lawyers teaching part time), according to a letter sent by the bar association to CU. . .
> In addition, CU ranks low for annual expenditures on law library materials— its $1.7 million is $1 million less than the average, according to the ABA.[23]

As is common with accrediting organizations, all the things cited as factors in the American Bar Association's accreditation concerns were *inputs* into the educational process, rather than the *output* of qualified graduates. But efficiency consists precisely in turning given inputs into more or better output. In the case of a law school, there is an external and objective measure of output quality, the ability of its graduates to pass the bar exam. While this is not the only possible measure of quality, it is a crucial measure because, without passing the bar exam, students cannot become lawyers. Students who aspire to more scholarly, more prestigious, or more policy-oriented goals have a variety of law schools to choose from, but students whose budgets limit their ability to pay high tuition for law school can afford only those law schools which keep tuition affordable by spending less for faculty, libraries, and buildings.

In the case of the University of Colorado's law school, complying with the ABA's demands involved spending more than $40 million for a new building, and this and other cost increases led to a rise in annual law school tuition from $6,700 to $16,738 for Colorado residents and to $30,814 for non-residents. This more than doubling of tuition in just a few years undoubtedly put the University of Colorado's law school beyond the financial reach of some students. It also protected high-cost law schools from the competition of the University of Colorado law school's previous low tuition, and made it more difficult for other low-cost law schools to arise to compete with high-cost law schools. In short, the ABA's accreditation standards and practices served much the same role as a protective tariff, insulating high-cost producers from the competition of low-cost producers.

Few law schools could risk operating without accreditation, as the Nashville School of Law has done, depending on its low tuition to attract students and depending on its graduates' ability to pass the state bar exam to maintain the institution's reputation. While graduates of the Nashville School of Law who have passed the state bar exam can practice law in Tennessee, and many have gone on to successful careers there, their law degrees from an unaccredited institution may not be accepted everywhere else.

While law schools are unusual in that there is an independent, objective, and career-relevant test of their graduates' education— and therefore a check on the relevance of the accrediting agency's criteria— other accrediting agencies for colleges and universities tend to have *input* criteria much like those of the ABA, with little or no regard to *output* quality, and with similar indulgences of the preconceptions of members of the accrediting agency.

Such practices reinforce the barriers against less expensive forms of higher education. Thus traditional academic institutions, which have inherited large costs from the past, such as tenure for many professors or large libraries with expensive upkeep, are protected from the competition of lower-cost newcomers who can avoid the costs of such practices through the use of electronically available books and journals and a high proportion of non-tenured faculty. The net result is that there are fewer competitive pressures to reduce tuition or even to inhibit continuing rises in tuition.

It should also be noted that the people who make the decisions on which accreditation is based are mostly people whose full-time careers are on the staffs of existing academic institutions. For example, more than four-fifths of the people on the board of the Middle States Commission on Higher Education work for the academic institutions that this organization accredits.[24] This built-in conflict of interest is common with other academic accrediting agencies that have the power to reject institutions which operate differently, and at lower costs, than the existing institutions they work for. In 2007, for example, the various regional accrediting associations had more than 3,500 professors and administrators as volunteers, compared to fewer than 150 full-time staff members.[25]

The limited time and resources available to the accrediting agencies virtually dictate that these agencies focus on readily measurable criteria, rather than attempt to assess the intellectual quality of college and university graduates. As the president of Rice University put it, "the accreditors are not interested in what or how the students learn, but how many square feet of classroom space we have per student."[26]

The requirement of accreditation in order to receive federal money puts enormous leverage in the hands of the accreditation agencies, especially since federal aid grew more than sixty-fold from academic year 1963–64 to academic year 2008–2009,[27] enabling the accrediting agencies to impose their own arbitrary preconceptions on the institutions they evaluate, including demographic "representation" of various groups among students and faculty. The accreditors of the American Bar Association have specified the number of square feet required for each law professor's office.[28]

Despite misuses of the accreditation process, some standards of quality control are obviously required. Many diploma mills set up essentially to bring in federal dollars in student aid were shut down when they failed to meet accreditation standards. Moreover, no one should assume that either profit-seeking or non-profit institutions automatically live up to quality standards, or even standards of honesty. A number of lawsuits claim that unaccredited, for-profit institutions have misled students into believing that their credits would be automatically transferable to other institutions and their degrees recognized, when in fact neither claim was true. The ways in which non-profit academic institutions also mislead students have been the subject of many books and articles, and Nobel laureate George J. Stigler observed, "the typical college catalogue would never stop Diogenes in his search for an honest man."[29]

Academic Careers

The particular job security policies in American colleges and universities have their own peculiar consequences, often quite different from the goals of these policies. Academics who have been employed a given number of years at a given college or university must either be promoted to a position with permanent tenure or let go. This is called the "up or out" system. It means more job security for those who go up but less job security for those who are forced out— less not only compared to their more fortunate academic colleagues, but less compared to people of similar ages in other sectors of the economy without such job security systems.

Because academic job security systems leave colleges and universities with long-term commitments that can easily cost millions of dollars for each tenured faculty member, this can lead to more stringent requirements for continued employment than if no such commitment were implied. Untenured faculty members (usually assistant professors) whose current work is considered to be perfectly satisfactory will nevertheless often be let go— not have their contracts renewed— when time comes for the "up or out" decision, when there is not yet sufficient evidence to be confident that they will in future years progress to the higher performance levels expected of senior faculty members, notably in scholarly research.

Nor is there any reason to believe that the next crop of assistant professors will be any better than those dismissed, even though turnover has costs to the institution as well as to the individuals concerned. The reason for the turnover is to comply with the standards of the American Association of University Professors without getting stuck permanently with costs of millions of dollars per faculty member.

At the highest-rated universities, it is common for *most* assistant professors to be terminated before time for them to become associate professors, since there has seldom been enough time for them to have produced the high levels of research quantity and quality required for senior positions at such institutions. In short, the goal of a policy— in this case, greater job security— turns out to have little to do with the actual end result of that policy, which is less job security than most people of similar ages have in other sectors of the economy where there are no such policies as those surrounding academic tenure.

This academic promotions system also helps explain a common but paradoxical phenomenon at many universities— the outstanding young teacher who is terminated, often to the consternation of his students, who may even mount organized protests, usually in vain. A former dean at Harvard noted "the widely held undergraduate opinion that their favorite teachers are systematically denied tenure."[30] It is even common on some campuses to hear the "teacher of the year" award referred to as "the kiss of death" for young faculty members. That is because outstanding teaching is very time-consuming, in terms of creating high-quality courses and preparing outstanding lectures in these courses, as well as giving individual attention to students who may be having trouble understanding the material. This often leaves insufficient time for a junior faculty member to do the amount and quality of research required for getting tenure at a top university. Such institutions often fill their senior positions by hiring those people who have already produced the requisite quantity and quality of publications somewhere else.

The top-level universities in prestige— based primarily on research— are usually top-level in faculty salaries as well. The salaries of full professors at Stanford and Princeton averaged more than $180,000 per year in academic year 2008–2009, and full professors at Harvard averaged more than $190,000. Meanwhile, full professors at four-year colleges in general averaged under $90,000, though full professors at the elite of the four-year colleges— Amherst and Swarthmore, for example— averaged more than $120,000.[31] Faculty salaries, like an institution's prestige, do not indicate where a student is likely to get the best undergraduate education. In many fields, such as mathematics or economics, getting a solid grounding in the introductory course is a prerequisite for mastering the higher level courses that build on that foundation. Is a high-priced professor who is one of the top scholars in the world likely to be better at teaching introductory courses— or even likely to agree to teach at such an elementary level at all?

Often the choice for students contemplating which kind of academic institution to attend may be between being taught such courses by competent professors at a small liberal arts college or being taught by transient junior faculty members, or even by graduate students, at a large and prestigious research university. The transience of both junior faculty members and graduate students means that they must be preparing, usually through research, to enhance their prospects of getting a desirable job somewhere else, in addition to spending time canvassing the job market and traveling to interviews.

Whether all the students they are teaching in introductory courses really master partial derivatives in mathematics or the elasticity of demand in economics may not be as high a priority to them as to some professor who is already established at a liberal arts college, and who is at such an institution precisely because of the professor's preference for teaching over research. A study of how faculty members divide their time between teaching and research found that the various duties involved in teaching took up less than half the working time of the faculty at research universities and nearly two-thirds of the working time of faculty at liberal arts colleges.[32]

THE STUDENTS

There are approximately 18 million students attending colleges and universities in the United States. These include nearly 5 million attending two-year institutions, either full-time or part-time, approximately 8 million attending four-year institutions full-time and nearly 1.7 million more attending part-time, plus more than 3 million graduate students.[33] A growing proportion are people older than the usual college-age population. While the number of college students younger than 25 increased by about 71 percent between 1970 and 2005, the number of college students who were 25 or older increased by 183 percent over those same years.[34]

The student population as a whole is of course not scattered randomly among colleges as a whole. Students choose colleges and colleges choose students— and there are facts and fallacies involved in both choices.

Choices Among Colleges

Since a college's academic prestige, and especially that of a university, depends primarily on its professors' research and publications, students will not necessarily get a better education at the more prestigious institutions with the higher paid faculty. Various studies have shown students at small liberal arts colleges doing as well as, or even better than, students from prestigious research universities on tests such as those for medical schools, and a higher percentage of the liberal arts college students going on to receive Ph.D.s.[35] The four institutions with the highest percentage of their graduates going on to receive Ph.D.s are all small colleges with fewer than 2,000 undergraduates each: Cal Tech, Harvey Mudd, Swarthmore, and Reed. Cal Tech and Harvey Mudd have fewer than a thousand undergraduates each. Small colleges in fact dominate the top ten. Grinnell College has a higher percentage of its graduates go on to receive Ph.D.s than does either Harvard or Yale.[36]

One of the biggest fallacies about academic institutions is that attendance at big-name colleges and universities is virtually essential for reaching the top in later life. But, of the chief executive officers of the 50 largest American corporations surveyed in 2006, only four had Ivy League degrees and just over half graduated from state colleges, city colleges, or a community college.[37] Some did not graduate at all, including Michael Dell of Dell computers and Bill Gates of Microsoft.

How much colleges in general add to economic or other success in later life is not easy to determine, and the methods often used can easily overstate the effect of college, and especially the effect of the more prestigious colleges. These methods would be valid if the people attending prestigious and non-prestigious institutions were comparable to begin with, so that their later differences in incomes and occupations after graduation could be attributed to what happened in college. But the students cannot be assumed to be comparable.

If students who enter Harvard, for example, have higher qualifications than the students who enter Podunk State, then later differences between the graduates of the two institutions cannot be arbitrarily attributed to differences in the education received in these two places. If Harvard graduates are more likely to continue on to medical school, law school, or other postgraduate study, then their later incomes are likely to be raised still further above those of the graduates of Podunk State. Ideally, the comparison should be made between people who went to Harvard and people who were admitted to Harvard but chose instead to go to Podunk State. Unfortunately, this is likely to produce samples too small for statistical analysis, and those who make such choices may not be typical of the students at either institution.

Studies have been made of people with comparable test scores who attended prestigious and non-prestigious colleges and universities, in order to try to determine the "value added" by the institutions themselves. Some such studies indicate that the more prestigious institutions do add value and others indicate that they do not. But seldom, if ever, do these studies indicate that the value added is as great as the raw statistics might suggest, without making allowances for the differences among the students themselves.

A widely repeated claim that going to college adds more than a million dollars to one's lifetime income is based on lumping all kinds of colleges and universities together. A finer breakdown showed that the *gross* lifetime income difference between a high school graduate and a college graduate ranged from just over half a million dollars at a private open admissions college to more than two million dollars for graduates of the most selective private institutions. However, the *net* lifetime income difference— taking into account tuition and lost earnings while in college— fell to about $150,000 for those graduating from private open-admissions colleges to about half a million dollars for graduates of the most selective private institutions. Dividing these sums by a 50-year career would lead to $3,000 a year for graduating from the former, which must be further discounted for the delay in receiving this amount.

A finer breakdown by specific institutions found the net pay-off from graduating from the University of Georgia was far higher than the net pay-off from graduating from Harvard, and the University of Delaware had a better pay-off than any Ivy League college. None of this takes into account the field in which one receives a degree. Ten years after graduation, those whose degrees were in business or engineering earned twice as much as those whose degrees were in education.[38]

Not only may the students themselves differ, so may the families they come from. If affluent or wealthy people are more likely to send their children to prestigious colleges and universities, then the incomes of those students in later life may reflect their greater career opportunities as a result of their family connections, a greater likelihood of being able to afford to go on to postgraduate study, or their greater income from the earnings of inherited assets, rather than their earnings from what they may have learned at the more prestigious colleges or universities.*

"Value Added" by College

Similar problems arise when trying to determine the value of going to college at all, as compared to going to work after finishing high school— or not finishing high school. It is common to compare the incomes of college graduates with the incomes of high school graduates, high school dropouts,

---

* Much may also depend on whether statistics cite median income or mean income. If the latter, then the class in which I graduated from Harvard would probably have had a high mean income, even if most of us held minimum wage jobs, since that class included a Rockefeller and the Aga Khan.

or others, and then attribute the much higher incomes of the college graduates to the education received in college. But people whose education stops before college cannot be assumed to be the same in orientation, values, priorities, or ability as people who go on to college. Therefore income differences between them cannot be automatically attributed to what was taught in college. Another way of looking at this is that a given individual, with given ability, given preferences, etc., cannot assume that the difference between going to one institution rather than another will be as great as statistics on other people attending different institutions.

A further complication is that many— if not most— people who drop out of high school later resume some form of education, whether in academic institutions or by studying a trade or acquiring certification from courses given by Microsoft, Oracle, Adobe, or other computer companies. Is the income of dropouts who later resumed their education elsewhere to be counted in the statistics on the incomes of dropouts? Are the incomes of dropouts who later go on to earn a Ph.D. without ever getting a high school diploma (such as the author of this book) to be included in the statistics on the incomes of dropouts? Or is the term "dropout" to be reserved solely for those who never resume any further education?

As a practical guide to those considering when to discontinue their academic education, at least temporarily, it makes a big difference whether particular statistics make such distinctions. Given the greater difficulty and higher costs of following particular individuals over time, it is very doubtful if most statistics— or perhaps any— make such distinctions. This means that the incomes of people who dropped out of high school and later received an academic degree without bothering to go back and get a high school diploma are very unlikely to be counted in statistics on the incomes of high school dropouts.

The Admissions Process

The college admissions process, like other decision-making processes within the academic institutions, reflects not only the non-profit nature of colleges and universities, but also the particular incentives facing those who make particular decisions. The most fundamental fact about the college admissions process is the high rate of rejection of applicants by big-name institutions. As of 2008, Harvard rejected 93 out of every 100 applicants, Yale rejected 92 percent and Columbia rejected 91 percent. More than 80 percent of applicants were rejected by Bowdoin, Georgetown, Dartmouth and Brown.[39] In light of this, it might seem strange that prestigious colleges, with several times as many applicants as places available for them, would spend vast sums of money recruiting students across the country and even overseas. Yet high school seniors who may never have thought of applying to Harvard or Stanford can find themselves receiving unsolicited mail from these and other well-known academic institutions, urging them to consider applying. As one dean of admissions described the process:

> For a high school student unaccustomed to getting stacks of letters, there can be a feeling of instant popularity. How many students have been contacted by a Stanford or an Oberlin and have concluded, "They must want me!"[40]

In reality, one of the incentives for recruiting so many students is precisely to be able to reject the great majority of them— thereby preserving the prestige of the college as "selective" in the rankings by *U.S. News & World Report* and publishers of various other college guides, since selectivity is measured by how small a percentage of applicants are admitted. Another incentive is to satisfy faculty demands for brighter students by providing a larger pool, from which more students with high academic qualifications can be skimmed.

High rejection rates by many well-known colleges and universities mean that many students find it necessary to apply to a number of academic institutions, in hopes of getting admitted to at least one. The institutions that they apply to often include at least one that they have no intention of attending, unless they are unable to get into any of their preferred colleges or universities. In short, the uncertainties that academic institutions create because of their high rejection rates lead students to make multiple applications that have costs in both money and time. Moreover, these multiple applications create uncertainties in college admissions offices as to how many of those admitted will actually show up to enroll.

These uncertainties create costs in money and time to both students and colleges. Because Vanderbilt University, for example, built a dormitory to house 1,550 freshmen, that was the number that the admissions office was charged with putting into that dormitory, leaving no empty rooms—meaning no missing tuition money, no missing dormitory rent money and, at the same time, no freshman unable to be housed in that dormitory among other freshmen. "My margin for error," said a Vanderbilt admissions official, "was literally not one student."[41] Since Vanderbilt and other institutions are uncertain about how many of the students they admit will in fact choose to accept their offers, this leads to various strategies involving waiting lists, early decisions and other means of trying to get just the right number of enrolled freshmen.

None of these strategies is foolproof or without costs. Some years ago, when Dickinson College found that not enough of the students it admitted actually enrolled, it sent admissions offers to students on its waiting list—but not enough of them enrolled to fill the freshman class. As a result, Dickinson in later years increased the proportion of applicants that it admitted, despite risking an adverse effect of this on the college's "selectivity" rating in the college guides. As an admissions official at Dickinson put it, "I'm more willing to sacrifice our acceptance rate up front than to come in low."[42]

While students or their parents may think that getting admitted to a particular college or university is a matter of meeting or not meeting their academic standards, that is by no means necessarily so. Because of highly subjective criteria used by college admissions officials, no given student can feel assured of being admitted to any given college or university, regardless of that student's academic record or test scores.

More than half of the applicants for Amherst's class of 2011 who scored between 750 and 800 on the math SAT were rejected, while 20 students who scored below 550 were accepted.[43] At Brown University, even students with a perfect 800 math score were accepted for the class of 2012 only 26 percent of the time, while more than two dozen students with math scores below 500 were accepted.[44] Similar patterns are common at other selective colleges and universities, where many rejected students may have better academic qualifications than other students who were accepted, because of the admissions committees' highly subjective judgments.

Nevertheless, rejected students may feel that some inadequacies of theirs were responsible for their rejection, and take it personally, as an admissions dean observed:

> Recipients of rejection letters, no matter how unrealistic their prospects may have seemed to objective observers, are often stunned. Just ask anyone who has been a high school guidance counselor during the month of April. I have been there. As a counselor, I felt the pain. As an admission dean, I have caused the pain.[45]

The actual selection process reflects the priorities and interests of an internal constituency within the college or university— namely, the admissions office staff— since there is no external constituency, such as stockholders or prospective stockholders in a corporation, to react adversely to an inefficient use of resources. Far-flung recruiting efforts, including visits to high schools across the country and the maintenance of on-going relationships with particular high school counselors, require far larger admissions office staffs and far larger budgets than would be required otherwise, if colleges simply waited for students to apply and selected those with the best academic records or test scores. *The Chronicle of Higher Education* reported, for example, that Northern Michigan University "has 14 admissions-staff members, who have visited a total of 1,500 high schools and fairs this year."[46] Even at a small liberal arts college like Ohio Wesleyan, officials referred to "the thousands of high school counselors with whom we are in some contact."[47]

Admissions criteria and practices reflect not only a rationale for a far larger staff than would be required if objective criteria were considered sufficient for selecting among applicants, these criteria and practices can also create a sense of importance among admissions office staffers who see themselves as applying deep insights about such subjective things as "leadership potential" and "commitment" among the applicants, and the dispensing of rewards for such things as having overcome adversity or having engaged in activities arbitrarily defined as "community service."

Since ethnic "diversity" is one of the prevailing notions among admissions committees, these committees are able to create whatever demographic mix they like, as yet another decision made possible by being in a non-profit organization, where there are no stockholders or other external monitors to be concerned about the economic or educational costs of such admissions committee decisions. Among the results of such unchecked decisions is that, because Asian and Asian American students tend to be "over-represented" in colleges, especially the highest-ranked colleges, admission committees seeking to create demographic "diversity" have fewer incentives to admit such individuals and perhaps incentives to limit the number of students of Asian origin who are admitted, as some colleges in times past limited the number of Jewish students admitted, even when they were academically better qualified than non-Jewish students who were admitted.

A study of Asian applicants to the University of Michigan, for example, found that those accepted averaged 50 points higher than accepted white students on combined SAT scores, 140 points higher than Hispanic students accepted there and 240 points higher than the black students who were accepted. In 2006, an Asian American student with perfect SAT test scores and near-perfect scores on physics, chemistry and calculus tests was turned down by Stanford, M.I.T. and three Ivy League universities, even though he was admitted to Yale and Harvard.[48] Nor was his case unique. Being highly subjective, admissions criteria are unlikely to be consistent from one college to another, so that a particular student being turned down at one institution while being accepted at a higher-ranked institution is by no means unheard of.

Subjective criteria give members of admissions committees bigger budgets, more power and more sense of importance than if objective criteria were predominant. Again, in this as in many other things, the non-profit nature of academic institutions enables internal constituencies to serve their own interests with fewer constraints than in institutions more dependent for their survival on simultaneously satisfying customers and investors.

It is not a matter of conjecture that admissions office staffs could be much smaller. For most of the history of academic institutions, they were in fact far smaller. Right after the Second World War, for example, the admissions staff at Harvard consisted of one admissions officer and a part-time secretary.[49] Today, even a small college can have a dozen or more full-time admissions officers plus a substantial clerical staff to deal with all the paperwork generated by the admissions office's activities across the country. As more and more money became available for higher education over the years, including government subsidies for even private institutions, the expansion of bureaucratic empires followed.

Unlike private, profit-seeking enterprises, where there are rewards for accomplishing a given task with a minimum number of people and resources, incentives for officials in a non-profit organization are often just the opposite— to use as many people and as large a budget as higher officials can be persuaded to authorize, since the responsibilities of managing a larger staff and a more substantial budget become reasons to expect higher pay and more importance within the institution. As a former dean of admissions at Stanford said, "If we only admitted students based on SAT scores, I wouldn't have a job."[50] She would certainly not have had as large a staff or budget. Whether deliberately or not, college admissions officials have every incentive to turn the applicant selection process into something esoteric and highly subjective, requiring large numbers of people working long hours and traveling thousands of miles a year to confer with high school counselors and students across the nation.

Here, as elsewhere in academia, there is no external check on the validity of the decisions made or the cost in money or lost intellectual talent. There are no owners or stockholders to demand that they get "the most bang for the buck."

Any academic administrator who sought to test the validity of the criteria used by the admissions office— by, for example, admitting half the entering class by objective criteria and the other half by the decisions of the admissions office, and then seeing how the two halves compared later, at graduation time— would stir up a hornet's nest of opposition that would do his or her own career little good and perhaps much harm. Given the incentives and constraints, the path of least resistance for an academic administrator is to let sleeping dogs lie— here as in many other aspects of academic governance— since there are few offsetting personal benefits from greater institutional efficiency, whether in money terms or in terms of meeting the proclaimed educational goals of the institution.

The Cost of College

The cost of going to college can easily be under-estimated or over-estimated. Tuition is often over-estimated when tuition at expensive private colleges and universities is repeatedly cited in the media, even though 56 percent of students in 2008–09 were enrolled in four-year institutions whose tuitions were less than $9,000 per year.[51] Although tuition is more than $30,000 at some well-known colleges that are often mentioned in the media, these tuitions are not only atypical, but are often not actually paid by even half the students who attend, because so many students receive discounts known as "financial aid."

Even in an era of high and rising college tuitions, the biggest cost of going to a college will in many cases not consist of the tuition being paid but the cost of foregoing opportunities to earn income from a full-time job. The average tuition at state colleges and universities is often less than the annual income from an entry-level job, and the tuition at community colleges is almost invariably less. The cost of attending college also includes the growing costs of books but does *not* include the full costs of room and board, since students would have to be housed and fed whether they went to college or not. Only to the extent that these costs are higher on campus can they be considered part of the cost of a college education. In short, money outlays do not measure the total costs of going to college, which can be higher or lower, depending on the institution and the circumstances.

Many lament that the costs of going to college can leave graduates with substantial debts to pay off in later years— and that these debts can be especially burdensome for those who go into occupations with modest pay. Politicians are likely to be responsive to such laments, especially in election years. However, many or most of the discussions of such issues ignore the role of costs and prices in the economy, and proceed as if anyone whose desires are constrained by economics should have those constraints removed by government— which is to say, by shifting those costs to the taxpayers.

Despite what *The Chronicle of Higher Education* has called "high-pitched campaigns" depicting student debt as "a national crisis," about one third of all college students graduate with no debt at all and the average debt among the others is about $20,000— "just below the starting price of a 2009 Ford Escape."[52] No one thinks that the debt incurred in buying an automobile is so crushing that taxpayers must subsidize the purchase of cars. Moreover, the debt from a college education is repaid just once, while most Americans buy more than one automobile in a lifetime. Finally, it is by no means certain that the average taxpayer makes more money than the average college graduate, so the case for forcing taxpayers to subsidize people with better economic prospects than themselves cannot invoke the usual arguments about helping the less fortunate.

As for the argument that the burden of debt is heavier for those who enter lower paying occupations, this ignores the whole role of prices in allocating scarce resources, including expensively educated human beings. It would be an exercise in futility to print money if people's decisions were not to be influenced by it. After all, the money itself is not wealth— otherwise the government could make us all rich just by printing more of it. Money is simply an artificial device to provide incentives for economic behavior affecting the production of real wealth. If people are automatically to be enabled to make their choices independent of monetary considerations, then there has been an enormous waste of paper and ink in printing money.

Seldom is the argument made that nobody should have to take rates of pay into account when choosing among occupations. More usually, there is an assumption that some especially prescient third parties can determine which special occupations "really" meet society's "needs" and therefore should be subsidized through compulsory exactions from the taxpayers. Such arbitrary choices, made by third parties who pay no price for being wrong, are considered to be either economically or morally superior to choices made by people who pay their own money for what they want and thereby determine which products, industries, and occupations will be remunerated to what extent.

ACADEMIC COSTS

In financial discussions, costs and prices are sometimes confused. In the academic world, costs are what colleges and universities pay to their employees and to suppliers of everything from electricity to office supplies, in order to carry on their various activities. Prices are what academic institutions charge other people, whether for educating students, doing research for the government or private industry, or other activities such as staging sports events or publishing books and academic journals. The most prominent of these prices is tuition, and it has become a very prominent item in many families' budgets, together with the other expenses of sending a student to college.

As a former dean of Harvard put it, "A single year's bill at most private universities, not just the top-tier ones, is now about the same as the median U.S. household income."[53] Tuition of more than $30,000 a year is charged not only by all eight Ivy League institutions and by such comparable institutions as Stanford, M.I.T. and the University of Chicago, but also by George Washington University, Hampshire College, Chapman University, and Occidental College, among other less celebrated places.[54] This does not of course include food, housing, and other college expenses.

While the incomes of academic institutions must cover their costs, as with other institutions, whether profit-seeking businesses or non-profit organizations, there are some financial factors at work peculiar to colleges and universities.

Although "cost" is a short and apparently simple word, it conceals a wide variety of complications, whether in an academic or a non-academic context. Costs refer to the expenses incurred to produce goods and services; prices are what the consumers of those goods and services are charged. Price control laws, for example, can reduce prices without having the slightest effect on

costs— which is one of the reasons for the adverse effects of such laws.*
Even when we are clear that what we want to consider are costs of
production, there may be no such thing as "the" cost of producing a given
good or service. Mass production brings down the cost per unit of many
goods, so the cost per unit of producing many things depends on how many
units are produced.

In economics, "costs" usually refer to the inherent or lowest cost of
producing a given quantity and quality of goods and services. Otherwise,
any outlays of money, whether caused by inefficiency, irresponsibility, or
corruption, would be counted as production costs. But, as already noted,
there are academic policies and practices which inflate the actual financial
outlays of colleges and universities well beyond these inherent costs, whether
these policies and practices originate within academic institutions or are
imposed from the outside by accrediting agencies, the American Association
of University Professors, or others.

Among the inherent costs of running a college or university are of course
the costs of educating students and the costs of employing faculty members.
In neither case are there the kinds of incentives to restrain costs as there are
in profit-based enterprises.

Costs of Educating Students

Anything colleges and universities choose to spend money on is called a
"cost" by them— and can then be used to justify raising tuition and calling
upon the government and other donors to help cover "rising costs." These
"costs" have included the building of a high-tech center six miles away from
the campus of the University of Texas at Austin, creation of overseas
campuses by the University of Evansville in England and by the University
of Dallas in Rome, as well as the creation of overseas student centers in
Europe and South America by Stanford. *The Economist* magazine reported
that Ohio University has a student center "which contains a 250-seat
theatre, a food court and a five-storey atrium." At a cost of more than $130

---

* See Chapter 3 of my book *Basic Economics*.

million, Princeton established a new residence complex for 500 students, in which each student's room "has triple-glazed mahogany casement windows made of leaded glass" and the "dining hall boasts a 35-foot ceiling gabled in oak," according to *BusinessWeek* magazine.[55]

Even when a university expenditure is for a genuine academic purpose, that does not necessarily represent a benefit to college students. New science laboratories being added on many university campuses are an example:

> Even many undergraduates studying science will have limited access to the benefits of the new campus labs, which are there mostly for the benefit of faculty members and their graduate students.[56]

When increased voluntary spending is called "rising costs," and becomes a basis for raising tuition, seeking more taxpayer money, or even dipping into the principal of endowments, then the kinds of economic constraints faced by competing business enterprises are clearly not operating in the academic world.

Against that background, it is possible to understand the proliferation of campus amenities such as bowling alleys and posh lounges, all counted as costs of education. Indiana University of Pennsylvania, for example, began spending $270 million for new dormitories described in *The Chronicle of Higher Education* as "swanky."[57] College dormitories in general have been described by *The Chronicle of Higher Education* as "cushier" than in the past.[58] Other amenities have also grown more elaborate and costly:

> Last year the *Dallas Morning News* reported that Baylor University increased the height of its planned rock-climbing wall from 41 to 52 feet after learning that Texas A&M University's was 44 feet. Then the University of Houston built a climbing wall that was 53 feet high, and even that was later surpassed by the University of Texas at San Antonio.[59]

Those atypical academic institutions which depend solely on making a profit for their survival seldom offer the kinds of amenities offered by non-profit colleges and universities. As one study put it:

> For-profits operate in modest but comfortable buildings in many locations, rather than in one large, centralized campus. Enrollments are often measured in the hundreds or, at most, a few thousand, on any given campus. Almost all of their facilities are directly related to instruction or

administration— there are few, if any, of the recreational facilities, art galleries, concert halls, research laboratories, or libraries that are features of the typical university campus.[60]

The education offered by profit-seeking colleges and universities is not only more cost-conscious but also tends to be more focused on courses that create occupational skills, such as computer programming, business management, and other subjects that are valued in the job market, rather than courses on philosophy, anthropology and the like.[61] In short, they tailor what they supply to what is in demand by paying customers, the same as other profit-based businesses do.

Given the inhibitions against price competition in academia created by accrediting agencies and the American Association of University Professors, as well as the availability of taxpayers' money to meet "rising costs," and the ability to tap endowment money as "needed," non-profit colleges exhibit the kind of non-price competition through competing amenities once found in the airline industry (which often gave out toiletries kits or free glasses of wine, for example) back in the days when it was insulated from competition by government regulation. After deregulation, the entry of new and lower-cost airlines brought the disappearance of many airline amenities. But academic institutions are protected by, among other things, accrediting agencies which treat many amenities and perquisites as costs that newcomers must incur in order to get the accreditation needed to attract both students and government money.

Costs are especially elusive in the case of academic institutions because most are producing joint products, including teaching and research. *There is no such thing as the average cost of a joint product.* There is an average cost of raising a pig but there is no average cost of producing bacon, which is produced jointly with ham, pork chops, and pigskin. In the academic world, where the same professors, the same libraries, the same science labs, and the same computer facilities are all used for producing both teaching and research, any division of their costs between these two activities is arbitrary.

There is another sense in which determining the costs of teaching and research is difficult: When the average teaching load at many universities was reduced over the years from 12 semester hours to 6 semester hours, that required the hiring of twice as many faculty members to teach a given number of courses. Although the additional costs might be attributed to teaching in the institution's accounting records, in fact a key reason for reduced teaching loads has been to provide more time for professors to do more research.

Academic institutions often make the argument that their costs for educating a student are greater than the price they charge as tuition, which some take as a sign of the altruism of a non-profit institution. But, since teaching is one of the joint products of an academic institution, along with research and other ancillary activities, the meaning of such a statement is elusive.

No one would take seriously a similar statement by the owners of the New York Yankees, if they said that fans who go to Yankee Stadium do not pay the full cost of running the baseball team, and left the inference that their organization was an altruistic institution. The joint products being sold by the club owners include live performances of baseball games at Yankee Stadium, televised broadcasts of those games, the selling of advertising space at the park and the renting out of Yankee Stadium for other entertainment when the baseball team is not in town and during the off-season. Given the multiple sources of revenue from all these activities, there is no reason at all why fans who buy tickets at the ball park should cover all the costs of running the organization that fields a baseball team at Yankee Stadium.*

Similarly, there is no reason why students should pay all the costs of all the activities at a university. Yet people take seriously such statements as that by the provost of Stanford University that tuition covers only 58 percent of the cost of educating a student,[62] even though there is no definitive way of determining how much of the expenditures of Stanford or any other multi-purpose institution can be attributed to the teaching of students. *The Chronicle of Higher Education* calculated how much of the cost of educating a student was paid by the student by "dividing each institution's total annual budget by its enrollment." It then concluded that students at state research

---

* In addition, the presence of fans in the stands enhances the spectacle for television viewers beyond what it would be if the game were played in a silent and empty ball park. The spectators are like movie extras, except that, instead of being paid like extras, they are paying to be present.

universities pay only 47 percent of the costs of such institutions[63]— as if all these institution's costs come from educating students.

If the argument is taken literally that colleges and universities lose money on every student, then it would be hard to explain why these institutions spend so much time and money recruiting students, and why the number of students admitted to a given institution tends to increase over time.* But these things make sense when taking into account the fact that the *incremental* costs of adding students may be quite low. Once classrooms, dormitories, libraries, sports arenas, and other campus facilities have been built, the cost of having more students using them can be very modest. Put differently, when a college does not have enough of the students it admitted actually enroll to fill up the dormitories, the empty rooms are unlikely to reduce the cost of dormitory upkeep as much as the missing students' missing tuitions and missing room rents reduce the college's revenues. As *The Chronicle of Higher Education* once put it:

> As competition for new students grows tougher, college presidents are treating admissions directors like football coaches, firing those who can't put the numbers on the board.[64]

This is not the kind of behavior to expect if colleges are in fact losing money on their students. Colleges are at least as anxious to recruit students as the New York Yankees are to get fans to come to Yankee Stadium, even though in both cases the price of admission does not cover all the costs of the organization. Price discounts known as "financial aid" in academia make economic sense in this situation. As a book co-authored by a college president and a university dean put it:

> Just as airlines have come to learn that a seat filled at a deep discount is a better deal than an empty seat, so colleges have come to see that a student with a big institutional grant still brings more net revenue than an empty seat in a classroom or an unoccupied bed in a dormitory.[65]

---

* Harvard was more than 200 years old before it graduated a class of as many as a hundred students. Harry R. Lewis, *Excellence Without a Soul*, p. 27.

Among colleges with more applicants than they can admit, it would be possible to admit only students who can pay the full list price tuition but this would conflict with faculty desires, the institution's public relations, and the prevailing ideas among people in college admissions offices, where even merit-based scholarships are often deplored as "buying students" with high qualifications, as distinct from awarding need-based scholarships to students whose academic qualifications may not be as high. Moreover, the fact that there are no owners or investors to monitor the effects of decisions on institutional income means that admissions offices are freer to indulge their own views. A common view in academia is that "merit aid constitutes another reward to students who have already garnered a greatly disproportionate share of the nation's resources."[66]

This raises a fundamental question as to what admissions policies, as well as financial aid policies, are meant to accomplish— whether these policies are meant to allow admissions office personnel to dispense largesse, whether in money or in kind, in accordance with their own arbitrary social notions, or to invest the institution's financial and academic resources where there will be "the most bang for the buck" in terms of the intellectual quality of graduates coming out of the institution. In the absence of any bottom-line criterion for measuring the success or failure of admissions and financial aid policies, those who staff these offices become another internal constituency able to indulge themselves, with little or no regard to external institutional purposes and little or no monitoring of their decisions by others with a vested interest in institutional efficiency.

The Costs of Faculties

One of the major costs to colleges and universities is faculty tenure. When combined with laws against "age discrimination," tenure means virtually a lifetime guarantee of employment, even for those professors who do not keep up with the advances in their respective fields or who otherwise become less effective as teachers or scholars in their later years. They can usually be replaced only by paying them a substantial sum of money to retire. Short of replacing them, another alternative is to hire someone else to teach the same subjects taught by a professor who has not kept up with the latest developments in that professor's field. Such duplication of courses is expensive but it may be the only way that a university with highly rated departments can maintain its high reputation, instead of sending less qualified students out into the world because they were taught by professors whose knowledge lags behind that of professional colleagues elsewhere.

While there is little that colleges and universities can do about existing tenured faculty members, nevertheless after these professors retire or die, the academic institutions that employed them have the option to hire replacements with tenure or to hire replacements who will not have tenure nor be appointed to the kinds of positions from which people are in line for tenure under the "up or out" system. These non-tenure-track positions can be as part-time faculty or adjunct instructors, or lecturers who may be full-time but who are hired with contracts creating no expectation of tenure.

With the passing years, more and more institutions are hiring increasing numbers of faculty members who do not have tenure or an expectation of tenure. These include part-time faculty and also some full-time faculty members who are not in tenure-track positions. Over time, there has been a general trend toward having a higher proportion of the total faculty consist of people who are not eligible for tenure.[67] In 2010, the *New York Times* reported:

> In 1960, 75 percent of college instructors were full-time tenured or tenure-track professors; today only 27 percent are. The rest are graduate students or adjunct and contingent faculty— instructors employed on a per-course or yearly contract basis, usually without benefits and earning a third or less of what their tenured colleagues make.[68]

Part-time faculty are especially prevalent at lower-ranked colleges, community colleges and profit-based institutions. At the College of Dupage, for example, adjunct faculty outnumber full-time faculty by more than three to one. At a profit-based institution like the University of Phoenix, nearly all the faculty are part-time.

However, the widespread use of non-tenure-track faculty is not confined to the less prestigious institutions, by any means. There may also be a widespread use of non-tenure-track faculty at those elite institutions where many top scholars prefer not to teach undergraduates but to concentrate on more advanced work that is more rewarding for themselves, both intellectually and financially. A science professor at the University of Michigan once put the situation very bluntly when he said: "Every minute I spend in an undergraduate classroom is costing me money and prestige."[69] What this means for students is that these students may be attracted to some big-name institutions whose prestige is generated by professors who are unlikely to teach them, especially in their freshman year, and who in some cases are not likely to teach them unless and until they reach graduate school.

ACADEMIC REVENUES

The fact that an institution is non-profit in no way implies that it is indifferent to money or even that it is less assiduous in pursuing money than are businesses set up to make a profit. In many colleges and universities, junior faculty members cannot expect to be promoted to tenured ranks unless and until they bring in research grants, from which the institution takes a sizable share as overhead charges— on average about 44 percent on grants from the Department of Health and Human Services, for example.[70]

To some extent, these overhead charges represent a recovery of investments made earlier in faculty members' careers. According to *The Chronicle of Higher Education*, the University of Wisconsin at Madison spends an estimated "$1.2-million in start-up costs for each new professor." *The Chronicle of Higher Education* adds:

> It typically takes eight years for a professor to bring in enough research money to cover that cost. A professor who stays at Madison for 25 years after earning tenure brings in an average of about $13-million in research money. But the university loses many professors before they even pay off the initial investment.[71]

Given the large sums of money that a professor at a leading research university can bring in, it is easy to see why competition for such professors drives their salaries up at such universities, as compared to teaching colleges.

Government

Government is a major source of revenue for colleges and universities. As already noted, money received from government exceeds money received from students' tuition at four-year colleges in general and especially at research universities.[72]

Government subsidies for students whose families' incomes are not high enough to make college "affordable" create an incentive for colleges to keep tuition high enough to be *unaffordable* for large numbers of students. When the government's formula for awarding student aid subtracts a family's "expected contribution" (based primarily on family income) to a student's higher education from the prices charged by colleges, in order to determine how large the government subsidy will be, even a small college would forego millions of dollars in government money annually if it kept its tuition down within the range of what most families could afford. From the standpoint of the college's financial interests, it makes more sense to keep tuition unaffordable for most of its students and use the additional money this brings in from the government to upgrade campus amenities, in order to compete with other colleges that way, instead of competing on the basis of tuition.

The fallacy that keeps this perpetual tuition escalation going is ignoring the fact that subsidizing existing "costs" provides incentives for those "costs" to rise. One study has found that "public four-year institutions tended to raise tuition by $50 for every $100 increase in federal student aid."[73]

Academic institutions lobby Congress for money to be spent both on higher education in general and for money to be earmarked for their own particular institution. Since money earmarked in legislation for particular institutions are a way of by-passing the peer-review process by which federal agencies weigh competing requests for money, such earmarked funds are especially sought by institutions with lesser chances of getting grants on their merits in competition with more prestigious institutions. As a study noted, "the vast majority of university lobbying, and virtually 100 percent of lobbying by universities that are not among the top research institutions, is devoted to the pursuit of earmarks."[74] The lobbying process was described in the same study:

In January, a university's administrators meet with its lobbyist to formulate lobbying strategy for the upcoming fiscal year. They prioritize potential earmark requests by the likelihood of success and identify elected officials to lobby. They will typically target the representative and/or senators from the university's district and state. In March, the university begins to lobby the targeted representatives to include its request in the appropriations legislation. After the August recess, there is a push to get the request included in one of the 13 appropriations bills. The cycle ends in late autumn, as the appropriations bills are sent to the president.[75]

Universities engaged in lobbying for federal money spend an average of more than $100,000 a year each on such lobbying and receive back in federal money more than a million dollars each. Universities located in the district or state of a Congressional Representative or Senator who is a member of the House or Senate appropriations committee receive back even higher rates of return on their lobbying investments than the eight-fold return received by other universities. Again, being a non-profit institution does not mean less hotly pursuing money than enterprises whose incomes are called profit.

Money from outside sources— government, industry, foundations, and individual donors— are crucial for the research that in turn is crucial for both individual and institutional prosperity and prestige. Even richly endowed universities like Harvard and Yale, receiving millions of dollars annually from the earnings of their endowments that are invested in the financial markets, do not finance most of their research from their own money but from money received from government and other outside sources. In fiscal year 2004, for example, Yale University spent more than ten times as much money from the government as from its own money to finance its research and development— and Harvard spent none of its own money for that purpose, while spending $399 million in government money.[76]

Tuition and Financial Aid

While money from government exceeds tuition payments from students, revenue from tuition is not negligible. Although the official tuition is the same for everybody, in many of the more expensive colleges and universities, a majority of the students receive what is called "financial aid" in the form of discounts from those prices. In private industry, what is called tuition in academia would be called the list price, and giving different discounts according to income would be called "charging what the traffic will bear."

What being non-profit does mean is that institutional policies can adjust to fashions and pressures inside and outside academia more readily than a profit-based enterprise can in a competitive market. Thus, when universities with large endowments were under pressure from Congress to spend more of those endowments to reduce the costs of students attending college, Harvard led the way by announcing that it would cover the college costs of all students whose family's income did not exceed $60,000 a year. Private, profit-based enterprises could not afford to give away their goods or services like that. Whether that was the optimal use of Harvard's endowment, either from an educational standpoint or a social standpoint, is a question that need not be faced by those making such decisions, since there are no owners or investors to react when their financial interests are sacrificed.

Intercollegiate Athletics

Intercollegiate sports— especially football and basketball— are another source of considerable revenue for some colleges and universities. A number of colleges with big-time sports programs have had multi-year media contracts from companies paying tens of millions of dollars to broadcast their games. In 2009, Ohio State University signed a ten-year contract guaranteeing them a total of $110 million for their media and marketing rights.[77] However, these revenues seldom contribute anything toward the educational activities of these institutions.

A former president of Yale University summed up the situation succinctly: "I have yet to see the laboratory or library or dormitory built with football or basketball revenues."[78] On the contrary, these and other sports more commonly cost more money than they bring in, even though the top intercollegiate sports can bring in millions of dollars in gate receipts to a given college, and billions of dollars have been paid for the right to broadcast a college basketball tournament,[79] in addition to other money from other sources.

Although teaching and research are joint products, whose costs cannot be determined separately, most of the costs involved with intercollegiate sports are *not* costs incurred jointly with other academic activities. A stadium is seldom a site for research or the teaching of academic subjects. Even the academic coaching and advising of college athletes, in order to maintain their grades at a level that enables them to remain eligible to play, is often conducted by a separate staff and even in separate buildings from those used for the academic coaching and advising of other students.

In 2006, Ohio State University became the first academic institution to spend more than $100 million a year on its many athletic programs. However, with a top-ranked football team playing a bowl game, its $101.8 million in expenses was covered by $104.7 million in revenue that year.[80] At most colleges and universities, however, financial losses are the rule for athletic programs. Moreover, even those few colleges and universities whose sports programs cover their costs in a given year need not continue to do so. *The Chronicle of Higher Education* reported on the University of Oregon sports programs in 2007:

> Oregon proudly proclaims that it has recently joined the small handful of universities with self-supporting athletics departments. But university officials acknowledge that shrinking proceeds from a few bad seasons of football would be enough to put the department back in the red.[81]

Despite some "creative" accounting used to conceal how much some intercollegiate sports are costing, the head of the National Collegiate Athletic Association (NCAA) "acknowledged that, when properly accounted, fewer than 10 of the more than 1,000 college athletic departments run a surplus," according to the *New York Times*.[82] College baseball is the biggest money-losing intercollegiate sport, perhaps because there is little demand for the televising of college baseball games, in contrast to the demand for televising college football games, which can offset some of its costs. The median loss on college baseball programs in 2004–2006 was nearly $700,000 a year.[83]

The NCAA is a nationwide cartel, whose guiding principle is that none of the vast sums of money involved in intercollegiate sports shall be paid to the student athletes who play the games at the risk of their bodies. Meanwhile, those who direct these athletic contests from the sideline can be handsomely rewarded. More than a hundred years ago, when Harvard hired its first paid football coach, his salary "was 30 percent more than the best-paid Harvard professor received and was comparable to Eliot's salary after his almost forty years as president."[84] Such patterns remain common today, except that it is now more common for football coaches to be paid *more* than the presidents of their respective universities.[85]

Even a college's top recruiters of high school football players can earn more than $200,000 a year, which is more than the average salary of a full professor at Harvard.[86] In 2007, 21 Division I institutions spent more than a million dollars each on recruiting athletes, with the University of Tennessee at Knoxville spending more than $2 million. Even most Ivy League universities, which are not part of high-stakes Division I athletics, spent between three-quarters of a million and one million dollars each recruiting athletes.[87]

It might seem strange, if not irrational, for a college or university to be paying huge salaries to those who are directing an activity that is usually losing money on net balance. But, again, it is necessary to distinguish what is beneficial from the standpoint of the institution as a whole from what is beneficial from the standpoint of those particular individuals in charge of making particular decisions within that institution. Moreover, short-run economics differs from long-run economics.

In the short run, a sports stadium and other athletic facilities have already been built, so the only costs that matter are the *incremental* costs of maintaining and operating these facilities, which may be a small fraction of the total costs that include the cost of building such facilities. The revenues that a successful sports program can bring in— whether in gate receipts, television rights, bowl game money, etc.— may easily exceed the incremental costs of keeping the athletic program alive and successful. On the other hand, if the football or basketball team is a chronic loser in its games, all these sources of revenue may fall drastically, and fail to cover even the incremental costs of running an athletic program.

Obviously, for every unbeaten team there must be several teams that they have beaten, and total wins and losses must always be the same for college teams as a whole, leaving few teams with the kinds of impressive records that keep stadiums filled and television rights for their games in demand.

Given these incentives and constraints, hiring a coach who is likely to produce a winning season may be worth paying a very large salary.

In the long run, however, the stadium and other athletic facilities will need costly renovation or rebuilding. From a purely economic standpoint, the college or university might be better off at that point to discontinue intercollegiate athletic programs that are costing more money than they are bringing in. However, from the standpoint of a college or university president, is it worth stirring up a hornet's nest of outrage from students, alumni and perhaps even some faculty members, by discontinuing a football or basketball program that the president has been repeatedly authorizing for years? A college or university president has few incentives to think in long-run terms beyond the president's own term in office. Moreover, the president's term in office can be cut short precisely by outraging various constituencies of the institution.

When even a small, academically oriented liberal arts college like Birmingham-Southern dropped out of Division I athletic competition down to Division III, where they would compete against other small, academically oriented liberal arts colleges, there were student protests and local newspapers criticized the decision, even though the athletic budget of $6.5 million was 15 percent of the college's total budget.[88] If an uproar could be created at an institution not known historically as a football or basketball powerhouse, for merely dropping down into a less prominent athletic division, it can be imagined what the reaction could be from abandoning intercollegiate sports altogether.

Since universities participating in intercollegiate athletics are non-profit organizations, there are no stockholders to complain about the inefficiency of subsidizing money-losing activities, much less mount a campaign to get rid of a chief executive who is reducing the return on their investment. In a profit-based enterprise, any money-losing operation is a threat to the institution's long-run economic position— and that long-run threat is reflected *immediately* in its stock price, in a lowered rating of its bonds, and in a growing reluctance of banks or other financial institutions to lend them money. It is significant that the relatively few academic institutions that are run for profit, including the University of Phoenix, which has more students than any non-profit university, do not have football teams or stadiums.*

At the heart of these and many other institutional decisions in the academic world is the fact that few, if any, individuals have a direct personal interest in the long-run economic or educational consequences of decisions made by officials of most colleges and universities. Students are passing through in a few years, professors move easily from one institution to another, and few college or university presidents today stay at the same institution for decades, as Charles Eliot once did at Harvard or as Nicholas Murray Butler did at Columbia and Robert Hutchins did at the University of Chicago.

Presidents of lower-ranked colleges or universities may aspire to become presidents of higher-ranked institutions, and presidents of the latter may aspire to high positions in the political or foundations worlds. But seldom is there a long-term commitment to a given institution today that would provide incentives for students, faculty, or administrators to take a long-term view of the consequences for the institution of the decisions currently being made, whether in intercollegiate athletics or in other aspects of decision-making in higher education.

It should also be noted that, although spokesmen for the National Collegiate Athletic Association depict intercollegiate athletes as students first and athletes second, Division I football players spend an average of 44.8 hours per week on athletics, and even participants in intercollegiate golf average 40.8 hours a week on this sport.[89] Tighter academic standards for college athletes have led many colleges and universities to establish expensive programs of academic advisers exclusively for their athletes. According to *The Chronicle of Higher Education*:

> Since 1997, the budgets for academic services for athletes at more than half of the 73 biggest athletics programs in the country have more than doubled, on average, to more than $1-million a year. One program spent almost $3-million in 2007— an average of more than $6,000 per athlete.[90]

---

* The University of Phoenix has paid to put its name on a stadium, as other commercial enterprises do as an advertising device, but the University of Phoenix did not incur the costs of building that stadium, as non-profit academic institutions do.

These tutoring facilities exclusively for college athletes had annual budgets ranging up to nearly $3 million at the University of Oklahoma in academic year 2007–08 and have been housed in buildings ranging in size up to more than 20,000 square feet in at least a dozen institutions and more than 50,000 square feet at the University of Alabama at Tuscaloosa and at Louisiana State University at Baton Rouge.[91]

Among the biggest beneficiaries of intercollegiate athletics are professional football and basketball leagues, for whom college athletics has been aptly characterized as "a cost-free minor league." It has been estimated that, if colleges were economically based operations, they could charge professional football and basketball leagues more than $100 million for serving as the source of their players.[92]

Other Sources of Revenue

Among the other sources of revenue for academic institutions are the earnings from their endowments and proceeds from the sale of their bonds. The most richly endowed get from 20 to 40 percent of their operating revenue from the earnings on their endowment and/or from spending some of the principal. In some years, Princeton has gotten nearly half its budget from its endowment. The typical college, however, gets only about 5 percent of its operating revenues from its endowment, the *Wall Street Journal* reported in 2009. Bond sales also bring in money to meet current cash flow requirements, though this money is not revenue but simply a loan that will have to be repaid. During the economic downturn, Princeton received a billion dollars this way and Harvard a billion and a half.[93]

SUMMARY AND CONCLUSIONS

Many of the economic and educational decisions made at colleges and universities seem inexplicable as the actions of institutions pursuing either the best interests of the students or the best interests of the institutions themselves. However, the actions of academic institutions are much more readily understood as responses to the incentives and constraints facing the various autonomous decision-makers such as professors, administrators, trustees, athletic coaches and others pursuing their own self-interests. Such internal conflicts of interest with the over-all purposes of the institution as a whole are much more readily constrained in a profit-seeking enterprise, where the difference between profit and loss is the difference between survival and extinction— and where stockholders and outside financial institutions react quickly to both the short-run and long-run implications of decisions made within profit-seeking enterprises.

Institutional investors in private businesses, such as banks and Wall Street financial institutions, are especially likely to have the expertise and experience that individual stockholders may lack, and so serve as an especially keen watchdog on corporate efficiency. While much can be concealed from corporate stockholders, what is hard to conceal is the bottom line— how the profitability of a given company compares to the profitability of other companies in the same or other industries. There is no such bottom line in the non-profit academic world, either financially or in terms of the quality of the education produced. Institutional investors in academic institutions are often other non-profit organizations such as foundations or government agencies, which themselves lack the personal stakes which business investors have.

Where the ultimate test is satisfying paying customers and investors, rather than people inside the organization or their like-minded peers elsewhere, there are inherent limits on the extent to which self-indulgences among insiders are likely to be tolerated. Non-profit organizations like colleges and universities, however, receive much money from people whose desires do not count— not only taxpayers but also deceased donors who have contributed either to the institution's endowment or to particular academic programs. Even living donors may have little recourse, except through costly and protracted litigation with uncertain outcomes, when the purpose for which they donated money is not followed and the money is diverted to other purposes, including purposes antithetical to the donor's intent.

As much as academic institutions may seek earmarked funds from government, they discourage the earmarking of funds from donors, so as to leave themselves freer to spend the money entrusted to them for whatever they feel like spending it on. When both campus amenities for student and faculty research are subsidized by government, the taxpayers are in effect paying for academic institutions to compete against one another for relative prestige, an essentially zero-sum competition. While the results of some research is valuable to society at large, many knowledgeable people inside and outside the academic world have complained that much— perhaps most— of the research is of little value to anyone beyond those who must pad their résumés to advance their careers.

Since so much of this research is subsidized by government, foundations, and other outside sources, there is little check or limit on how far to carry the research, such as would apply in the case of a business which had to make sure that the return on its investment in research covered the costs of the research. There is also little economic constraint on a university's output of students with degrees, since the inability of college or university graduates to get jobs in some fields is their problem, not the problem of the institutions that awarded their degrees. In a number of fields, complaints that students receiving their Ph.D.s find it difficult to get jobs in their professions have been made for years— sometimes decades— without any reduction in the numbers of Ph.D.s awarded by universities to accommodate supply to demand. At one time, there were more than a hundred applicants for every teaching position in history, and even more in English and philosophy.[94]

Government subsidies are a factor in this continued overproduction of degrees, in disregard of the limits of demand, because these subsidies relieve universities of many of the huge costs of training graduate students especially, and relieve these graduate students of having to face the question of whether there is enough demand in the job market for the kinds of skills they are studying to acquire. Government research grants support many graduate students, both while they are working toward their doctorates and afterwards, because postdoctoral grants continue to support them at the universities after they complete their degrees and cannot find employment.

While this problem has long been especially acute in the humanities, it also exists in the sciences. "In physics nearly 70 percent of newly minted

Ph.D.'s go into temporary postdoctoral positions," *The Chronicle of Higher Education* reported in 2007.[95] In other words, government subsidies reduce incentives for the universities to supply fewer doctorates when there is less demand in the fields in which these degrees are awarded.

In general, the way that higher education is financed— including the non-profit status of most academic institutions— gives decision-makers in academia far greater latitude in deciding what to do than is the case in enterprises whose survival depends on accommodating both those who receive their goods and services and those who supply the money which makes the production of those goods and services possible. It is therefore not very surprising that many of the decisions made in the academic world serve the interests of those who make those decisions more so than the interests of the institutions that employ them, much less the interests of the larger society from which academics draw their resources.

Even in times of financial stringency, academic priorities are revealed by what things are cut and what things are not. One college president satirically analogized what happens in a time of academic financial crisis on campus to what happens on a sinking ship, where the college president is in the role of the captain, the faculty are the crew, and students are the passengers:

> All in all, it was akin to a ship hitting an iceberg, and the captain announcing as the boat sinks that his highest priority is to save the crew. The next priority is to avoid any inconvenience as the ship goes down by continuing all activities— the midnight buffet, the bingo game, and the shuffleboard tournament. The third priority is to repair the ship. And the fourth and final priority, should time permit, is to save the passengers.[96]

Chapter 5

INCOME FACTS AND FALLACIES

> *Measuring the growth of incomes or the inequality of incomes is a little like Olympic figure skating— full of dangerous leaps and twirls and not nearly as easy as it looks. Yet the growth and inequality of incomes are topics that seem to inspire many people to form very strong opinions about very weak statistics.*
>
> *Alan Reynolds*[1]

Mark Twain said that there are three kinds of lies— "lies, damned lies, and statistics." Income statistics are classic examples of numbers that can be arranged differently to suggest, not merely different, but totally opposite conclusions. Among the bountiful supply of fallacies about income and wealth are the following:

1. Except for the rich, the incomes of Americans have stagnated for years.
2. The American middle class is growing smaller.
3. Over the years, the poor have been getting poorer.
4. Corporate executives are overpaid, at the expense of both stockholders and consumers.

There are statistics which can be cited to support each of these propositions— and other statistics, or even the same statistics looked at differently— that can make these propositions collapse like a house of cards. Despite an abundance of statistical data collected by the Bureau of the

Census, other government agencies, and a variety of private research enterprises, controversies rage on, even though the numbers themselves are seldom in dispute. It is the analyses— or the fallacies— that are at issue.

Some of the most misleading fallacies come from confusing the fate of statistical categories with the fate of flesh-and-blood human beings. Statistical data for households, income brackets, and other statistical categories can be very misleading because (1) there are often different numbers of people in each category and (2) individuals move from one category to another. Thus the statistical category "top one percent" of income recipients has received a growing share of the nation's income in recent years— while the actual flesh-and-blood taxpayers who were in that category in 1996 actually saw their income go *down* by 2005. What makes it possible for both these apparently contradictory statements to be true is that more than half of the people who were in the top one percent at the beginning of the decade were no longer there at the end. As their incomes declined, they dropped out of the top one percent.

The same principle applies in the lower income brackets. The share of the national income going to the statistical category "lowest 20 percent" of taxpayers has been declining somewhat over the years but the actual flesh-and-blood human beings who were in the bottom 20 percent in 1996 had their incomes increase by an average of 91 percent by 2005. This nearly doubling of their incomes took more than half of them out of the bottom 20 percent category.[2]

INCOME STAGNATION

What might seem to be one of the easiest questions to answer— whether most Americans' incomes have been growing or not— is in fact one of the most hotly disputed.

Household Income

It has often been claimed that there has been very little change in the average real income of American households over a period of decades. It is an undisputed fact that the average real income— that is, money income adjusted for inflation— of American households rose by only 6 percent over the entire period from 1969 to 1996. That might well be considered to qualify as stagnation. But it is an equally undisputed fact that the average real income per person in the United States rose by 51 percent over that very same period.[3]

How can both these statistics be true? Because the average number of individuals per household has been declining over the years. Half the households in the United States contained six or more people in 1900, as did 21 percent in 1950. But, by 1998, only ten percent of American households had that many people.[4]

The average number of persons per household not only varies over time, it also varies from one racial or ethnic group to another at a given time, and varies from one income bracket to another. As of 2007, for example, black household income was lower than Hispanic household income, even though black per capita income was higher than Hispanic per capita income, because black households average fewer people than Hispanic households. Similarly, Asian American household income was higher than white household income, even though white per capita income was higher than Asian American per capita income, because Asian American households average more people.[5]

Income comparisons using household statistics are far less reliable indicators of standards of living than are individual income data because households vary in size while an individual always means one person. Studies of what people actually consume— that is, their standard of living— show substantial increases over the years, even among the poor,[6] which is more in keeping with a 51 percent increase in real per capita income than with a 6 percent increase in real household income. But household income statistics present golden opportunities for fallacies to flourish, and those opportunities have been seized by many in the media, in politics, and in academia.

A *Washington Post* writer, for example, said, "the incomes of most American households have remained stubbornly flat over the past three decades,"[7] suggesting that there had been little change in the standard of living. A *New York Times* writer likewise declared: "The incomes of most

American households have failed to gain ground on inflation since 1973."[8]
The head of a Washington think tank was quoted in the *Christian Science
Monitor* as declaring: "The economy is growing without raising average living
standards."[9] Harvard economist Benjamin M. Friedman said, "the median
family's income is falling after allowing for rising prices; only a relatively few
at the top of the income scale have been enjoying any increase."[10]

Sometimes such conclusions arise from statistical naivete but sometimes
the inconsistency with which data are cited suggests a bias. Long-time *New
York Times* columnist Tom Wicker, for example, used per capita income
statistics when he depicted success for the Lyndon Johnson administration's
economic policies and family income statistics when he depicted failure for
the policies of Ronald Reagan and George H. W. Bush.[11] Families, like
households, vary in size over time, from one group to another, and from one
income bracket to another.[12]

A rising standard of living is itself one of the factors behind reduced
household size over time. As far back the 1960s, a Census Bureau study
noted "the increased tendency, particularly among unrelated individuals, to
maintain their own homes or apartments rather than live with relatives or
move into existing households as roomers, lodgers, and so forth."[13] Increased
real income per person enables more people to live in their own separate
dwelling units, instead of with parents, roommates, or strangers in a rooming
house. Yet a reduction in the number of people living under the same roof as
a result of increased prosperity can lead to statistics that are often cited as
proof of economic stagnation. In a low-income household, increased income
may either cause that household's income to rise above the poverty level or
cause overcrowding to be relieved by having some members go form their
own separate households— which in turn can lead to statistics showing two
households living below the poverty level, where there was only one before.
Such statistics are not inaccurate but the conclusion drawn can be fallacious.

Differences in household size are very substantial from one income level
to another. U.S. Census data show 39 million people living in households
whose incomes are in the bottom 20 percent of household incomes and 64
million people living in households in the top 20 percent.[14] Under these
circumstances, measuring income inequality or income rises and falls by

households can lead to completely different results from measuring the same things with data on individuals. Comparing households of highly varying sizes can mean comparing apples and oranges. Not only do households differ greatly in the numbers of people per household at different income levels, the number of *working* people varies even more widely.

In the year 2000, the top 20 percent of households by income contained 19 million heads of households who worked, compared to fewer than 8 million heads of households who worked in the bottom 20 percent of households. These differences are even more extreme when comparing people who work full-time and year-round. There are nearly six times as many such people in the top 20 percent of households as in the bottom 20 percent.[15] Even the top *five* percent of households by income had more heads of household who worked full-time for 50 or more weeks a year than did the bottom *twenty* percent. In absolute numbers, there were 3.9 million heads of household working full-time and year-round in the top 5 percent of households and only 3.3 million working full-time and year-round in the bottom 20 percent.[16]

There was a time when it was meaningful to speak of "the idle rich" and the "toiling poor" but that time has long past. Most households in the bottom 20 percent by income do not have *any* full-time, year-round worker and 56 percent of these households do not have anyone working even part-time.[17] Some of these low-income households contain single mothers on welfare and their children. Some such households consist of retirees living on Social Security or others who are not working, or who are working sporadically or part-time, because of disabilities or for other reasons.

Household income data can therefore be very misleading, whether comparing income differences as of a given time or following changes in income over the years. For example, one study dividing the country into "five equal layers" by income reached dire conclusions about the degree of inequality between the top and bottom 20 percent of households.[18] These equal percentages of *households*, however, were by no means equal percentages of *people*, since the poorest fifth of households contain 25 million fewer people than the fifth of households with the highest incomes. Increasing income inequality over time also becomes much less mysterious in an era when people are paid more for their work, because this means that people who don't work as much, or at all, lose opportunities to share in this income rise. In addition to differences among income brackets in how many heads of household work, there are even larger differences in how many total members of households work. The top 20 percent of households have four times as many workers as the bottom 20 percent, and more than five times as many full-time, year-round workers.[19]

No doubt these differences in the number of paychecks per household have something to do with the differences in income, though such facts often get omitted from discussions of income "disparities" and "inequities" caused by "society." The very possibility that inequality is not caused by society but by people who contribute less than others to the economy, and are correspondingly less rewarded, is seldom mentioned, much less examined. But not only do households in the bottom 20 percent contribute less work, they contribute far less skills, based on education. While nearly 60 percent of Americans in the top 20 percent graduated from college, only 6 percent of those in the bottom 20 percent did so.[20] Such glaring facts are often omitted from discussions which center on the presumed failings of "society" and resolutely ignore facts counter to that vision.

Most statistics on income inequality are very misleading in yet another way. These statistics almost invariably leave out money received as transfers from the government in various programs for low-income people which provide benefits of substantial value for which the recipients pay nothing. Since people in the bottom 20 percent of income recipients receive more than two-thirds of their income from transfer payments, leaving those cash payments out of the statistics greatly exaggerates their poverty— and leaving out in-kind transfers as well, such as subsidized housing, distorts their economic situation even more. In 2001, for example, cash and in-kind transfers together accounted for 77.8 percent of the economic resources of people in the bottom 20 percent.[21] In other words, the alarming statistics on their incomes so often cited in the media and by politicians count *only 22 percent of the actual economic resources at their disposal.*

Given such disparities between the economic reality and the alarming statistics, it is much easier to understand such apparent anomalies as the fact that Americans living below the official poverty level spend far more money than their incomes[22]— as their income is defined in statistical studies. As for stagnation, by 2001 most people defined as poor had possessions once considered part of a middle class lifestyle. Three-quarters of them had air-conditioning, which only a third of all Americans had in 1971. Ninety-seven percent had color television, which less than half of all Americans had in 1971. Seventy-three percent owned a microwave, which less than one percent of Americans owned in 1971, and 98 percent of "the poor" had either a videocassette recorder or a DVD player, which no one had in 1971. In addition, 72 percent of "the poor" owned a car or truck.[23] Yet the rhetoric of the "haves" and the "have nots" continues, even in a society where it might be more accurate to refer to the "haves" and the "have lots."

No doubt there are still some genuinely poor people who are genuinely hurting. But they bear little resemblance to most of the millions of people in the often-cited statistics on households in the bottom 20 percent. Much poverty is imported across the southern border of the United States that immigrants cross, legally or illegally, from Mexico. The poverty rate among foreign nationals in the the United States is nearly double the national average.[24] Homeless people, some disabled by drugs or mental problems, are another source of many people living in poverty. However, the image of "the working poor" who are "falling behind" as a result of society's "inequities" bears little resemblance to the situation of most of the people earning the lowest 20 percent of income in the United States. Despite a *New York Times* columnist's depiction of people who are "working hard and staying poor"[25] in 2007, Census data from that same year showed the poverty rate among full-time, year-round workers to be 2.5 percent.[26]

Workers' Incomes

Some people deny that American workers' incomes have risen at all in recent times. Such claims require a careful scrutiny of statistics. Here again, there are heated disputes over very basic facts that are readily documented in statistics. A *Washington Post* editorial, for example, said that in a quarter of a century, from 1980 to 2004, "the wages of the typical worker actually fell slightly." Many others, writing in similarly prominent publications and in books, have repeated similar claims over the years. But economist Alan Reynolds, referring to those very same years, said "Real consumption per person increased 74 percent"— and others have likewise categorically rejected the claims that workers' incomes have not risen. Such complete contrasts and contradictions have been common on this issue,[27] with both sides citing official statistics.

Here, as elsewhere, we cannot simply accept blanket assertions that "statistics prove" one thing or another, without scrutinizing the definitions used and noting what things have been included and excluded when compiling numbers.

In the case of statistics claiming that workers' incomes have not risen significantly— or at all— over the years, these data exclude the value of job benefits such as health insurance, retirement benefits and the like, which have been a growing share of employee compensation over the years.[28] Moreover, "workers" lump together both full-time and part-time employees— and part-timers have been a growing proportion of all workers. Part-time workers receive lower weekly pay than full-time workers, both because they work fewer hours and because they are usually paid less per hour. While the real hourly earnings of production workers declined somewhat in the last two decades of the twentieth century, the real value of the total compensation package received by those workers continued to rise during that same period.[29]

In short, the weekly earnings of part-time workers drag down the statistical average of workers as a group, even though part-timers' work adds to both national output and to their own families' incomes. It is not that full-time workers are paid less than before, but that more part-time workers' earnings are being averaged in with theirs statistically. Thus increased prosperity can be represented statistically as stagnating worker compensation because average weekly pay as of 2003 is very similar to what it was 30 years earlier. The difference is that the average weekly hours have declined over that span of time, due to more part-time workers being included in the statistics, and because more of workers' compensation is now being taken in the form of health insurance, retirement benefits and the like.

Even so, the money income of full-time wage and salary workers increased between 1980 and 2004 and so did real income—either by 13 percent or 17 percent, depending on which price index is used.[30] Counting health and retirement benefits, worker compensation rose by nearly a third between 1980 and 2004, even though this still excludes "the statistically invisible returns inside IRA and 401(k) plans."[31]

The way real income is computed tends to understate its growth over time. Since real income is simply money income divided by some price index to take account of inflation, everything depends on the accuracy and validity of such indexes. The construction and use of these indexes is by no means an exact science. Many leading economists regard the consumer price index, for example, as inherently— even if unintentionally— exaggerating inflation. To the extent that the price index over-estimates inflation, it under-estimates real income.

The inflationary bias of the consumer price index results from the fact that it counts the prices of a given collection of goods over time, while those goods are themselves changing over time. For example, the price of automobiles is increasing but so are the features of these automobiles, with today's cars routinely including air conditioning, stereos, and many other features that were once confined to luxury vehicles. Therefore not all the rise in the price of automobiles is simply inflation. If Chevrolets today contain many features once confined to Cadillacs, the rise in the price of Chevrolets over the years to become similar to the price of Cadillacs in the past is not all inflation. When similar cars cost similar prices, that is not inflation just because the similar cars had different names in different eras.

Another inflationary bias to the consumer price index is that it counts only those things that most people are likely to buy. Reasonable as that might seem, what people will buy obviously depends on the price, so new products that are very expensive do not get included in the index until after their prices come down to a level where most people can afford them, as typically happens over time, so that things like laptop computers and videocassette recorders that were once luxuries of the rich have now become readily affordable to vastly larger numbers of people. What this means statistically is that price increases and price decreases over time are not equally reflected in the consumer price index.

How much difference does this make in estimating real incomes over time? If a price index estimates 3 percent inflation and statistics on money income are reduced accordingly to get real income, then if a more realistic estimate is 2 percent, that one percentage point difference can have very serious effects on the resulting statistics on real income. The cumulative effect of a difference of one percentage point per year, over a period of 25 years, has been estimated to statistically understate the real annual income of an average American by nearly $9,000 at the end of a quarter century.[32] That is yet another contribution to the fallacy of stagnating real incomes, even when those incomes are rising.

One of the perennial fallacies is that the jobs being lost in the American economy— whether to foreign competition or to technological change— are high-wage and the new jobs being created are low-wage jobs, flipping hamburgers being a frequent example. But seven out of ten new jobs created between 1993 and 1996 paid wages above the national average.[33] Economist Alan Reynolds used consumption data as the most realistic indicator of living standards— and found that consumption in real terms had increased by 74 percent over the period during which workers' pay had supposedly stagnated.[34]

There are other, more technical, fallacies involved in generating statistics that are widely cited to support claims that workers' pay has stagnated.[35] But we have already seen enough to get a general idea of what is wrong with those statistics. Why so many people have been so eager to accept and repeat the dire conclusions reached is another question that goes beyond the realm of economics.

INCOME INEQUALITY

Ultimately, we are concerned with people rather than statistical categories, and especially our concern is with the standard of living of people. Since the affluent and the wealthy can take care of themselves, people of modest or low incomes are a special focus. Obvious as all this might seem, much ingenuity has gone into concocting statistical alarms having little or nothing to do with the standard of living of actual flesh-and-blood human beings.

One widely quoted study, for example, used income tax data to show dramatically growing income inequality among "tax units," leaving the impression that there was a similarly sharp increase in income inequality among human beings. Some tax units coincide with individuals, some coincide with married couples, and some coincide with neither, because some of these tax units are businesses. Comparisons among such heterogeneous categories are comparisons of apples and oranges. In some media translations of these studies, these tax units are often referred to loosely as "families."[36] But a couple living together and filing separate income tax returns are not two families, and to record their incomes as family incomes means artificially creating two statistical "families" averaging half the income of the real family.

Tax laws changed significantly during the period when this dramatic increase in statistical inequality occurred, so that some income that had previously been taxed as business income was now being taxed as personal income, particularly at the highest income levels, where business income is an especially large share of total income. In other words, money that would previously not have been counted as personal income among the higher-income tax units was now counted, creating the statistical impression that there was a dramatic change in real income among real people, when in fact there was a change in definitions used when compiling statistics. This study mentioned such crucial caveats in a footnote but that footnote was seldom, if ever, quoted in the many alarming media accounts.[37]

Just as income statistics greatly under-estimate the economic resources available to people in the lower income brackets, steeply progressive income taxes substantially *over*-estimate the actual economic resources at the disposal of people in the upper income brackets. Most income statistics count income before taxes and leave out both cash transfers and in-kind transfers from the government. Since most of the taxes are paid by people earning above-average incomes and most of the income of people in the lowest income bracket comes from government transfers, income statistics exaggerate the differences in actual standards of living. Disparities between *A* and *B* will always be greater if you exaggerate what *A* has and understate what *B* has. Yet that simple fallacy underlies much of the political, media, and even academic alarm over income "disparities" and "inequities."

Concern over poverty is often confused with concern over differences in income, as if the wealth of the wealthy derives from the poverty of the poor. But this is just one of the many forms of the zero-sum fallacy. Since the United States contains several times as many billionaires as any other country, ordinary Americans would be among the most poverty-stricken people in the world if the wealth of the wealthy derives from the poverty of the poor. Conversely, billionaires are much rarer in the most poverty-stricken parts of the world, such as sub-Saharan Africa. Some people have tried to salvage the zero-sum view by claiming that wealthy people in wealthy countries exploit poor people in poor countries. That fallacy will be examined in the discussion of Third World countries in Chapter 7. But, first, poverty and inequality require separate analysis and careful definitions.

"The Rich" and "The Poor"

Even such widely used terms as "the rich" and "the poor" are seldom defined and are often used in inconsistent ways. By "the rich," for example, we usually mean people with large accumulations of wealth. However, most statistics used in discussions of "the rich" are *not* about accumulations of wealth, but are about the current flow of income during a given year. Similarly, "the poor" are usually defined in terms of current income, rather than in terms of how much wealth they have or have not accumulated. Income and wealth are not only different in concept, they are very different in terms of who has how much of each. Among the people with low incomes who are *not* poor are the following:

1. Wives of affluent or rich men and husbands of affluent or rich women

2. Affluent or wealthy speculators, investors, and business owners whose enterprises are having an off year, and who may even be losing money in a given year

3. People who graduate in the middle of the year from high schools, colleges, or postgraduate institutions, and who therefore earn only one-half or less of what they will be earning the following year

4. Doctors, dentists, and other independent professionals who are just beginning their careers, and who have not yet built up a sufficient clientele to pay office and other expenses with enough left over to create an income at all comparable to what they will be making in a few years

5. Young adults still living in the homes of affluent or wealthy parents, rent-free, or living elsewhere at their parents' expense, while they explore their possibilities, work sporadically or in low-paid entry-level jobs, or as volunteers in philanthropic or political enterprises

6. Retirees who have no rent to pay or mortgage payments to make because they own their own homes, and who have larger assets in general than younger people have, even if the retirees' current income is low.

None of these is what most people have in mind when they speak of "the poor." But statistics do not distinguish between people whose current incomes are low and people who are genuinely poor in the sense that they are an enduring class of people whose standards of living will remain low for many years, or even for life, because they lack either the income or the wealth to live any better. Similarly, most of the people whose current incomes are in the top 10 or 20 percent are not rich in the sense of being people who have been in top income and wealth brackets most of their lives. Most income statistics present a snapshot picture as of a given moment—and their results are radically different from those statistics which follow the same given individuals over a period of years.

For example, three-quarters of those Americans whose incomes were in the *bottom* 20 percent in 1975 were also in the *top* 40 percent at some point during the next 16 years.[38] In other words, a large majority of those people who would be considered poor on the basis of current incomes as of a given year later rise into the top half of the income recipients in the country. Nor is this pattern peculiar to the United States. A study in Britain followed thousands of individuals for six years and found that, at the end of that period, nearly two-thirds of those individuals whose incomes were initially in the bottom 10 percent had risen out of that bracket. Other studies showed that one-half of the people in Greece and two-thirds of the people in Holland who were below the poverty line in a given year had risen above that line within two years. Studies in Canada and New Zealand showed similar results.[39]

More recent data on Americans, based on income-tax returns, show similar patterns, even more dramatically and in greater detail. Among people who were 25 years old and older who filed income tax returns in 1996, and who were initially in the bottom 20 percent, their incomes had risen by 91 percent by 2005. Meanwhile, people of the same description whose incomes were in the top one percent in 1996 had a *drop* in income of 26 percent by 2005.[40] In short, the picture of the rich getting richer and the poor getting poorer that is repeated endlessly in the media and in politics is directly the opposite of what the income tax data show. Yet both pictures are based on official statistics whose accuracy is not in dispute.

The difference is that one set of statistics— such as those from the Bureau of the Census— compares changes in the income received in particular *income brackets* over the years while other statistics, such as income tax data from the Treasury Department, compare income changes among *given individuals* over the years. The crucial difference is due to individuals moving from one income bracket to another over time. More than half the people tracked by the Internal Revenue Service data moved to a different quintile between 1996 and 2005.[41] When people in the bottom 20 percent of income-tax filers nearly doubled their incomes in a decade, many were no longer in the bottom income bracket any more. Similarly, when people in the top income bracket in a given year had their income decline by about one-fourth during the same decade, many of them dropped out of the top bracket.

It might be thought that surely those in the top one percent of income recipients, and especially those in the top one-hundredth of one percent, are an enduring class of the truly rich. In reality, however, Treasury Department data based on income tax returns show that more than half the people who were in the top one percent in 1996 were no longer there in 2005 and that three-quarters of the taxpayers who were in the top one-hundredth of one percent in 1996 were no longer there by 2005.[42] A spike in income for any of a number of reasons can put someone in that rarefied income stratum in a given year— for example, the sale of a home, receiving an inheritance, cashing in stocks or bonds accumulated over a period of years, or hitting the jackpot in Las Vegas. But such things are no guarantee of a continuing income at that level. There are genuinely rich people, just as there are genuinely poor people, but "snapshot" statistics on income brackets can be grossly misleading as to how many such people there are. Comparing what happens to statistical categories over time— in this case, income brackets— is not the same as comparing what happens to flesh-and-blood individuals over time, when those individuals are moving from one category to another.

Ironically, sports statistics are dealt with more carefully than statistics on more weighty things such as income and wealth. Not only are data on the same individuals over time more common in sports statistics than in statistics on income, in sports there is less confusion between abstract categories and flesh-and-blood human beings. No one imagines that the San Francisco 49ers football team of today is the same as the 49ers of ten years ago, though it is common to act as if the top one percent of income recipients are the same people over the years, so that one can speak of how "the rich" are getting a higher proportion of the national income, even when the flesh-and-blood human beings who initially constituted the top one percent of income recipients— "the rich"— in 1996 actually had a substantial *decline* in their income over the decade. Too often statistics about abstract statistical categories, such as income brackets, are used to reach conclusions and make public policy about flesh-and-blood human beings.

Given the transience of individuals in low income brackets, it becomes easier to understand such anomalies as hundreds of thousands of families with annual incomes below $20,000 living in homes worth $300,000 or more.[43] In addition to such exceptional people, the *average* person in the lowest fifth in income spends about twice as much money annually as his or her annual income.[44] Clearly there must be some supplementary source of purchasing power— whether savings from previous and more prosperous years, credit based on past income and future prospects, unreported illegal income, or money supplied by a spouse, parents, the government, or other benefactors.

Despite many depictions of the elderly as people struggling to get by, households headed by people aged 70 to 74 have the highest average wealth of any age bracket in American society. While the average *income* of households headed by someone 65 years old or older is less than half that of households headed by someone 35 to 44 years old, the average *wealth* of these older households is nearly three times the wealth of households headed by people in the 35 to 44 year old bracket— and more than 15 times the wealth of households headed by people under 35 years of age.[45] Of the income of people 65 and older, only 24 percent comes from earnings, while 57 percent comes from Social Security or other pensions.[46] This means that "income distribution" statistics based on *earnings* grossly understate the incomes of the elderly, which are four times as high as their earnings.

This does not even count the money available to elderly homeowners by tapping the equity in their homes with "reverse mortgages." The money received by borrowing against the equity in their homes is not counted as income, since these are loans to be repaid posthumously by their estates. But the economic reality is that money available by transferring home equity into a current flow of dollars serves the same purposes as income, even if it is not counted in income statistics.

Despite media and political depictions of the elderly as mired in poverty and having to eat dog food in order to afford medicine, in 2007 the poverty rate among persons 65 years old and older was below the national average. Moreover, fewer than two percent of them were without health insurance.[47] The elderly have lower than average incomes, since many are retired, but they are far from poor otherwise. Eighty percent of people 65 and older are either homeowners or home buyers. Of these 80 percent, their median monthly housing costs in 2001 averaged just $339. That includes property taxes, utilities, maintenance costs, condominium and association costs for people with such living arrangements, and mortgage payments for those who do not own their homes outright. Eighty-five percent of their homes have air-conditioning.[48] Not only are housing costs lower in these age brackets, retirees of course do not have the daily transportation and other costs of going to and from work.

The elderly tend to have higher medical costs but the net cost to them depends on the nature of their medical insurance coverage, including Medicare. Whatever their net costs of living, their economic situation compared to younger groups cannot be determined simply by comparing their average earnings, or even average incomes.

If "the poor" are ill-defined by statistics on current income, so are "the rich." Seldom is any specific amount of money— whether as wealth or even income— used to define who is rich. Most often, some *percentage* level— the top 10 or 20 percent, for example— is used to label people as rich. Moreover, laws to raise taxes on "the rich" are almost invariably laws to raise the taxes on particular income brackets, without touching accumulations of wealth. But the incomes of those who are declared to be rich by politicians or in the media are usually far below what most people would consider rich.

For example, as of 2001 a household income of $84,000 was enough to put those who earned it in the top 20 percent of Americans. A couple making $42,000 each is hardly what most people would consider rich. Even to make the top 5 percent required a household income of just over $150,000— that is, about $75,000 apiece for a working couple.[49] As for individuals, to reach the top ten percent in individual income required an income of $87,300 in 2004.[50] These are comfortable incomes but hardly the kinds of incomes that would enable people to live in Beverly Hills or to own a yacht or a private plane.

The different ages of people in different income brackets— with the highest average incomes being among people 45 to 54 years old— strongly suggests that most of the people in upper income brackets have reached that level only after having risen from lower income levels over the course of their careers. In other words, they are no more of a lifetime class than are "the poor." Despite heady rhetoric about economic disparities between classes, most of those economic differences reflect the mundane fact that most people start out in lower-paid, entry-level jobs and then earn more as they acquire more skills and experience over the years. They are transients in particular income brackets, rather than an enduring class of either rich or poor. The same individual can be in statistical categories with each of these labels, at different times of their lives.

There are various ways of measuring income inequality but a more fundamental distinction is between inequality at a given time— however that might be measured— and inequality over a lifetime, which is what is implied in discussions of "classes" of "the rich" and "the poor" or the "haves" and "have-nots." Given the widespread movement of individuals from one income level to another in the course of a lifetime, it is hardly surprising that lifetime inequality is less than inequality as measured at any given time.[51] Moreover, medical interns are well aware that they are on their way to becoming doctors, as people in other entry-level jobs do not expect to stay at that level for life. Yet measurements of income inequality as of a given time are what dominate discussions of income "disparities" or "inequities" in the media, in politics, and in academia. Moreover, a succession of such measurements of inequality in the population as a whole over a period of years still misses the progression of individuals to higher income brackets over time.

To say that the bottom 20 percent of households are "falling further behind" those in the upper income brackets— as is often said in the media, in politics, and among the intelligentsia— is not to say that any given flesh-and-blood individuals are falling further behind, since most of the people in the bottom 20 percent move ahead over time to rise into higher income brackets. Moreover, even when an abstract statistical category is falling behind other abstract statistical categories, that does not necessarily represent a declining real per capita income, even among those people transiently within that category. The fact that the share of the bottom 20 percent of households declined from 4 percent of all income in 1985 to 3.5 percent in 2001 did not prevent the real income of the households in these brackets from rising— quite aside from the movement of actual people out of the bottom 20 percent between the two years.[52]

Even when discussions of "the rich" are in fact discussions of people who have large accumulations of wealth— as distinguished from high levels of current income— much of what is said or assumed is incorrect. In the

United States, at least, most of the people who are wealthy did not inherit that wealth as part of a wealthy class. When *Forbes* magazine's annual list of the 400 richest people first appeared in 1982, people with inherited wealth were 21 percent of that 400— which is to say, nearly four-fifths of these rich people earned the money themselves. By 2006, fewer than 2 percent of the 400 wealthiest people on the *Forbes* magazine list were there because of inherited wealth. Despite the old saying that "the rich get richer and the poor get poorer," the number of billionaires in the world declined from more than a thousand to less than eight hundred in 2008, while the number of American millionaires fell from 9.2 million to 6.7 million.[53]

The "Vanishing" Middle Class

One of the perennial alarms based on income statistics is that the American middle class is declining in size, presumably leaving only the small group of the rich and the masses of the poor. But what has in fact been happening to the middle class?

One of the simplest statistical illusions has been created by defining the middle class by some fixed interval of income— such as between $40,000 and $60,000— and then counting how many people are in that interval over the years. If the interval chosen is in the middle of a statistical distribution of incomes, that may be a valid definition *so long as the midpoint in that distribution of incomes does not change.* But, as already noted, American incomes have been rising over the years, despite strenuous statistical efforts to make incomes seem to be stagnating. As the statistical distribution of incomes shifts to the right over the years (see the graphs on the next page), the number of people in the income range originally in the center of that distribution declines. In other words, the number of middle class people declines when there is a fixed definition of "middle class" in a country with rising levels of income.

The simple situation illustrated in these two graphs— a general rise in incomes— has generated large and recurring waves of journalistic and political rhetoric deploring an ominous shrinking of the middle class, implicitly defined as a reduction in the numbers of people between the income levels represented by perpendicular lines *a* and *b* on these graphs.

Let the top graph illustrate the initial distribution of income, with incomes between line *a* and line *b* being defined as "middle class" incomes:

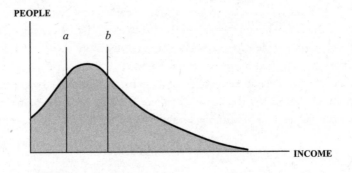

Now let the graph below illustrate an increase in median income:

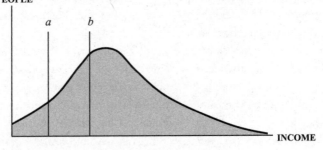

The fact that there are now fewer people within the fixed income brackets between *a* and *b* that *previously* defined the middle class does not mean that the middle class is disappearing when the median income increases. Despite the simplicity of this fallacy, people who should know better (and perhaps do know better) have been depicting this reduction in the number of people within fixed income brackets as something dire. Economist Paul Krugman, for example, has said:

> By almost any measure the middle class is smaller now than it was in 1973. . . . There is now a pervasive sense that the American Dream has gone astray, that children can expect to live worse than their parents.[54]

The insinuation is that the statistical distribution of incomes has shifted to the left, when in fact all the evidence shows that it has shifted to the right. Yet Professor Krugman was by no means alone in his depiction of a shrinking middle class. The same theme has been echoed over the years in such prominent publications as the *New York Times*, the *Washington Post*, and *The Atlantic* magazine.[55]

One of the complications of making income comparisons over time— especially time as long as a generation— is that inflation can move people into higher income brackets without their actual purchasing power or standard of living rising. To avoid that problem, real income (money income adjusted for inflation) can be compared. Using real income data, there is no question that the income distribution has shifted to the right. That is, real income has increased, not just money income. As of 2007, for example, just over half (50.3 percent) of all American households had incomes of $50,000 and up. Back in 1967, on the other hand, just over one-third (33.7 percent) had incomes with that same purchasing power. Moreover, in 1967 most of that third (20.6 percent of all households) had incomes equivalent to from $50,000 to $74,999 in real purchasing power in 2007 dollars. By 2007, however, more people were concentrated at the top of this range, rather than at the bottom of the range.

In 2007, those whose incomes were $100,000 and over were more numerous than those in the $50,000 to $74,999 bracket. In fact the whole income distribution moved to the right— low-income households as well as high-income households. In 1967, 18.3 percent of the households had money income equivalent to less than $15,000 in 2007 purchasing power. But the proportion of the households with incomes that low had shrunk to 13.2 percent by 2007.[56] The claim that the rich were getting richer and the poor were getting poorer was simply false. A rising tide had lifted all boats.

Executives' Pay

The high pay of corporate executives in general, and of chief executive officers in particular, has attracted much popular, media, and political attention— much more so than the similar or higher pay of professional athletes, movie stars, media celebrities, and others in very high income brackets. The median pay of chief executive officers of corporations important enough to be listed in the Standard and Poor's index in 2006 was $8.3 million a year. While that is obviously many times more than most people make, it is exceeded by the income of women's golf star Michelle Wie ($12 million), tennis star Maria Sharapova ($26 million), baseball star Alex Rodriguez ($34 million), basketball star Kobe Bryant ($39 million) and golfing great Tiger Woods ($115 million).[57] Even the highest paid corporate CEO, earning $71.7 million a year,[58] made less than a third of what Oprah Winfrey makes.

Yet it is rare— almost unheard of— to hear criticisms of the incomes of sports, movie, or media stars, much less hear heated denunciations of them for "greed." While "greed" is one of the most popular— and most fallacious— explanations of the very high salaries of corporate executives, when your salary depends on what other people are willing to pay you, you can be the greediest person on earth and that will not raise your pay in the slightest. Any serious explanation of corporate executives' salaries must be based on the reasons for those salaries being *offered*, not the reasons why the recipients desire them. Anybody can desire anything but that will not cause others to meet those desires. Why then do corporations go so high in their bidding for top executive talent? Supply and demand is probably the quickest short answer— and any fuller answer would probably require the kind of highly specific knowledge and experience of those corporate officials who make the decisions as to whom to hire and how much pay to offer. Given the billions of dollars at stake in corporate decisions, $8.3 million a year can be a bargain for someone who can reduce mistakes by 10 percent and perhaps save the corporation $100 million.

Some have argued that corporate boards of directors have been overly generous with the stockholders' money and that this explains the high pay of corporate CEOs. To substantiate this as a *general* explanation would require more than a few specific examples. This theory could be tested as a general explanation by comparing the pay of CEOs in corporations owned by a large number of stockholders, most of whom are in no position to keep abreast of— much less evaluate— decisions made within these corporations, versus the pay of CEOs of corporations owned and controlled by a few huge financial institutions with both expertise and experience, and spending their own money.

It is precisely these latter corporations which offer the highest pay of all for chief executive officers.[59] These giant financial institutions do not have to justify their decisions to public opinion but can base these decisions on far greater specific knowledge and professional experience than that of the public, the media, or politicians. They are the least likely to pay more than they have to— or to be penny-wise and pound-foolish when choosing someone to run a business where billions of dollars of the institutional investors' own money are at stake. While various activists have urged a larger voice for stockholders in determining the pay of CEOs in publicly held corporations, significantly the mutual funds that invest in such corporations have opposed this,[60] just as major financial institutions that invest in privately held corporations are less concerned with corporate executives' pay than with getting executives who can safeguard their investments and make them profitable.

Although many outsiders have expressed incredulity and non-comprehension at the vast sums of money paid to various people in the corporate world, there is no reason why those people should be expected to comprehend why A pays B any given sum of money for services rendered. Those services are not rendered to third party observers, most of whom have neither the expertise nor the specific experience required to put a value on such services. Still less is there any reason why they should have a veto over the decisions of those who *do* have the expertise and experience to assess the value of the services rendered. For example, the director of the company that publishes the *Washington Post* assessed the recommendations of one member of his board of directors this way: "Mr. Buffet's recommendations to management have been worth— no question— billions."[61]

It is very doubtful whether Mr. Buffet's compensation from the Washington Post Company alone runs into billions of dollars but it may well run into enough millions to cause third party onlookers to exclaim their incredulity and perhaps moral outrage. The source of moral outrage over corporate compensation is by no means obvious. If it is based on a belief that individuals are overpaid for their contribution to the corporation, then there would be even more outrage toward people who receive hundreds of millions of dollars for doing nothing at all, when they simply inherit fortunes. Yet inheritors of fortunes are seldom resented, much less denounced, the way corporate CEOs are. Three heirs to the Rockefeller fortune, for example, have been elected as popular governors of three states.

Two things seem especially to anger critics of high corporate executive salaries: (1) the belief that their high compensation comes at the expense of consumers, stockholders, and/or employees and (2) the multimillion dollar severance pay package often given to executives who have clearly failed. But, like anybody who is hired anywhere, whether in a high or low position, a corporate CEO is hired precisely because the benefits that the CEO is expected to confer on the employer exceed what the employer offers to pay. If, for example, an $8.3 million a year CEO saves the corporation $100 million as expected, then the stockholders have lost nothing and are in fact better off by more than $90 million. Neither have the consumers nor the employees lost anything. Like most economic transactions, the hiring of a corporate CEO is not a zero-sum transaction. It is intended to make both parties better off.

It would be immediately obvious why the zero-sum view is wrong if someone suggested that money paid to George C. Scott for playing the title role in the movie *Patton* was a loss to stockholders, moviegoers, or to lower-level employees who performed routine tasks during the making of the movie. Only if we believe that *Patton* would have made just as much money without George C. Scott can his pay be regarded as a deduction from the money otherwise available to stockholders, moviegoers, and other people employed making the movie. Much has been made of the fact that corporate executives make many times the pay of ordinary workers under them— the number varying according to who is making the claim— but no one would bother to figure out how many times larger George C. Scott's pay was than that of movie extras or people who handled lights or carried film during the production of *Patton*.

The most puzzling and most galling aspect of corporate executives' compensation, for many people, are the multimillion dollar severance payments— the "golden parachutes"— paid to CEOs who are clearly being gotten rid of because they failed. For example, in 2007 the chief executive officer of Merrill Lynch received a "retirement" package of "in excess of $160 million," according to the *Wall Street Journal*, which called it "an obscenely rich reward for failure," since Merrill Lynch lost $7.9 billion in mortgage-related transactions under his leadership.[62]

Since human beings are going to make mistakes, whether hiring an entry-level, unskilled employee or a corporate CEO, the question is: What options are available when it becomes clear that the CEO is a failure and a liability? Speed may be the most important consideration when someone is making decisions which may be losing millions— or even billions— of dollars. Getting that CEO out the door as soon as possible, without either internal battles within the corporation or lawsuits in the courts, may be well worth many millions of dollars. Merrill Lynch's $160 million "retirement" package for its departing CEO may have been a bargain to prevent losses of another $7.9 *billion*.

This is not a unique situation, even if the sums of money involved are larger in a multibillion dollar corporation than in other situations that people are more familiar with. Aging university professors who have not kept up with recent developments in their fields may be offered a lucrative early retirement package, in order to replace such professors with people who have mastered the latest advances. Similarly, many a married person has paid very substantial sums of money to get a divorce— perhaps larger in proportion to income compared to what a corporation pays to bring a bad relationship to an end.

In this and other situations, putting an end to a relationship may be just as valuable, or even more valuable, than the initial beginning of the relationship once seemed. As with the original hiring decision, neither stockholders nor consumers nor other employees are worse off for the payment of a large severance package, if that cuts losses that would be even bigger if the failed CEO stayed on. Nor need the original hiring decision have been mistaken when it was made. Times change and individuals change over the years, so that a CEO who was perfect for the circumstances that existed at the time of hiring may be out of touch with very different conditions that evolve in later years.

When Sewell Avery was head of U.S. Gypsum from 1905 to 1931 and then head of the Montgomery Ward retail store chain after 1931, he was regarded as one of the premier business leaders in the country. However, during his later years, when conditions in retailing became quite different,[63] there were complaints about his leadership of Montgomery Ward, and bitter internal struggles to try to get rid of him. When he finally left, the value of Montgomery Ward stock shot up immediately. It might well have been a bargain for the stockholders, the customers, and the employees to have paid Avery enough to get him to leave earlier, since a badly run company hurts all of these people.

Third party observers may find it galling that some people seem to be rewarded handsomely for failing. But third parties are neither paying their own money nor are in a position to know how much it is worth to be rid of someone. When an individual pays dearly to divorce a spouse who is impossible to live with, that too might be seen as rewarding failure. But does any third party presume to say that the decision to divorce was wrong, much less feel entitled to be morally outraged, or to call on government to stop such things?

Social Mobility

We have already noted one kind of economic and social mobility, the movement of people out of the lowest income brackets in the course of their own working lifetime. A major study at the University of Michigan has followed the same individuals— tens of thousands of them— over a period of decades. Among individuals who are actively in the labor force, only 5 percent of those who were in the bottom 20 percent in income in 1975 were still there in 1991, compared to 29 percent of those in the bottom quintile in 1975 who had risen to the *top* quintile by 1991.[64] More than half of those in the bottom quintile in 1975 had been in the top quintile at some point during these years.[65] However, as we have also seen, not everyone is working, especially in the lowest income brackets. The rises of those who are working indicates what opportunities there are. How many people take advantage of those opportunities is another question.

There is another kind of socioeconomic mobility that many have written about— the extent to which people born in low-income families rise to higher income or occupational levels than those of their parents. Here a number of things get confused with one another, including the amount of opportunity available versus the amount of opportunity used. Much discussion of social mobility is based on the concept of "life chances"— the likelihood that someone born into given socioeconomic circumstances will grow up to achieve some given economic or occupational level. Sometimes causation is confused with blame, as when any attempt to point out factors in any social group which inhibit their progress is called "blaming the victim," presumably the victim of "society."

Many factors, however, involve no blame, and may be due to neither the individual nor to society, but to circumstances. For example, someone born deaf is unlikely to become a musician, even though Beethoven continued to write music after losing his hearing. Physical or mental handicaps beyond the individual's control may reduce the likelihood of utilizing various opportunities that are otherwise available in a given society. Cultural values, inherited socially rather than biologically, may also reduce the statistical *probability* of advancing in income or occupations, even when the *opportunity* to do so is available— and no given individual chooses which culture to be born into. Even sophisticated statistical analyses of probabilities of people from various groups achieving various income or occupational levels often equate low probabilities with high barriers created by others.

A child raised in a home where physical prowess is valued more than intellectual prowess is unlikely to have the same goals and priorities as a child raised in a home where the reverse is true. Some have seen such circumstances as examples of "barriers" and "privileges." For example, a *New York Times* article that said it is "harder to move up from one economic class to another" and that this was due to a new kind of privilege:

> Merit has replaced the old system of inherited privilege, in which parents to the manner born handed down the manor to their children. But merit, it turns out, is at least partly class-based. Parents with money, education and connections cultivate in their children the habits that the

meritocracy rewards. When their children then succeed, their success is seen as earned.[66]

In a similar vein, the head of the Russell Sage Foundation conceded that the "old system of hereditary barriers and clubby barriers has pretty much vanished" but regarded these barriers as now being replaced by "new ways of transmitting advantage."[67]

Failure to make a distinction between *external* impediments to individual advancement and *internal* differences in individual orientation makes attempts to determine or measure empirically the opportunities available an exercise in futility or confusion. For example, when a study shows that "only" 32 percent of sons of fathers in the bottom quarter of income earners reached the top half of income earners by their early thirties,[68] that statistic tells us nothing about whether this was due to external barriers or internal orientations. Moreover, statistics from this widely reported study arbitrarily omit any upward mobility that occurs to males after their early thirties, all upward mobility by women, and any movement upward that does not get as far as the top half. What purpose this serves is open to speculation.

To the extent that blaming "society" is more or less the default setting for explaining differences in social mobility among income classes, ethnic groups, or among other segments of society, this itself shifts attention away from internal factors which inhibit many individuals from using opportunities that are available. By reducing awareness of such internal impediments to advancement, this approach reduces the chances of changes in such internal impediments— and thereby reduces the very chances for lower income people to advance that these studies claim to be concerned about.

SUMMARY AND CONCLUSIONS

Some very plain and straightforward facts about income and wealth have been obscured by fallacies based on vague and inconsistent words, garnished with misleading statistics. There is, after all, nothing very mysterious about the fact that inexperienced young people, beginning their working careers, are unlikely to be paid as much as older, more experienced and more skilled people with proven track records. Nor is there anything very hard to understand about the fact that households in which fewer people are working at all are unlikely to receive as much money as households in which people who work full-time and year-round are the norm. Nor should it be surprising that some people are paid millions of dollars when their decisions can affect a corporation's profit-and-loss statement by billions of dollars.

A hasty leap from statistical categories to economic realities underlies many fallacies about income and wealth. When more than two-thirds of the economic resources available to people in the bottom 20 percent of income earners get left out of income statistics because they are transfers in cash or in kind from government, that is a serious discrepancy between statistics and reality. Similarly when three-quarters of the economic resources available to the elderly do not get counted in statistics on earnings. Nor are these random discrepancies. Almost invariably, such widely publicized statistics overstate poverty and understate standards of living. When income statistics leave out both taxes on people in upper income brackets and transfers to people in lower income brackets, they exaggerate inequalities as of a given time. When they fail to follow given individuals over time, they exaggerate lifetime inequality, as well as enabling observers to speak of people who are transiently in various income brackets as if they are enduring "classes."

To say that some people have less probability of achieving a given income or occupational level is too often automatically equated with saying that "society" puts barriers in their path. This precludes *a priori* the very possibility that there might be internal reasons for not doing as well economically as some other people. Moreover, this is not just a matter of an abstract judgment. To the extent that there may in fact be internal reasons for not achieving as much as others, directing attention away from those reasons has the practical effect of reducing the likelihood that those reasons will be addressed and the potential for advancement improved. In short, those who are lagging are offered a better public image instead of better prospects.

Claims by some that they cannot understand or justify large income differences ("disparities," "inequities") are another version of the presumption that third parties are the best judges— as if people's incomes, like their housing arrangements, should be judged by what a tableau they present to outsiders, rather than how they reflect the choices and mutual accommodations of those directly involved. Such third-party presumptions are often based on an awareness of being part of a more educated group having, on average, more general knowledge than most other people— and an *unawareness* that the *total* knowledge of all the others vastly exceeds theirs, as well as being more specific knowledge relevant to the decisions at hand. No third parties can possibly know the values, preferences, priorities, potentialities, circumstances, and constraints of millions of individuals better than those individuals know themselves.

Sometimes the presumptions are moral, rather than intellectual. Third parties who take on the task of deciding who "really" deserves how much income often confuse merit with productivity, quite aside from the question whether they have the competence to judge either. In no society of human beings has everyone had the same probabilities of achieving the same level of productivity. People born into families with every advantage of wealth, education, and social position may be able to achieve a high level of productivity without any great struggle that would indicate individual merit. Conversely, people who have had to struggle to overcome many disadvantages, in order to achieve even a modest level of productivity, may show great individual merit. But an economy is not a moral seminar authorized to hand out badges of merit to deserving people. An economy is a mechanism for generating the material wealth on which the standard of living of millions of people depend.

Pay is not a retrospective reward for merit but a prospective incentive for contributing to production. Given the enormous range of things produced and the complex processes by which they are produced, it is virtually inconceivable that any given individual could be capable of assessing the relative value of the contributions of different people in different industries or sectors of the economy. Few even claim to be able to do that. Instead, they express their bafflement and repugnance at the wide range of income or wealth disparities they see and— implicitly or explicitly— their incredulity that individuals could differ so widely in what they deserve. This approach has a long pedigree. George Bernard Shaw, for example, said:

> A division in which one woman gets a shilling and another three thousand shillings for an hour of work has no moral sense in it: it is just something that happens, and that ought not to happen. A child with an interesting face and pretty ways, and some talent for acting, may, by working for the films, earn a hundred times as much as its mother can earn by drudging at an ordinary trade.[69]

Here are encapsulated the crucial elements in most critiques of "income distribution" to this day. First, there is the implicit assumption that wealth is collective and hence must be divided up in order to be dispensed, followed by the assumption that this division currently has no principle involved but "just happens," and finally the implicit assumption that the effort put forth by the recipient of income is a valid yardstick for gauging the value of what was produced and the appropriateness of the reward. In reality, most income is *not* distributed, so the fashionable metaphor of "income distribution" is misleading. Most income is earned by the production of goods and services, and how much that production is "really" worth is a question that need not be left for third parties to determine, since those who directly receive the benefits of that production know better than anyone else how much that production is worth to them— and have the most incentives to seek alternative ways of getting that production as inexpensively as possible.

In short, a collective decision for society as a whole is as unnecessary as it is impossible, not to mention presumptuous. It is not a question of rewarding input efforts or merits, but of securing output at values determined by those who use that output, rather than by third party onlookers. If the pleasure gained by watching a child movie star is valued more highly by millions of moviegoers than the benefits received by a much smaller number of people who benefit from buying the product of the drudgery of that child's mother, by what right is George Bernard Shaw or anyone else authorized to veto all these people's choices of what to do with their own money?

Although one person's income may be a hundred or a thousand times greater than another's, it is of course very doubtful that one person is a hundred or a thousand times more intelligent or works a hundred or a thousand times as hard. But, again, *input* is not the measure of value. *Results* are.

The absence of Tiger Woods from various golf tournaments in the United States for several months, due to a knee operation in 2008, led to declines in television audiences ranging from 36 percent for the World Golf Championship to 55 percent for the PGA Championship.[70]

In a multibillion dollar corporation, one person's business decisions can easily make a difference of millions— or even billions— of dollars, compared to someone else's decisions. Those who see paying such a person $10 million or $20 million a year as coming at the expense of consumers or stockholders have implicitly accepted the zero-sum view of economics. If the value of the services rendered exceeds the pay, then both consumers and stockholders are better off, not worse off, whether the person hired is a corporate CEO or a production line employee.

Would anyone say that the pay of an airline pilot comes at the expense of passengers or of the airline's stockholders, when both are better off as a result of the services rendered? Would anyone even imagine that one pilot is as good as another when it comes to flying a commercial jet airliner with hundreds of people on board, so that getting some crop-duster pilot at lower pay to fly the jet would make the stockholders and the passengers better off? Yet that is the kind of reasoning, or lack of reasoning, that is often applied when discussing the pay of corporate CEOs— and virtually no one else in any other field, including professional athletes or entertainers who earn similar or higher incomes. Perhaps the most fallacious assumption of all is that third parties with neither experience nor expertise can make better decisions, on the basis of their emotional reactions, than the decisions of those who have both experience and expertise, as well as a stake in the results.

Despite the popularity of the phrase "income distribution," most income is *earned*— not distributed. Even millionaires seldom simply inherited their fortunes.[71] Only a fraction of the income in American society is actually distributed, in such forms as Social Security checks or payments to welfare recipients, for example. Most income is "distributed" only in the figurative statistical sense that the incomes of different people are in varying amounts that can be displayed in a curve on a graph, as in the previous discussion of middle class incomes. But much of the rhetoric surrounding variations in income proceeds as if "society" is collectively deciding how much to hand out to different individuals. From there it is a small step to arguing that, since "society" *distributes* income with given results today that many do not understand or like, there should be a simple change to distributing income in a different pattern that would be more desirable.

In reality, this would by no means be either a simple or innocuous change. On the contrary, it would mean going from an economic system in which most people are paid by those particular individuals who benefit from their goods and services— at rates of compensation determined by supply and demand involving those consumers, employers, and others who assess the benefits received by themselves— to an economy in which incomes are in fact distributed by "society," represented by surrogate, third-party decision-makers who determine what everyone "deserves." Those who think that such a profound change would produce better economic or social results can make the case for such a change. But making such a case explicitly is very different from gliding into a fundamentally different world through verbal sleight of hand about "income distribution."

Chapter 6

RACIAL FACTS AND FALLACIES

Almost all expressions now connected with race and colour can be described as 'escape words'— that is attempts, usually unsuccessful, to avoid giving offence or to deflect in advance accusations of prejudice.

Paul Johnson[1]

Few subjects produce more fallacies than race. Some might even say that race itself is a fallacy, in a world where racial intermixtures keep increasing, well beyond the levels of earlier times, even while the stridency of separate racial identities becomes louder.

Indigenous American Indians were once referred to as "the vanishing Americans," because of their dwindling proportions in the growing population of the United States, but their official numbers have in recent years increased at a rate far beyond any biological reality, because more and more people with some fraction of American Indian ancestry now choose to identify themselves as members of that group. It is much the same story halfway around the world in New Zealand, where there are great numbers of Maoris whose ancestries are at least as Caucasian as they are Maori. Among black Americans, there are relatively few people of unmixed African ancestry and there have always been some individuals like Walter White, once head of the NAACP, who were considered to be Negroes or blacks more or less as a matter of convention, despite their Caucasian features and blue eyes.

Rising rates of intermarriage have reduced the biological significance of racial differences, even as their political significance has increased. The intermarriage rate for blacks was just under one percent in 1963 but was 12 percent in 1993.[2] The 1990 census showed that just over one-fourth of Japanese American marriages were intermarriages, as were 60 percent of American Indian marriages.[3] Among Jewish Americans, the intermarriage rate rose to 57 percent by 1985–1990.[4] Yet these were also years of ever more strident separate racial or ethnic "identity" trends.

Race can be discussed as a social reality with a biological component. The consequences of that social reality have been very serious, however, and continue to be so. So are the consequences of the fallacies surrounding race. Among these fallacies are that race was the basis of slavery, and that racism is the main reason for black-white differences in incomes and in all the other aspects of life that depend on income. Moreover, there is often an implicit assumption that racism and discrimination are so closely linked that they go up or down together, when in fact as we shall see, some times and places with more racism have been known to have less discrimination— and discrimination can exist without racism. Lurking in the background of some discussions of race is the question whether races differ in innate intelligence, a question that has generated fallacies among those on both sides of this issue.

GROUP DIFFERENCES

It has often been common to compare a given group, such as blacks in the United States, with the national average and regard the differences as showing a special peculiarity of the group being compared, or a special peculiarity of policies or attitudes towards that group. But either conclusion can be misleading when the national average itself is just an amalgamation of wide variations among many ethnic, regional and other groups. While the black and white populations of the United States have long differed in various economic and social variables— in income, years of schooling, life expectancy, unemployment rates, crime rates, and scores on a variety of tests— so have other groups differed widely from one another and from the national average in countries around the world.

One of the most overlooked, but important, differences among groups are their ages. The median age of black Americans is five years younger than the median age (35) of the American population as a whole, but blacks are by no means unique in having a median age different from the national average or from the ages of other groups. Among Asian Americans, the median age ranges from 43 for Japanese Americans to 24 for Americans of Cambodian ancestry to 16 for those of Hmong ancestry.[5] Incomes are highly correlated with age, with young people usually beginning their working lives earning much less than older and more experienced workers. Therefore gross comparisons of incomes among racial or ethnic groups can be misleading when the median ages of groups can differ by a decade or even a quarter of a century. Nor are age differences the only differences among Asian Americans. While 61 percent of Japanese Americans were born in the United States, fewer than a third of the Asian Americans of Chinese, Filipino, Vietnamese, Korean, or Asian Indian ancestry were.[6] Native-born citizens are obviously more familiar with the opportunities available in the society and better able to take advantage of those opportunities.

Educational differences are likewise as great among American ethnic minorities as they are between minorities and the larger population. Among high school graduates aged 16 to 21, just under half of those who were black or Hispanic were enrolled in college, while nearly four-fifths of Asian Americans were.[7] Although Hispanics have overtaken blacks numerically as part of the population, blacks still receive more doctorates than Hispanics. While the Asian American population is only a fraction of the size of either the black or the Hispanic population, Asian Americans receive more doctorates than Hispanics and nearly as many as blacks.[8] In short, an even distribution of groups is by no means common, whether in age, education, or other characteristics.

Nor is the United States unique in the nature or magnitude of economic or social differences among racial or ethnic groups. Income differences between the Chinese and Malay populations of Malaysia, for example, have long been greater than income differences between blacks and whites in the United States.[9] So have economic differences between different tribes in Nigeria or between Asians and Africans in East Africa.

Various groups around the world have differed in everything from alcohol consumption per capita to IQs. Indeed, differences have been the norm and identical economic or social outcomes have been rare to non-existent. That is why singling out any given group for comparison with the national average can be misleading if it suggests that the situation of the group in question is peculiar, rather than being part of a worldwide pattern of wide variations from group to group. This is not to say that intergroup differences don't matter. Some of these differences matter greatly.

What are the reasons behind these disparities? Perhaps a more fundamental question might be: *What reason was there to expect these groups to be the same in the first place?* Geography, demography, history and culture have all differed among groups in countries around the world.[10] We have already seen how widely the median ages of groups can vary, even within a given country and how much difference there is in native birth within Asian Americans alone. The same is true in other countries and between one country and another. The median age in Germany and Italy is forty, while in Yemen and Afghanistan it is below twenty.[11]

Put differently, there are many opportunities for fallacies. Many of those fallacies arise from implicitly assuming that the various groups are comparable in skills, experiences, or attitudes, so that statistical disparities among them can only be explained by the different ways that the society around them treats them. Many, if not most, societies have discriminated among groups throughout most of history. But that discrimination has not been the only factor at work producing intergroup differences and the challenge is to assess the effects of all the factors involved. Moreover the relative weights of different factors do not remain the same over time, so some consideration of history is also necessary.

HISTORY

Perhaps the biggest fallacy about the history of racial and ethnic minorities is that the passage of time reduces the hostility and discrimination they face. In many countries, minorities have faced greater

hostility and discrimination in a later period than in earlier periods. In other
countries, the reverse has been true. But the passage of time alone does not
automatically produce either result.

The Role of Time

Back at the end of the fifteenth century, Jews expelled from Spain fled
primarily to the Islamic countries of the Middle East, where they were
generally treated better than they were in Europe— and far better than they
would be treated in the same Middle Eastern countries in the twentieth
century. Jews became prominent as physicians in the Ottoman Empire and
it was not uncommon in the seventeenth century for Sultans of the
Ottoman Empire to have Jewish physicians present, or even predominant,
on their medical staffs,[12] or for Jews to be used as translators for Ottoman
envoys to European countries.[13] Jews were so common as customs officials
that many of the Ottoman customs receipts from that era were written in
Hebrew.[14] In the Ottoman economy, Jews were prominent in roles ranging
from peddlers in villages to international traders.[15]

However, as the age of the Ottoman Empire's pre-eminence in military,
cultural, and scientific achievements gave way to centuries in which
European countries overtook them in all these respects, the confident and
cosmopolitan toleration of minorities within the Ottoman Empire gave way
to an era of Ottoman anxiety about dangers from without and within, and
to xenophobia that greatly restricted and endangered Jews and other
minorities. By the early twentieth century, Jews were persecuted worse in the
Middle East than anywhere else, until the rise to power of the Nazis in
Germany. The Nazis' racism in general and their anti-Jewish doctrines and
policies in particular found many Middle Eastern sympathizers both before
and during the Second World War. By the time the modern state of Israel
was created after that war, hatred of Jews was already widespread in Middle
Eastern countries that had once been part of the Ottoman Empire.

Within an even shorter span of time, the island nation of Sri Lanka, off
the coast of India, went from being a country whose good relations between
majority and minority had become a model for intergroup harmony to one

with a decades-long civil war taking tens of thousands of lives. During the first half of the twentieth century, there was not a single riot between the Sinhalese majority and the Tamil minority. But, during the second half of that century, there were many such riots, marked by unspeakable atrocities, and ultimately degenerating into a civil war that was still not completely ended as the twenty-first century dawned.

Other such examples could be found in many countries and in many periods of history. In Bohemia, Germans and Czechs co-existed peacefully for centuries, until the rise of Czech nationalism, climaxed by the creation of the new nation of Czechoslovakia after the First World War, led to discrimination against Germans and then to a German backlash that led ultimately to the Munich crisis of 1938, when the Czechs were forced to relinquish the predominantly German Sudetenland to Nazi Germany. After Germany later took over all of Czechoslovakia, the Germans in that country then joined in the Nazis' persecution of Czechs. After the defeat of Germany in World War II, Germans in Czechoslovakia were expelled by the millions, often under brutal conditions that led to many deaths.

Such retrogressions in intergroup relations were not unknown in the United States, though not usually to such extremes. The predominantly German Jewish population of the United States was far better assimilated and accepted before the arrival of millions of unassimilated Eastern European Jews in the late nineteenth and early twentieth centuries led to a social backlash against all Jews that resulted in restrictions against Jews in places where such restrictions had not existed before. Black Americans, meanwhile, were far better accepted in Northern cities at the end of the nineteenth century than they would be in the first half of the twentieth century, after massive migrations of less assimilated Southern blacks caused a similar backlash that created new restrictions against all blacks. Northern cities in which blacks had lived largely dispersed among whites saw in the early twentieth century the rigid residential segregation patterns that would create the black ghettoes which quickly became the norm.

It would be as fallacious to depict racial retrogression as an inevitable result of the passage of time as to depict racial progress as something happening automatically over time. Much racial progress occurred in the second half of the twentieth century in the United States, especially for blacks. Since this was not something that happened automatically, it is important to understand the causes and the timing. It is especially important to scrutinize the evidence because many individuals and organizations have a vested interest in claiming credit for progress, and incessantly repeated claims can sometimes be mistaken for facts.

Progress and retrogression are not always separated in different eras. There can be much progress in some respects during the same time when there is retrogression in other respects. That was especially true among black Americans in the second half of the twentieth century.

Before the landmark Supreme Court decision in *Brown v. Board of Education* in 1954, the racial segregation of schools was required in all the Southern states that had once formed the Confederacy, as well as in Missouri, Texas, Oklahoma, and the District of Columbia— and racial segregation of the schools was permitted in Wyoming, Arizona, and New Mexico. All such laws were nullified by the Supreme Court decision and, over the next decades, the practice of racial segregation in the schools was dismantled. The Civil Rights Act of 1964 outlawed racial segregation in both public and private enterprises and institutions, and forbad employment discrimination as well. The Voting Rights Act of 1965 outlawed practices which had disenfranchised black voters in the South and the 1970s saw "affirmative action" take on the meaning of preferential hiring of minority workers.

These major legal landmarks of the civil rights revolution have often been credited with the economic and political advances of the black population. Certainly the Voting Rights Act was responsible for a huge increase in black voting in the South and the subsequent skyrocketing of the number of black elected officials throughout the region. But history tells a very different story as regards the economic advancement of blacks.

The percentage of black families with incomes below the poverty line fell most sharply between 1940 and 1960, going from 87 percent to 47 percent over that span, *before* either the Civil Rights Act of 1964 or the Voting Rights Act of 1965 and well before the 1970s, when "affirmative action" evolved into numerical "goals" or "quotas." While the downward trend in poverty continued, the pace of that decline did not accelerate after these legal landmarks but in fact slackened. The poverty rate declined from 47 percent to 30 percent during the decade of the 1960s and then only from 30 percent to 29 percent between 1970 and 1980.[16] However much credit has been claimed for the civil rights laws of the 1960s or the War on Poverty programs of that same decade, the hard facts show that blacks' rise out of poverty was more dramatic before any of these government actions got under way.

There was a similar historical trend as regards the rise of blacks into professional, managerial, and other high-level occupations. The number of blacks in white collar occupations, managerial and administrative occupations doubled between 1940 and 1960, and nearly doubled in professional occupations. Meanwhile, the number of blacks who were farm workers in 1960 was only one-fourth of the number who were in 1940.[17] These favorable trends continued after 1960 but did *not* originate in the 1960s. As regards the group preferences and quotas— "affirmative action"— which began in the 1970s, they produced little or no effect on the relative sizes of black and white incomes. The median black household income was 60.9 percent of the median white household income in 1970— and never rose above that, or as high as that, throughout the decade of the 1970s. As of 1980, median black household income was 57.6 percent of median white household income.[18]

The facts are clear but the fallacies persist that it was the civil rights laws, the "war on poverty" programs of the 1960s, and affirmative action which caused the rise of blacks out of poverty and their ascent into middle class occupations.

Slavery

In addition to its own evils during its own time, slavery has generated fallacies that endure into our time, confusing many issues today. The distinguished historian Daniel J. Boorstin said something that was well known to many scholars, but utterly unknown to many among the general public, when he pointed out that, with the mass transportation of Africans in bondage to the Western Hemisphere, "Now for the first time in Western history, the status of slave coincided with a difference of race."[19]

For centuries before, Europeans had enslaved other Europeans, Asians had enslaved other Asians and Africans had enslaved other Africans. Only in the modern era was there both the wealth and the technology to organize the mass transportation of people across an ocean, either as slaves or as free immigrants. Nor were Europeans the only ones to transport masses of enslaved human beings from one continent to another. North Africa's Barbary Coast pirates alone captured and enslaved at least a million Europeans from 1500 to 1800, carrying more Europeans into bondage in North Africa than there were Africans brought in bondage to the United States and to the American colonies from which it was formed.[20] Moreover, Europeans were still being bought and sold in the slave markets of the Islamic world, decades after blacks were freed in the United States.[21]

Slavery was a virtually universal institution in countries around the world and for thousands of years of recorded history. Indeed, archaeological evidence suggests that human beings learned to enslave other human beings before they learned to write. One of the many fallacies about slavery— that it was based on race— is sustained by the simple but pervasive practice of focussing exclusively on the enslavement of Africans by Europeans, as if this were something unique, rather than part of a much larger worldwide human tragedy. Racism grew out of African slavery, especially in the United States, but slavery preceded racism by thousands of years. Europeans enslaved other Europeans for centuries before the first African was brought in bondage to the Western Hemisphere.

The brutal reality is that vulnerable people were usually taken advantage of wherever it was feasible to take advantage of them, regardless of what race or color they were. The rise of nation states put armies and navies around some people but it was not equally possible to establish nation states in all parts of the world, partly because of geography. Where large populations had no army or navy to protect them, they fell prey to enslavers, whether in Africa, Asia or along unguarded stretches of European coastlines where Barbary pirates made raids, usually around the Mediterranean but sometimes as far away as England or Iceland.[22] The enormous concentration of writings and of the media in general on slavery in the Western Hemisphere, or in the United States in particular, creates a false picture which makes it difficult to understand even the history of slavery in the United States.

While slavery was readily accepted as a fact of life all around the world for centuries on end, there was never a time when slavery could get that kind of universal acceptance in the United States, founded on a principle of freedom, with which slavery was in such obvious and irreconcilable contradiction. Slavery was under ideological attack from the first draft of the Declaration of Independence[23] and a number of Northern states banned slavery in the years immediately following independence. Even in the South, the ideology of freedom was not wholly without effect, as tens of thousands of slaves were voluntarily set free after Americans gained their own freedom from England.

Most Southern slaveowners, however, were determined to hold on to their slaves and, for that, some defense was necessary against the ideology of freedom and the widespread criticisms of slavery that were its corollary. Racism became that defense. Such a defense was unnecessary in unfree societies, such as that of Brazil, which imported more slaves than the United States but developed no such virulent levels of racism as that of the American South. Outside Western civilization, no defense of slavery was necessary, as non-Western societies saw nothing wrong with it. Nor was there any serious challenge to slavery in Western civilization prior to the eighteenth century.

Racism became a justification of slavery in a society where it could not be justified otherwise— and centuries of racism did not suddenly vanish with the abolition of the slavery that gave rise to it. But the direction of causation was the direct opposite of what is assumed by those who depict the enslavement of Africans as being a result of racism. Nevertheless, racism became one of the enduring legacies of slavery. How much of it continues to endure and in what strength today is something that can be examined and debated. But many other things that are considered to be legacies of slavery can be tested empirically, rather than being accepted as foregone conclusions.

The Black Family

Some of the most basic beliefs and assumptions about the black family are demonstrably fallacious. For example, it has been widely believed that black family names were the names of the slave masters who owned particular families. Such beliefs led a number of American blacks, during the 1960s especially, to repudiate those names as a legacy of slavery and give themselves new names— most famously boxing champion Cassius Clay renaming himself Muhammad Ali.

Family names were in fact *forbidden* to blacks enslaved in the United States,[24] as family names were forbidden to other people in lowly positions in various other times and places— slaves in China and parts of the Middle East,[25] for example, and it was 1870 before common people in Japan were authorized to use surnames.[26] In Western civilization, ordinary people began to have surnames in the Middle Ages.[27] In many places and times, family names were considered necessary and appropriate only for the elite, who moved in wider circles— both geographically and socially— and whose families' prestige was important to take with them. Slaves in the United States *secretly* gave themselves surnames in order to maintain a sense of family but they did not use those surnames around whites. Years after emancipation, blacks born during the era of slavery remained reluctant to tell white people their full names.[28]

The "slave names" fallacy is false not only because whites did not give slaves surnames but also because the names that blacks gave themselves were not simply the names of whoever owned them. During the era of slavery, it was common to choose other names. Otherwise, if all the families belonging to a given slave owner took his name, that would defeat the purpose of creating separate family identities. Ironically, when some blacks in the twentieth century began repudiating what they called "slave names," they often took Arabic names, even though Arabs over the centuries had enslaved more Africans than Europeans had.[29]

A fallacy with more substantial implications is that the current fatherless families so prevalent among contemporary blacks are a "legacy of slavery," where families were not recognized. As with other social problems attributed to a "legacy of slavery," this ignores the fact that the problem has become much worse among generations of blacks far removed from slavery than among generations closer to the era of slavery. Most black children were raised in two-parent homes, even under slavery, and for generations thereafter.[30] Freed blacks married, and marriage rates among blacks were slightly *higher* than among whites in the early twentieth century.[31] Blacks also had slightly higher rates of labor force participation than whites in every census from 1890 to 1950.[32]

While 31 percent of black children were born to unmarried women in the early 1930s, that proportion rose to 77 percent by the early 1990s.[33] If unwed childbirth was "a legacy of slavery," why was it so much less common among blacks who were two generations closer to the era of slavery? One sign of the breakdown of the nuclear family among blacks was that, by 1993, more than a million black children were being raised by their grandparents, about two-thirds as many as among whites, even though there are several times as many whites as blacks in the population of the United States.[34]

When tragic retrogressions in all these respects became painfully apparent in the second half of the twentieth century, a "legacy of slavery" became a false explanation widely used, thereby avoiding confronting contemporary factors in contemporary problems.

These retrogressions were not only dramatic in themselves, they had major impacts on other important individual and social results. For example, while most black children were still being raised in two-parent families as late as 1970, only one third were by 1995.[35] Moreover, much social pathology is highly correlated with the absence of a father, both among blacks and whites, but the magnitude of the problem is greater among blacks because fathers are missing more often in black families. While, in the late twentieth century, an absolute majority of those black families with no husband present lived in poverty, more than four-fifths of black husband-wife families did not.[36] From 1994 on into the twenty-first century, the poverty rate among black husband-wife families was below 10 percent.[37]

It is obviously not simply the act of getting married which drastically reduces the poverty rate and infant mortality rate among blacks, or among other groups, but the values and behavior patterns which lead to marriage and which have a wider impact on many other things.[38]

Culture

As already noted, races can differ for reasons that are not racial, because people inherit cultures as well as genes. So long as one generation raises the next, it could hardly be otherwise. Many of the social or cultural differences between American blacks and American whites nationwide today were in antebellum times pointed out as differences between white Southerners and white Northerners. These include ways of talking, rates of crime and violence, children born out of wedlock, educational attainment, and economic initiative or lack thereof.[39]

While only about one-third of the antebellum white population of the United States lived in the South, at least 90 percent of American blacks lived in the South on into the twentieth century. In short, the great majority of blacks lived in a region with a culture that proved to be less productive and less peaceful for its inhabitants in general. Moreover, opportunities to move beyond that culture were more restricted for blacks.

While that culture was regional, both blacks and whites took the Southern culture with them when they moved out of the South. As one small but significant example, when the movement for creating public schools swept across the United States in the 1830s and 1840s, not only was that movement more successful in creating public schools in the North than in the South, those parts of Northern states like Ohio, Indiana and Illinois that were settled by white Southerners were the slowest to establish public schools.[40]

The legacy of the Southern culture is more readily documented in the behavior of later generations than is the legacy of slavery, which some distinguished nineteenth century writers said explained the behavior of antebellum Southern whites,[41] and which later writers said explained the behavior of blacks. In reality, the regional culture of the South existed in particular regions of Britain in centuries past, regions where people destined to settle in the American South exhibited the same behavior patterns before they immigrated to the South.[42] They were called "crackers" and "rednecks" before they crossed the Atlantic— and before they ever saw a slave. As a well-known Southern historian said, "We do not live in the past, but the past in us."[43]

Educational and intellectual performance is a readily documented area where the persistence of culture can be tested. As late as the First World War, white soldiers from various Southern states scored lower on mental tests than black soldiers from various Northern states.[44] Not only did black soldiers have the advantage of better schools in the North, they also had an opportunity for the Southern culture to begin to erode in their new surroundings. Over the years, much has been made of the fact that blacks score lower than whites nationwide on mental tests. From this, some observers have concluded that this is due to a racial difference and others have concluded that this is due to some deficiency or bias in the tests. But neither explanation would account for white Southerners' mental test scores in the First World War.

Whatever the sources of the lower educational or intellectual attainments among blacks, there are major economic and social consequences of such differences.

For many years, blacks received a lesser quantity and lower quality of education in the Southern schools that most attended. But, even after the quantity gap was eliminated by the late twentieth century, the qualitative gap remained large. The test scores of black seventeen-year-olds in a variety of academic subjects were the same as the scores of whites several years younger.[45] That is obviously not a basis for expecting equal results in an economy increasingly dependent on mental skills.

Crime and Violence

The history of crime and violence among blacks contradicts many widespread beliefs about the causes of that crime and violence. Poverty, unemployment, and racial discrimination are frequently listed among the prime "root causes" of riots and other criminality among blacks. Many are so convinced of this that they see no reason to examine the factual historical record.

Crime among black Americans, like crime among white Americans, was declining for years *prior* to the decade of the 1960s, with its landmark civil rights laws and its "war on poverty" programs. But it was during the 1960s that crime rates began skyrocketing among both blacks and whites, and it was precisely *after* the historic civil rights laws were passed that blacks began rioting in cities across the country. Within days of the passage of the Voting Rights Act of 1965, the first of hundreds of riots that would rack cities across the country over the next four years began in the black neighborhood of Los

Angeles known as Watts. These riots did not begin where blacks were poorest or most oppressed, which was still the South. Indeed, Southern cities seldom suffered the riots that struck many Northern cities and devastated many black neighborhoods in those cities.[46] Thirty four people died in the Watts riots but 43 were killed when blacks rioted in Detroit two years later.

Although Detroit had the worst of the riots that struck virtually every Northern city during the latter part of the 1960s, the poverty rate among Detroit's black population was only half of that of blacks nationwide, its homeownership rate among blacks was the highest in the country, and its unemployment rate was 3.4 percent— lower than that among *whites* nationwide.[47] Detroit did not have a massive riot because it was an economic disaster area. It *became* an economic disaster area after the riots, as did black neighborhoods in many other cities across the country. Moreover, riot-torn neighborhoods in these cities remained disaster areas for decades thereafter, as businesses became reluctant to locate there, reducing access to both jobs and places to shop, and both black and white middle class people left for the suburbs.

Whatever the causes of these waves of riots, whether as background factors or as immediate precipitating incidents, they were clearly *not* the factors that have been repeated endlessly but fallaciously. The worst ghetto riots occurred precisely at those times and places where the things that were supposed to prevent riots were most prevalent, including officials promoting welfare state policies and restraining the police. Conversely, riots were least destructive, and sometimes non-existent, in places and times where officials took an opposite view.

As already noted, Southern cities were far less often struck by urban riots. Among Northern cities, Chicago was one of the cities least affected by ghetto riots. It had no such riots in 1967. The following year, when riots swept across the country in the wake of the assassination of Martin Luther King, Chicago's Mayor Richard J. Daley issued a highly publicized "shoot to kill" order to his police that was denounced by many, but deaths from riots in Chicago were a fraction of what they were in cities like Detroit where more humane and sympathetic expressions were used and the police were restrained. Nationally, the most and worst urban ghetto riots occurred during the Johnson administration but there was not one major urban riot during the entire eight years of the Reagan administration. Yet such hard facts did not make a dent in fashionable beliefs, then or now. Both politicians and activists have a vested interest in racial fallacies, which attribute the advancement of blacks to politicians and activists, and blame others for the retrogressions.

ECONOMICS

Gross income differences between groups can easily lead to fallacious conclusions if various demographic, educational, and other differences are ignored. Unfortunately, many racial comparisons are like comparisons of apples and oranges, since races differ in many ways besides race. They differ not only in age and family size but also in education and in the proportion of their respective populations that are working, among other differences. As with comparisons of women and men, comparing truly comparable individuals of different races often produces very different results from gross intergroup comparisons.

Gross comparisons of racial and ethnic groups are only a starting point in the process of trying to understand the factors at work in producing differences in incomes and occupations at a given time, as well as changes over time.

The U.S. census in 2000 showed that the median earnings of blacks was $27,264 in 1999, compared to a national average of $32,098, so that blacks as individuals earned 85 percent of what Americans in general earned. As families, however, blacks earned only 66 percent of the national average for families. That is because the average black family has fewer people than American families in general, since a higher proportion of black families lack fathers. When comparing black married couples with other married couples, however, blacks earned 88 percent of the national average for married couples— $50,690, compared to a national average of $57,345.[48]

Among Asian Americans, the 2000 census showed that their median individual earnings exceeded the national average— $40,650 for Asian American men compared to $37,057 for all American men. As individuals,

Asian Americans earned 10 percent *more* than the national average. As families, they earned 19 percent more— $59,324, compared to a national average of $50,046.[49] Part of this is due to the fact that Asian American families tend to include fathers more often than the families of Americans in general.[50] With Asian Americans as with blacks, their incomes have not always been as high— relative to the national average— as today. With both, assessing the role of racial discrimination involves a consideration of history as well as economics.

For perspective, we also need to consider racial and ethnic groups in other countries. In Malaysia, for example, the Malay majority averaged less than half the income of the Chinese minority throughout the last quarter of the twentieth century, even though the Chinese were in no position to discriminate against the Malays, and in fact there were widespread government programs giving preferential treatment to Malays. In Sri Lanka, the Tamil minority likewise had higher incomes than the country's majority population, the Sinhalese, until laws and policies severely discriminating against the Tamils, beginning in the 1950s, enabled the Sinhalese to overtake the Tamils in income by 1973.[51] In general, discrimination must take its place among the various other factors behind intergroup economic differences. How much of a factor can vary from group to group, from country to country, and from one time period to another.

Employment Discrimination

"Discrimination" is one of those words that is often used and seldom defined. Bias, prejudice, and discrimination are often lumped together, as if they were pretty much the same thing. But bias and prejudice are attitudes— things inside people's heads— while discrimination is an overt act taking place outside, in the real world. That is not a small distinction when analyzing economic differences, which are things visible in the real world. Nor can we simply assume that more bias or prejudice translates automatically into more discrimination— or that discrimination would not exist in the absence of bias or prejudice. What is overlooked in such fallacious assumptions is the *price* that has to be paid by someone who turns his subjective feelings into an overt act.

Imagine someone who owns a golf course in a country where racial discrimination is perfectly legal— and that this owner has a bias or prejudice against blacks. With an international tournament scheduled to be played at this golf course, would the owner pay no price for excluding Tiger Woods? The price to be paid would probably run into the millions, because the absence of Tiger Woods would reduce the worldwide television audience, on which advertising rates and revenues are based— thereby reducing how much television networks would pay the owner of the golf course to broadcast the tournament.

While it is easy to visualize the cost of discrimination in an example like this, there is usually a cost to be paid by anyone who competes in the marketplace in other situations. Employers who discriminate against job applicants from particular groups usually have to either pay more, in order to attract additional workers from other groups to take their place, or else lower the job qualifications required, in order to make more of the existing job applicants eligible. Either way, that costs money, whether in higher pay or in lower productivity from less qualified workers. If the discriminating employer is competing with other producers of similar products, then those competitors who have either less racial partiality or who care more about money can hire more qualified workers from the rejected groups without having to pay the additional costs paid by the employer who rejected them. In a competitive market, these cost differences translate into differences in profit rates and can even translate into a difference between survival and bankruptcy.

Do the costs of discrimination actually change behavior in the real world? Hard evidence indicates that it does. Even in South Africa during the era of white rule and official racial apartheid policies that limited or forbad the employment of blacks in particular jobs or industries, white employers in competitive industries often hired blacks in greater numbers or in higher occupations than the law allowed. A South African government crackdown in the construction industry alone led to fines imposed on hundreds of companies for such violations of the apartheid laws.[52] There is no reason to suppose that these employers had less racial bias or prejudice than the politicians who passed the apartheid laws. The difference was that passing such laws cost politicians nothing, but discrimination against blacks cost competitive businesses money.

Similar economic principles apply when landlords discriminate against certain groups who want to become tenants, or when lenders discriminate against members of such groups who wish to borrow.

This is not to say that no discrimination ever takes place. For one thing, all economic transactions need not take place in competitive industries or in profit-seeking enterprises. Before racial discrimination became illegal and socially unacceptable in the United States, non-profit organizations like universities, foundations, and hospitals could discriminate more readily, and against more groups, because their survival did not depend on making a profit, and the implicit costs of their decisions were paid out of the endowments and donations supplied by others.

Similarly, government enterprises around the world have tended to be more discriminatory, because their costs of discrimination are paid by the taxpayers, rather than by those who do the discriminating. In some eras this discrimination has been against minorities but in other eras there has been "reverse discrimination" against members of the majority, which is often phrased politically as "preferences" for members of selected minorities. Universities which seldom, if ever, hired black professors before the 1960s began the *preferential* hiring of black professors afterwards. Similarly with the employment practices of hospitals, foundations, government agencies and regulated public utilities, all of whom are cushioned in one way or another from the economic pressures of competition. Neither discrimination nor reverse discrimination costs them what such practices cost profit-based businesses in competitive industries.

Just as people with racial bias or prejudice may fail to discriminate when the cost of doing so is too high, someone with no racial antipathy at all may still discriminate by race if rates of crime, disease, or other undesirable characteristics differ from one racial group to another and alternative ways of sorting out individuals are more costly or less accurate. Indeed, *members of the same group* may discriminate against other people like themselves for this reason, as when black taxi drivers avoid picking up black male passengers after dark.

In short, race is used as a sorting device for decision-making, even by people who are not racists. Thus employers may be reluctant to hire young black males because these employers are aware of what a high proportion of them have been arrested or imprisoned, even if these employers have no antipathy to black people, as such, and readily hire older blacks or black females. A study of those employers who routinely check for prison records among all people who apply for employment found that these particular employers hired black males more often than other employers did.[53] That is, these particular employers no longer had to rely on using race as a sorting device, when they already had in place a more accurate (and more costly) sorting device that was in use for screening their job applicants in general. Distinguishing racism, as such, from the use of race as a sorting device complicates the problem of trying to determine how much racial discrimination exists.

It is also worth noting that one of the things that makes race such a widely used sorting device is that it is far less costly than other sorting devices, since race is immediately visible to the naked eye at no cost, unlike religion, education or other sorting devices that require more time, effort or expense. Many people have said that each person should be judged as an individual but virtually no one actually does that because the cost of acquiring sufficient knowledge about an individual is often far more than it is worth. Such costs can include not only financial costs but also physical dangers, including death. When you see a shadowy figure in an alley at night, that might be a kindly neighbor out walking his dog or a sadistic serial killer waiting to ambush another victim. It is not worth the cost of finding out which. In general, how finely it pays to sort depends on the costs and the benefits of doing so. At one time, many employment advertisements said "No Irish Need Apply." Such ads did not begin to disappear until the acculturation of Irish immigrants to the norms of American society reached the point where the benefits of sorting the Irish individually exceeded the costs of doing so.

With racial or ethnic minorities, as with women, the question of discrimination is not simply whether there is any, or how much, but also where it takes place. In both cases, the discrimination can begin in childhood, especially when it comes to schooling, so that there may be real differences in qualifications by the time individuals begin entering the job market as adults. For many years— indeed, generations— black children in the South attended schools where the expenditures per pupil were substantially lower than in white schools. In some parts of the South, per pupil expenditure was several times as high for white students as for black students.[54] In some places, the number of days in a school year differed, so that black and white students with the same number of years of schooling had very different quantities and qualities of education.

When, in adulthood, blacks and whites with the "same" education were paid different amounts during the Jim Crow era, it was by no means certain whether the difference represented employer discrimination or discrimination that occurred before the worker reached the employer, or some combination. In a later era, after such disparities in per pupil expenditures and in days of school attendance were either less or non-existent, the academic performances of the students themselves differed so much that, as already noted, an average black seventeen-year-old scored at a level achieved by white students who were years younger.[55] Here again, though for different reasons, comparisons of the incomes of blacks and whites with the "same" education were comparisons of apples and oranges, so that inferences of employer discrimination were still questionable.

Among the economic questions that can be raised about discrimination are: How much of it there is at a given time and place, how much has it changed over time, and how much of the economic differences between groups can be explained by it? One way to assess the last is by comparing truly comparable individuals from different racial or ethnic groups. Simple as that might seem in principle, it is not always easy in practice. Often the best we can do is to observe how gross differences between groups narrow when comparing individuals from those groups who are comparable in some important respects.

As far back as 1980, college-educated black married couples earned slightly *more* than white college-educated married couples.[56] As far back as 1969, young black males whose homes included newspapers, magazines, and library cards, and who had also gone on to obtain the same number of years of schooling as young white males, had the same incomes as their white counterparts.[57] This had not always been true. In earlier periods, such cultural factors had little weight,[58] suggesting that racial discrimination had more weight in earlier times. By 1989, blacks, whites, and Hispanics in the United

States of the same age (29) and with the same IQ (100) all had annual incomes within a thousand dollars of one another when they worked year-round.[59]

Seldom, if ever, do employers ask job applicants whether they come from homes with newspapers, magazines, and library cards. Nor are they likely to give job applicants IQ tests. Moreover, even if they did these unlikely things, employers who are racists are unlikely to care when the applicant is black or belongs to some other racial or ethnic group that the employer does not like. The fact that researchers today find such factors shrinking the racial difference in income to the vanishing point among comparable individuals suggests that racial discrimination by employers explains relatively little of the still large income differences between blacks and whites. In short, these racial income differences are not between individuals who are comparable on cultural variables but reflect the fact that these variables are themselves different between the races. Comparisons of comparable people can even reverse the conclusions suggested by gross statistics:

> A number of economists and sociologists investigating discrimination in the labor market have recently concluded that this is the principal reason why [blacks] don't have average incomes that are as high as those of whites. What looks like discrimination, this body of research suggests, is better described as rewarding workers with stronger cognitive skills. Thus a study of men twenty-six to thirty-three years old who held full-time jobs in 1991 found that when education was measured in the traditional way (years of school completed), blacks earned 19 percent less than comparably educated whites. But when the yardstick was how well they performed on basic tests of word knowledge, paragraph comprehension, arithmetical reasoning, and mathematical knowledge, the results were reversed. Black men earned 9 percent *more* than white men with the same education— as defined by skill.[60]

Even where race, as such, is not used as a sorting device, other sorting devices can have different impacts on people of different races. For example, to disqualify job applicants who have been convicted felons may disqualify a larger percentage of one group than another. Even to disqualify individuals who have tattoos or strange names can likewise affect a larger percentage of one group than another. Anti-discrimination laws make employers liable to legal action for policies or practices which have a "disparate impact" on different groups.

The burden of proof falls on the accused in these cases to demonstrate the validity of the particular criteria used. This reversal of the usual legal principle of putting the burden of proof on the accuser is often enough to predetermine the outcome, since the cost of proving effectiveness to the satisfaction of third parties with no experience can easily exceed the value of whatever is at issue in the lawsuit. For example, it can cost tens of thousands of dollars just to validate a mental test, with no guarantee that it will be validated to the satisfaction of third parties who are unlikely to be experts on mental tests, statistical analysis, or the industry involved. Such cases are often settled out of court by employers aware of the futility of trying to prove their innocence, even when they have not discriminated.

Consumer Discrimination

Employment discrimination is not the only kind of discrimination. There have been many allegations that businesses in ghetto neighborhoods charge higher prices or offer inferior goods and services, and that banks and other lending institutions discriminate against black applicants for loans, while check-cashing agencies charge unjustifiably high prices for performing a service that banks perform free of charge for their middle class customers. Data in support of such charges need to be scrutinized, like other data that seem convincing on the surface, but only on the surface.

There is little question that the prices charged by stores in low-income neighborhoods tend to be higher than prices charged by stores in middle-class neighborhoods. Moreover, the quality of perishable items like meat, fruits, and vegetables may also be lower, and there have been many complaints that the quality of service is not as high in low-income neighborhoods. Many who have studied such things in racial ghettoes conclude that this shows "exploitation" of consumers or racial discrimination or both.[61] An alternative economic explanation is that it costs more to operate stores in ghetto neighborhoods and that such costs are passed on to the consumers there. To the extent that higher costs cannot be fully passed on to the consumers, ghetto businesses would tend to be less profitable, and so such neighborhoods would attract fewer businesses in general. Moreover, the kinds of businesses they do attract are often businesses that would find it difficult to survive the competition in middle-class neighborhoods, whether because of lower efficiency or less courteous service.

While both the racism-and-exploitation theory and the economic theory are consistent with the observed differences between ghetto businesses and businesses in middle-class neighborhoods, there are empirical data which can test these theories against one another. First, it would need to be established that there are in fact differences in the cost of doing business in these different neighborhoods and what those differences are. As already noted in Chapter 2, the costs of delivering merchandise to stores is lower when a given amount of merchandise is delivered to one giant supermarket or "big box" store like Wal-Mart or Costco than to a large number of smaller stores scattered around town. Moreover, in so far as stores in ghetto neighborhoods face higher costs due to higher rates of shoplifting, vandalism, crime or violence, these costs are reflected in merchandise losses, repair costs, insurance costs, and costs of preventive devices like iron grates or security guards.

While higher prices charged to consumers recapture some of those costs, they may not capture all. A higher proportion of low-income consumers shop outside their own neighborhoods than is the case with middle-class customers, no doubt because some low-income consumers try to escape the higher prices charged locally in their neighborhood. Therefore the ability of stores within ghetto neighborhoods to recover all their extra costs by raising prices is limited by the prospect that even more of their customers will shop elsewhere if they raise their prices further. That in turn means that their profit rates are limited more so than that of stores in middle-class neighborhoods. A study of stores in low-income neighborhoods in Washington found that indeed prices were higher but that profit rates were *not* higher in these neighborhoods.[62] This might also explain the absence of many stores, and especially stores belonging to large supermarket chains, in ghetto neighborhoods. Ghetto stores may in fact be struggling to survive while being accused of "exploitation" and "greed."

It should also be noted that most people are not criminals, even in high-crime neighborhoods, but that those who are not pay the price in many ways for those among them who are. Yet the high prices they pay in stores are seldom attributed to the criminals who cause these high prices but are instead more likely to be attributed to the storekeepers who charge these prices. This particular fallacy is especially likely if the store owner is from a different racial or ethnic group. Moreover, where there are local politicians and community activists who are quick to denounce the police for taking forceful action against criminals or rioters, the police tend to become less vigorous in enforcing the laws in these neighborhoods, in order to protect their own careers, so that criminal elements have a freer hand, again at the expense of the local residents, both economically and otherwise.

It should also be noted that ghetto neighborhoods have not always been places largely deprived of stores and other businesses providing both services and jobs. In earlier eras, when crime rates were lower, and especially before the massive ghetto riots of the 1960s, there were many businesses operating in black communities that no longer do so, as noted in Chapter 2. That is also part of the large and lasting prices paid by ghetto residents. An additional factor today is that, in those few cases where low-price, big-box stores like Wal-Mart are considering locating in or near cities with large minority populations, they are often thwarted by the political opposition of labor unions, reinforced by allies they recruit by denouncing the non-union and other policies of such stores. These allies often consider themselves friends of minorities— one of many fallacies about race.

Lending Discrimination

Statistical differences between acceptance rates for black and white applicants for loans from financial institutions have been cited as bases for claims of racial discrimination. A nationwide study of mortgage lending statistics for 1990, published by the Federal Reserve Board in 1991, showed differences among various racial groups in the proportion of mortgage loan applications accepted and rejected. Most black, white, Hispanic and Asian applicants had their applications approved but the percentage denied conventional mortgage loans ranged widely from 34 percent for blacks to 13 percent for Asian Americans.[63] Although the study warned that it had no data on the applicants' net worth, credit history, employment history, and other factors normally weighed in decisions to grant or deny mortgage loan applications,[64] there were immediate claims that the study showed racial discrimination.

Jesse Jackson called it "criminal activity" that banks "routinely and systematically discriminate against African-Americans and Latinos in making mortgage loans."[65] A similar Federal Reserve Board study with similar results, published the following year, led to similar conclusions. The *Washington Post*, for example, reported that there was "overwhelming evidence" of discrimination in "our banking system."[66] Comments on both studies focussed on differences between blacks and whites— and sometimes Hispanics as well— but the statistics in these studies also included data on Asian Americans, and these latter data were almost invariably ignored.

In both the 1991 study and the 1992 study, whites were denied conventional home mortgage loans more often than Asian Americans.[67] Mortgage lending data for 2000 likewise showed blacks being denied conventional mortgages at a rate double that of whites— and whites being denied conventional mortgages at a rate nearly double that of Asian Americans.[68] Just as whites have higher credit scores than blacks, Asian Americans have higher average credit scores than whites.[69]

The same reasoning that led to the conclusion that blacks were being discriminated against in favor of whites would lead to the very questionable conclusion that whites were being discriminated against in favor of Asian Americans. But however questionable that conclusion, we cannot simply accept empirical evidence when it supports our preconceptions and reject that same evidence when it goes against those preconceptions. That would be adding to the many fallacies already surrounding race. Another study showed that Asian Americans took out expensive subprime loans less frequently than whites did— but again the media focus was on black-white differences in the use of costly subprime loans and again the conclusion was that racial discrimination in access to conventional loans explained the difference.[70]

Here, as with claims of job discrimination and consumer discrimination, gross statistics need to be scrutinized to ensure that the comparisons being made are not comparisons of apples and oranges. Although the data on mortgage loan applicants in the Federal Reserve studies did not include

their net worth, for example, other data on blacks and whites in general
showed very large differences in net worth, even when differences in income
are controlled.[71] So to say, as many did, that blacks and whites with the same
income were turned down at different rates is not to say that individuals of
equal credit standing were turned down at different rates, since net worth is
a weighty consideration in the granting or denial of mortgage loans.
According to an earlier survey, "the average white household held roughly
four times the amount of liquid assets as the average black household."[72]

This was only one of the ways in which the comparisons being made were
comparisons of apples and oranges. A 1992 study of mortgage lending in
Boston by the Boston Federal Reserve Bank showed that black, white, and
Hispanic applicants were not the same on a number of relevant factors:

> As reported in other surveys, black and Hispanic applicants have
> considerably less net wealth and liquid assets than whites. Black and
> Hispanic applicants also tend to have poorer credit histories than whites.
>   Blacks and Hispanics in Boston are substantially more likely than
> whites to be purchasing a two- to four-family home. The higher
> proportion of two- to four-family homes among denied applicants, for
> whites as well as for blacks and Hispanics, suggests that lenders perceive
> more risk associated with financing the purchase of such properties.[73]

One reflection of these and other differences is that different proportions
of the various groups applied for conventional mortgage loans, as
distinguished from government-backed mortgage loans. The government-
backed loans tend to be easier to qualify for and also tend to have lower
restrictions on the size of the loans that are available, thereby limiting how
expensive a house could be bought by someone without sufficient assets to
supplement the mortgage loan. Blacks' applications for government-backed
loans were 85 percent as numerous as their applications for conventional
loans, while whites applied for government-backed loans only 32 percent as
often as they applied for conventional loans, and Asians applied for
government-backed loans only 11 percent as often as for conventional loans.[74]

On virtually every variable for which there are data, the groups differ
markedly. For example, whites applied for loans to refinance their homes
more often than they applied for loans for home improvement, while with

blacks it was just the reverse.[75] Yet, here as in other cases, statistical disparities are readily taken as proof of racial discrimination, as if race is the only difference among the people being compared. Moreover, the omission of Asian Americans suggests that discordant data are being avoided, rather than being allowed to raise embarrassing questions about the whole approach of drawing implications from statistical disparities. This is not the only situation where statistical and other facts about Asian Americans are avoided, when such facts could undermine the prevailing and convenient explanation of racial differences.[76]

The study by the Federal Reserve Bank of Boston sought to control statistically for various factors, in order to determine what unexplained residual differences would remain after comparing blacks and whites with the same measured characteristics. The conclusion reached was that while blacks with the same measured characteristics as whites were turned down 17 percent of the time, they should have been turned down just 11 percent of the time if the same criteria were used. However, instead of a plain statement of a 6 percentage point unexplained differential, the conclusion was expressed quite differently:

> A black or Hispanic applicant in the Boston area is roughly 60 percent more likely to be denied a mortgage loan than a similarly situated white applicant. This means that 17 percent of black or Hispanic applicants instead of 11 percent would be denied loans, even if they had the same obligation ratios, credit history, loan to value, and property characteristics as white applicants. In short, the results indicate that a serious problem exists in the market for mortgage loans, and lenders, community groups, and regulators must work together to ensure that minorities are treated fairly.[77]

Thus a 6 percentage point unexplained differential was presented as a 60 percent greater chance of being denied a loan, since 17 percent is roughly 60 percent larger than 11 percent. But the problems of the Boston Federal Reserve study go beyond tendentious semantics. Like so many studies which hold particular variables constant, this one seemed to assume that either these were the only variables that mattered or that any other variables could be assumed to be the *same* as between blacks and whites— even though every variable actually investigated had turned out to be *different* between blacks and whites. Finally, when the records of specific banks were examined by others, it turned out that all the remaining difference in loan approval rates for apparently comparable blacks and whites were due to just one bank— and that bank was owned by blacks![78]

If the lending discrimination theory were correct, it would mean that blacks had to have higher credit-worthiness than whites in order to have their loans approved. That in turn would imply that subsequent default rates among blacks borrowers would be lower than among white borrowers. But empirical evidence from census data did not suggest a racial difference in default rates among the approved borrowers.[79] A writer for *Forbes* magazine explained the implications of this fact to the principal author of the Boston Federal Reserve Bank study, Alicia Munnell. When pressed, she agreed with his point that "discrimination against blacks should show up in lower, not equal, default rates— discrimination would mean that good black applicants are being unfairly rejected." But she called this "a sophisticated point"[80] and this discussion followed:

> FORBES: Did you ever ask the question that if defaults appear to be more or less the same among blacks and whites, that points to mortgage lenders making rational decisions?
> Munnell: No.
> Munnell does not want to repudiate her study. She tells FORBES, on reflection, that the census data are not good enough and could be "massaged" further: "I do believe that discrimination occurs."
> FORBES: You have no evidence?
> Munnell: "I do not have evidence. . . . No one has evidence."[81]

Even if there were no data on factors that affect mortgage lending, the mortgage lending discrimination charge would have a hard time passing the plausibility test. Let us assume, for the sake of argument, that every mortgage loan officer in every bank and every savings & loan association is white and that every one of them dislikes black people. What follows from that?

The mortgage loan officer is going to have to deal with black mortgage loan applicants, whether their loan applications are approved or disapproved— and these black applicants will probably never be seen again by anyone at the bank, whether their applications are approved or disapproved. Moreover, for neither black nor white applicants is approval a question of doing someone a favor. It is a question of making money from them. Does dislike of black people mean dislike of receiving their mortgage payment checks in the mail each month? Even in the worst years of racism in the Jim Crow South, very few white people refused to accept money in the mail from blacks.

During the period of the earlier study alleging mortgage loan discrimination, banks and savings & loan associations were struggling to avoid going bankrupt and many lost that struggle. To believe that they were turning down qualified blacks whose checks in the mail could have saved their hides is to believe that the mere knowledge that the checks coming in from people they never saw were from black people would have been enough for these bank officials to cut their own throats financially.

As for sub-prime lenders who charge higher interest rates to people with lower credit ratings, many— if not most— have had heavy losses in the millions of dollars. In 2001, the Bank of America abruptly shut down its subprime lending program after losing hundreds of millions of dollars.[82] Some subprime lenders have gone bankrupt, all the while being widely denounced for unconscionably exploiting the poor, when what they have done in fact has been to under-estimate how risky the loans were that they were making, so that even the higher interest rates they charged were not enough to cover those risks.

SUMMARY AND IMPLICATIONS

While gross data on differences among racial and ethnic groups are readily available, the inferences to be drawn from those data are highly varied and controversial. The very same set of data can yield radically different conclusions, depending on the arbitrary selection of data to be cited and the arbitrary selection of the groups to be compared. If, for example, one omits Asian Americans when comparing blacks and whites, one can miss the fact that the same reasoning which would lead to the conclusion that blacks are discriminated against would lead to the conclusion that whites are discriminated against because they not only are turned down for mortgage loans more frequently than Asian Americans, and have to resort to costly subprime loans more often than Asian Americans, a study of the 1990–91 downturn in employment showed that white workers were more likely to lose their jobs than were Asian American workers.[83] Either we believe that white employers are prejudiced against white workers or we admit that groups can differ from one another in characteristics relevant to economic decisions.

Questions about the existence, magnitude, and consequences of racial discrimination cannot be answered with gross statistics, nor even by some of the research methods commonly used. For example, there have been research projects which sent out black and white job applicants with the same objective qualifications, or black and white applicants for housing or loans with the same incomes, and then determined how often or how severely blacks were discriminated against by the difference in the rates at which these matched individuals were hired as employees or accepted as tenants, home buyers or borrowers.

The fallacy in this approach comes from ignoring the high cost of knowledge and the high costs of making wrong decisions. Neither objective job qualifications nor income tell the whole story for anyone of any race. Other sorting devices may be resorted to where acquiring more specific information is costly, such as seeking more detailed information from previous employers— which many former employers are reluctant to provide, given the legal risks they face when providing adverse information— or hiring private detectives to look into the private lives of job applicants, housing applicants, or applicants for loans. Among these sorting devices are hiring by recommendations from existing employees, who have incentives not to jeopardize their own standing with their bosses by recommending someone they know will be wrong for the job. Race, as we have already seen, can be used as a sorting device, even by people who have no hostility to a particular race, including other members of that same race.

If, in fact, there are differences among the races in the proportion of people who are desirable as employees, tenants, homeowners, or borrowers, then the use of race as a sorting device may disqualify many individually desirable people, *without imposing costs on the race as a whole, beyond the costs created by their own behavior.* No doubt there were many sober, hard-working, and productive Irishmen who were hurt, due to no fault of their own, during the era when many employers had signs that said, "No Irish Need Apply." But that is wholly different from saying that employment and income differences between the Irish as a whole and other Americans during that era represented discrimination rather than behavioral differences whose costs were reflected in employment differences. Determining whether economic differences between two groups as a whole are a result of discrimination is wholly different from determining whether individuals have been penalized for things they did not do and situations beyond their control. However much discrimination against individuals may be condemned, it cannot automatically explain income and employment differences between groups.

Somewhat similar conclusions were implicit in W.E.B. DuBois' nineteenth century study which concluded that if all white people lost their racial prejudices overnight, it would not make much difference to most black workers. Though "some few would be promoted, some few would get new places" nevertheless "the mass would remain as they are," until the younger generation began to "try harder," until the "idle and discouraged" were stimulated and the whole race "lost the omnipresent excuse for failure: prejudice."[84] Again, as with the Irish, there may be serious losses to blameless individuals without such losses being able to explain much about the over-all income or employment differences between two groups. No doubt DuBois himself was deprived of opportunities for which he was well qualified, in academia and elsewhere, because of race. But the point here is that such employment discrimination could not explain much of the very large black-white income and employment differential of his time, according to DuBois' study at the time. Differences in decisions made about matched samples of individuals are misleading as explanations of differences in the economic fate of whole groups, when those groups are by no means matched on the relevant factors.

Another way of looking at this is that in job markets, as in consumer markets, a sharp distinction must be made between those who create certain costs and those who react to those costs by passing the costs on to be paid by others. Just as costs created by criminals in low-income neighborhoods get passed on to be paid by local residents who are not criminals, so the costs created by less productive or more troublesome workers from a given racial or ethnic group get passed on to be paid by other workers from the same groups in the form of reduced job opportunities. Whether either of these actions is just is a moral question; whether these are the consequences that such circumstances lead to is an economic question.

At one time, it was widely recognized in the black community, as in the Irish or Jewish communities, that the negative impact of the behavior of some elements in their community adversely affected the other and larger elements of their community. Blacks, the Irish, and the Jews all had community organizations, both secular and religious, devoted to reducing the negative behavior of some, in the interest of all. But such efforts are reduced or undermined to the extent that all of a group's problems are blamed on outsiders, while group solidarity is maintained internally, even with wrong-doers, at all costs.

Data problems are by no means the sole, nor necessarily the principal, source of racial fallacies. Many people have a large vested interest in seeing racial problems in a particular way. Politicians and activists who have promoted a particular social vision of the reasons and remedies for racial disparities have their whole careers at stake, especially after they have portrayed politics and activism as the main sources of both past and future progress, contrary to hard evidence. Others have a heavy psychological or ideological investment in the prevailing vision, in which external causes predominate as explanations of group disparities in income and crime rates, among other things. These external causes range from employer discrimination to high prices in low-income neighborhoods to inadequate transportation to get to work.

Any questioning of these explanations may bring a charge of "blaming the victim." But the very question at issue is whether victimization is the explanation. As for blame, who can be blamed for inheriting a culture that existed before they were born? But, while nothing can be done about the past, much can be done in the present to prepare for the future. Whatever we wish to achieve in the future, it must begin by knowing where we are in

the present— not where we wish we were, or where we wish others to think
we are, but where we are in fact.

Both history and statistics reveal the fallacy of the "legacy of slavery"
explanation for current social pathology in America's black ghettoes. Senator
Edward Brooke, who grew up in Washington's black community in the 1920s
and 1930s summarized in a few words what many statistics confirm:

> For young people growing up in America today, stories of my youth
> will seem almost incomprehensible. It will require the suspension of their
> sense of reality to picture a time when large areas of Washington, D.C.,
> were truly safe, when families stayed together, neighbors helped one
> another, students were encouraged to study, and there were no drugs or
> drive-by shootings.[85]

The world that Senator Brooke described was generations closer to the
era of slavery than the generations pervaded by the ghetto social pathology
all too familiar in our own times. Moreover, many remarkably similar
pathologies have been found in a study of a white lower-class community in
Britain,[86] where none of the familiar explanations of slavery, racism or
discrimination apply. What lower-class white communities in Britain and
black ghettoes in the United States have in common is a pattern of social
pathologies that became pronounced in the latter half of the twentieth
century, when similar ideas and policies became dominant in both countries.
Britain was once one of the most law-abiding nations on earth but, by 1995,
its crime rate in most categories was higher than that in the United States.[87]
In both countries, politicians, activists, and ideologues who claimed to have
solutions instead made many problems worse than before.

Chapter 7

THIRD WORLD FACTS
AND FALLACIES

Contrasts between the prosperity of various Western nations and the dire poverty of some Third World countries arouse many emotions and provoke many inquiries into how such things can be. While such inquiries have turned up many facts, a failure to distinguish between causation and blame has produced many fallacies.

Since virtually unlimited numbers of sins can be found in the history of any branch of the human race, there will seldom be a lack of bad episodes that can be cited by those who seek to explain causation by blame. A book title captured much of this confusion: *How Europe Underdeveloped Africa.* Europeans certainly committed many sins in Africa— and North Africans committed not a few sins in Europe. North Africa's Barbary Coast pirates alone enslaved more Europeans than there were Africans taken in bondage to the United States, and North Africa's Moors invaded and subjugated Spain for centuries.

Such depredations and atrocities were by no means confined to Europeans and Africans. Asians, Arabs, Polynesians and the indigenous peoples of the Western Hemisphere all show a history very similar in this respect in its broad outlines, however much it differs in specific details from one part of the world to another. The confusion between blame and causation is likewise not confined to issues involving Europeans and Africans. Many blame the poverty in South America on North Americans or the poverty of India on British colonial rule in that subcontinent.

Sometimes, of course, blame and causation may coincide, just as a historic event may coincide with the spring equinox. But they are still two different things, despite such overlap. Spanish conquerors destroyed many indigenous economies and societies in the Western Hemisphere in the course of building a vast empire that stretched from the southern tip of South America all the way up to San Francisco, enriching Spain and impoverishing the indigenous populations of these regions. But, despite similar examples that could be cited in various parts of the world, the more fundamental question remains: Is that why *most* prosperous countries today are prosperous and why *most* poor countries are poor?

How could the conquerors have conquered in the first place, unless there were significant differences beforehand— whether economic, military, or whatever— between them and the conquered? Such questions are especially important when trying to explain how a country like Spain— not as large as Texas— could conquer territories many times its own size, with populations vastly outnumbering Spaniards, or how a number of European countries could do the same in Africa, or Japan do the same in East Asia in the first half of the twentieth century.

In short, even those who blame conquerors for the poverty of the conquered have still not disposed of the question of causation, for the preceding differences behind the conquests themselves remain to be explained. Moreover, there are prosperous countries whose conquests have been minor or non-existent, and countries mired in poverty that were never conquered. If the attempt to make causation synonymous with blame takes the form of blaming economic "exploitation"— however defined— for the poverty of the Third World, the great unanswered question then is: Why are those parts of the Third World least touched by contact with prosperous nations so often the most destitute of all?

Blame is much easier to understand than causation, more emotionally satisfying, and more politically convenient. But it is also a source of many fallacies. The complexities of causation must at least be examined before assuming that blame alone can explain Third World poverty. Many of the factors behind economic differences between different regions of the world have their origins in geography, for which neither the rich nor the poor can be blamed.

GEOGRAPHY

Geography encompasses many things— the configuration and fertility of the land, climate, natural resources, waterways, flora and fauna. All restrict or enhance the prospects of economic development, though seldom does any single factor determine the pace or magnitude of development.

It might seem strange that the configuration of the land could affect which peoples live in poverty and which achieve prosperity. But, as the distinguished French historian Fernand Braudel pointed out as a general rule: "Mountain life persistently lagged behind the plain."[1] Examples are not hard to find— the poverty and backwardness that long afflicted America's Appalachian region; in earlier centuries, the fact that people in Greece's mountains were the last to learn to speak Greek, just as the Scottish Highlanders did not learn to speak English until after the Scottish Lowlanders did; that the Islamic religion reached the people in the Rif mountains after the people on the land below had already become Muslims. It seems to be more than coincidence that the earliest known civilizations— in the Middle East, in India, and in China— all began in river valleys, and most of the great cities around the world were built on navigable waterways.

Although we tend to think of geography as fixed, what human beings can do with a given geographic environment changes over time as knowledge and experience grow, so that the advantages and disadvantages of particular environments, both absolutely and relative to other environments, can change profoundly over time. While the amount of natural resources in a particular environment might be considered to be given, what physical things can in fact function as natural resources depends entirely on what human beings know how to use. Waterfalls were not natural resources, but simply impediments to travel on waterways, before people invented water mills and later hydroelectric dams. Thus the relative geographic advantages and disadvantages of different regions that had, or did not have, waterfalls changed and therefore changed the prospects for prosperity or poverty for the inhabitants of those regions.

The presence or absence of petroleum, uranium, or other mineral deposits likewise had entirely different economic effects on the relative prospects of different regions and their inhabitants before and after ways of using these things became known. The heavy soils of Western Europe became more fertile than other soils only after ways were invented to harness horses or oxen so that farmers could effectively plow such soils. Meanwhile, no such developments were possible in the Western Hemisphere for thousands of years because there were no horses or oxen in the Western Hemisphere before the European invaders brought them. In an age when agriculture was the dominant economic activity over most of the planet, this meant that the economies of the indigenous peoples of the Western Hemisphere could not develop in the same way as economies on the vast Eurasian land mass, where the majority of the human race lived.

Because horses and oxen were also central to the transport of people and goods in Europe and Asia for thousands of years, this meant that land transport as well as agriculture could not be the same in the Western Hemisphere. Moreover, because the economically feasible magnitude of water transport depended on the capacity of land transport to handle cargoes when they reached port, there were not the same incentives and advantages to creating large, ocean-going vessels in the Western Hemisphere as there was in Europe or Asia. In short, whole ways of life had to be different in the two hemispheres because of geographic differences.

Perhaps the most profound effect of geography is in facilitating or impeding the interactions of peoples, not only economically but culturally. Since no one has a monopoly of new insights, the economic or other advancement of any given people depends in part on the extent to which they have access to the advances made by others. Geography plays a crucial role in determining how wide the cultural universe extends at any given place. For thousands of years, the peoples of the Eurasian land mass and the peoples of the Western Hemisphere were unaware of each others' existence, so that cultural interchanges were out of the question. The past few centuries in which they have been in contact with each other are a small fraction of the history of the human race, compared to the millennia in which they developed and elaborated separate and very different economies, cultures, skills, and values.

Similarly, peoples living on isolated islands in seas around the world have been cut off from the cultural interactions necessary to participate in the general advances of the human race. The indigenous people of the Canary Islands were of a Caucasian race, living at a stone-age level, when the Spaniards discovered them in the fifteenth century. The Australian aborigines were similarly isolated on their island-continent on the other side of the world before the British arrived. Geographic isolation has had a negative, and sometimes devastating, impact on economic and cultural development, whether that isolation has been absolute in some cases or relative in others.

Geographic differences can impose large differences in transportation costs, which in turn can facilitate cultural interactions among some peoples and inhibit or prevent it for others. Europe and Asia are regarded as separate continents, even though they are on one continuous land mass, because mountains and deserts separate Asians from Europeans, leaving them separate races with major cultural differences for thousands of years. While Europeans and Asians during that era were not separated as absolutely as the peoples of the Eurasian land mass in general were separated from the peoples of the Western Hemisphere, nevertheless economic interactions between Europeans and Asians were limited by transportation costs and their cultural interactions still more so, since the transportation and transplantation of human beings is more costly than the shipment of merchandise.

The vast Sahara Desert— comparable in size to the 48 contiguous United States— likewise, for thousands of years, separated the peoples of sub-Saharan Africa from the rest of the human race, not absolutely but to a very significant extent. As Fernand Braudel put it, "external influence filtered only very slowly, drop by drop, into the vast African continent South of the Sahara."[2] Moreover, many and severe internal geographic barriers separated many of the peoples of sub-Saharan Africa from one another,[3] fragmenting the region culturally, one sign of which are the great number of different African languages— 30 percent of all the languages in the world from only 13 percent of the world's population.[4] Wherever people have been isolated, whether by deserts or on distant islands in the sea or in remote mountain valleys, they have tended to lag behind the economic and cultural advances in the wider world.

Climate is also part of geography. In addition to the direct advantages and disadvantages of particular climates in terms of agriculture or diseases, climate can also affect the size of the cultural universe. People whose lands and waterways are frozen much of the year can seldom maintain trade or communications with the outside world as well as people in milder climates. Because climates usually vary more from north to south than they do over equal distances from east to west, knowledge of particular crops or the domestication and care of particular animals can travel far greater distances from east to west than from north to south. Such knowledge could travel all the way across Asia to places at similar latitudes in Europe, but knowledge of the flora and fauna in the temperate zone in South America could not travel a similar distance to the temperate zone in North America because they are separated by a very wide tropical zone where the flora and fauna have been very different.

Geographic variations can be extreme, even within a relatively limited area. Where moisture-laden winds blow across a mountain range, the rainfall on the windward side of those mountains can be several times as large as the rainfall on the leeward side, creating completely different conditions for agriculture on the two sides. Different vegetation also grows at different heights on the same mountains. Western Europe differs from Eastern Europe in climate, navigable waterways and in the mineral deposits necessary for industrialization— and it differs from Africa in all these respects even more so.[5]

The influence of geographic factors cannot be understood by looking at each factor in isolation because their interactions are often crucial. For example, while much of sub-Saharan Africa lacks beasts of burden that are common in Europe and Asia, the isolating effect of this is magnified by the dearth of navigable waterways and, in some places, difficult terrain for travel or transportation. The colorful sight of sub-Saharan Africans carrying large bundles on their heads is a sign of the severe limitations of transport which have handicapped that region for thousands of years.

What might be thought to be a crucial geographic factor in a country's economic fate— the presence or absence of saleable natural resources— turns out to have no such determining effect. Saudi Arabia is not only the world's largest producer of oil, that oil is so accessible that its cost of production is a small fraction of the price at which it sells on the world market. There are some extremely rich Saudis as a result but, for the country as a whole, its real income per capita is approximately half that of Singapore, which has virtually no natural resources, except for its harbor, and even has to import its drinking water from Malaysia. Israel, which has no significant amount of oil, has a higher real income per capita than most of the oil-rich Middle East countries.[6]

The world's largest producer of natural gas (Russia) is not even among the top 70 nations of the world in real income per capita. Neither is the world's largest producer of rubber (Thailand) or zinc (China). The world's largest producers of gold (South Africa) and copper (Chile) are 69th and 70th, respectively, in real income per capita.[7] The value of natural resources per capita in Uruguay and Venezuela is several times what it is in Japan or Switzerland but the real per capita income in Japan and Switzerland is about double that of Uruguay and several times that of Venezuela.[8] Geographic accessibility to the advances of the rest of the world seems to have had more effect on economic development than the possession of rich natural resources. Knowledge is, after all, what makes something a natural resource. The cave man lived amid the same physical resources we have today— and had them in greater abundance— but they were not natural resources in any economically meaningful sense until human beings acquired the knowledge to use them and the cultures to organize their use.

There is no need here to go into the detailed geography of Third World countries, much less to claim that geography is the sole determinant of their poverty. What is important is to understand that geography alone is enough to preclude any inherent economic sameness or equality among peoples or nations from being used as a benchmark or general presumption that would lead us to be shocked that there are differences and to look for mysterious or sinister reasons for those differences. There are also many other factors at work besides geography which influence the poverty or prosperity of nations. Because of other factors, some geographically very fortunate nations are nevertheless poverty-stricken and some much less geographically favored nations have prospered. We need to consider these other factors as well but, again, with no general presumption that peoples and nations around the world would have had the same economic outcomes except for some given factor.

HISTORY

When we refer to Third World nations, that may give the impression that there is a given set of countries very different from other countries. But that would be a fallacy. A list of either prosperous or poverty-stricken countries a hundred years ago would not contain all the same countries as today. As recently as the middle of the twentieth century, Singapore would have been among the poorest places on earth but today it is among the richest. Mid-nineteenth century Japan was a poor and backward nation and, as recently as the first half of the twentieth century, products made in Japan were usually regarded as poor quality imitations of similar products made in Europe or the United States. Yet today Japan's cars, cameras, and other products have set the standard for quality around the world, and the Japanese people are among the most prosperous. At the beginning of the twentieth century, Argentina was one of the ten most prosperous nations on earth— ahead of Germany or France— but it has long since lost that position. In the long view of history, all nations were Third World nations at some point or other in their evolution.

In short, what are identified as Third World nations today are simply countries whose economic levels lag behind those of most other countries. Some have always been poor and some have become poor, either absolutely or relative to rising living standards around the world. Some, such as China and India, have for some centuries been very poor but have, within the past generation or so, had unusually rapid economic growth rates that have lifted many millions of their people above these countries' official poverty lines. Within an even shorter span of time, the composition of the group of poorest nations has changed. As economist William Easterly has pointed out, "eleven out of the twenty-eight poorest countries in 1985 were *not* in the poorest fifth back in 1950."[9]

As noted in Chapter 5, comparing the relative incomes of statistical categories over time produces very different results from comparing the relative incomes of the same human beings over time. Likewise, comparing statistical categories of nations over time produces very different results from those of comparing the same nations over time. The World Bank, among others, has produced statistics showing that the ratio between the incomes of the 20 highest income countries and the 20 lowest income countries has grown over the period from 1960 to 2000, rising from about 23-to-one to about 36-to-one. Some have used such data to claim, among other things, that globalization increases the economic inequality between prosperous and poverty-stricken nations. But the directly opposite conclusion would be reached when comparing the *same* set of nations in 2000 as in 1960. The income ratio between the initially richest 20 nations and the initially poorest 20 *declined* from 23-to-one to less than ten-to-one.[10] Freer and rising amounts of international trade— globalization— was in fact one of the reasons why some nations rose out of the bottom 20.

Since all countries around the world began poor, what requires an explanation is not why there is poverty but how some countries rose out of poverty to become prosperous. No one knows who invented the wheel or what individual first began to plant crops instead of relying on gathering the spontaneous produce of nature. What is known is that such things appeared in some societies long before they appeared in others— and that they spread from one society to another, though not to all. The earliest known agriculture appeared in the Middle East and spread into those European societies located nearest the Middle East. Thus Mediterranean Europe, especially in the Eastern Mediterranean, was much more advanced in many ways than northern Europe. The ancient Greeks built magnificent structures such as the Parthenon but there was not a single building in the British Isles centuries later, when the Romans invaded. As Winston Churchill said, "We owe London to Rome."[11]

As late as the tenth century, A.D., a Muslim scholar could say that Europeans grow more pale the farther north they are, and also that the "farther they are to the north the more stupid, gross, and brutish they are."[12] However much such talk would be automatically dismissed as racism today, the fact is that he was there and we were not. Moreover, the enormous retrogression throughout Western Europe after the collapse of the Roman Empire, lasted many centuries, before the countries of Western Europe emerged as the new leaders of European civilization, displacing the countries of Mediterranean Europe. In Asia as well, the ancient civilization that developed around China's Yellow River spread not only across China but into other parts of Southeast Asia and to some extent Japan, and the products of China spread across the Eurasian landmass into Europe.

Places cut off from advances in the various leading civilizations of the world, whether for geographic or other reasons, tended to lag behind and to remain at levels of poverty that the more dynamic economies were leaving behind. Seventeenth century Japan adopted a national policy of deliberate isolation from the outside world that lasted until American warships entered Japanese waters in the middle of the nineteenth century and forced the Japanese to open their ports to the world. This painful episode provided a revelation to the Japanese of their own backwardness and weakness, creating an agenda of national economic development that dominated the country for generations to come.

Here was one of the rare examples of a country which saw in itself the sources of its own poverty— and therefore a need to change themselves in order to advance. Having never been conquered at that time, they could not blame colonialism and, having been isolated from international commerce and investment, they could not blame "exploitation" by foreigners. Operating on a vision radically different from that of many Third World nations today, Japan had one of history's most rapid and dramatic rises from poverty and backwardness.

In terms of leadership in science, technology, economic and political organization, and the arts, China was the leading nation in the world longer than any other nation in any other period of history. As late as the Middle Ages, China had the highest standard of living in the world. Yet, in more recent centuries, China has usually been a Third World nation, where recurrent famines took millions of lives, and only since the last quarter of the twentieth century has an accelerated growth rate begun to lift China out of that condition. Similarly, for centuries beginning in the Middle Ages, the Islamic world was well ahead of Europe in science, the arts, and militarily. But here too the relative positions of these two civilizations have reversed across a broad spectrum of social endeavors. In short, no nation or civilization has been permanently in the forefront of human advancement. But what has also never happened has been an economic equality across the spectrum of nations that many today regard as a norm, whose absence requires special and perhaps sinister explanations.

ECONOMICS

While contrasts between the economic levels of rich and poor nations are striking to the eye, these contrasts are truly staggering when seen in statistics. Real income per capita in Switzerland is more than three times that of Malaysia and 40 times that of Afghanistan, while the real income per capita of the United States is 50 times that of Afghanistan.[13] There are more than half as many automobiles owned in Germany, Switzerland, and Canada as there are adults and children in each of these countries, while in Ethiopia only one person out of a thousand owns a car.[14] The list of wide disparities goes on and on. However, some of these statistics need to be taken with a grain of salt.

In many Third World countries, much— if not most— of the economic activity takes place "off the books," because red tape and micro-managing laws and regulations make it too costly to do business legally. In India, for example, it has been estimated that only 10 percent of the country's working population work in the formal or legally recognized sector.[15] Even aside from that, per capita income data are often not comparable because populations differ greatly in age between Third World countries and more prosperous countries. The median age in Germany, Italy, and Japan is more than forty, while many Third World countries— from Angola to Zambia— have median ages below twenty. Not only do young people usually earn less than middle-aged people, in countries around the world, much production in higher income countries goes to deal with the special problems of older people.

More than one-fourth the populations of Germany, Italy, and Japan are more than 60 years old.[16] The additional production of things needed to cope with the infirmities of age— crutches, walkers, and medications ranging from Geritol to Viagra— make older people better off than they would be without these aids but *not* better off than young people who do not need them. If there were some feasible way to make adjustments in the data to take account of all such things, the statistical differences between more prosperous nations and poorer nations would then more accurately reflect the differences in real standards of living. The differences would still be there but not as extreme as the statistics make them appear.

Since all countries were once at least as poor as Third World countries are today, what needs to be explained is not poverty but the creation of wealth—and the things that increase or decrease the ability to create wealth.

Law and Order

One of the common denominators of prosperous times and places has been law and order. Put differently, times and places where it has been difficult to establish law and order have seldom prospered. Sometimes geography has been the problem. Mountainous regions have often been lawless regions, simply because the cost of providing police or military control in isolated and thinly populated areas is often so much more than the cost of establishing and maintaining control in lowland plains. Wherever government authority breaks down for whatever reason, as in Western Europe after the collapse of the Roman Empire, economic stagnation or even retrogression is seldom far behind. It has been estimated that it was a thousand years after the collapse of the Roman Empire before the standard of living in Europe rose again to the level that it had achieved in Roman times.

The same thing can be seen on a smaller scale in American black ghettoes where the devastating riots of the 1960s not only destroyed existing businesses but kept out many new businesses for more than a generation since then. Even despotic laws, as under Genghis Khan or in the Ottoman Empire, have fostered economic prosperity when these laws have been dependable, rather than capricious or corrupt. One of the hallmarks of many Third World countries, especially those with otherwise favorable economic prospects in terms of natural resources or other favorable geographic factors, has been ineffective, capricious, or corrupt law enforcement.

Nigeria, for example, has oil and better navigable waterways than most of sub-Saharan Africa, but has repeatedly been ranked among the world's most corrupt nations, if not *the* most corrupt. The same geographical fragmentation of sub-Saharan Africa which more directly handicapped Africa's economic development has also done so indirectly by making the establishment of law and order over wide areas difficult to achieve. As a study of the effect of culture on economic development put it:

> If you are really looking for societies characterized by unrestrained greed and weak government, sub-Saharan Africa is the place to find them. . .
> The "governments" of these countries are corrupt businesses, more akin to the Mafia than to public services.[17]

Countries fragmented into areas under the arbitrary rule of local warlords— whether Afghanistan today or the clan chiefs in the Scottish highlands in centuries past— have likewise remained mired in poverty. Law and order involve more than physical security, essential as that is. For economic activities that take some time, property rights are a prerequisite, so that those who farm or invest in business can feel assured that the fruits of their activities will be theirs. Even people who own no property have a large stake in property rights, if they are to be employed in an economy made prosperous by the presence of property rights.

Perhaps the easiest way to understand the role of property rights is to see what happens in their absence. Even in countries where property rights have not been formally abolished, the costs of legally validating ownership of a home, a farm, or a business may be prohibitively expensive, relative to the average income level in a given country. This is in fact a common situation in Third World countries. *The Economist* magazine has estimated that, in Africa, only about one person in ten works in a legally recognized enterprise or lives in a house that has legally recognized property rights. In Egypt an estimated 4.7 million homes have been built illegally. In Peru, the total value of the country's real estate that lacks property rights has been estimated to be more than a dozen times greater than all the foreign direct investments ever made in the country during its entire history. A similar prevalence of economic assets not recognized by the legal system has been found in other Third World countries.[18]

Such lack of legal recognition is not a mere formality. It is a crippling handicap for those seeking to rise from poverty to prosperity, whether as individuals or as nations. Many of the great corporate enterprises of the world began at an extremely modest level, such as those already achieved by innumerable entrepreneurs in the Third World. The Hewlett-Packard corporation, for example, began in a garage that was rented with borrowed money; the J.C. Penney department store chain was begun by a man who grew up in worse poverty than most people on welfare today; the NBC broadcast network was begun by a man who had to support himself as a teenager by hawking newspapers on the street. The list could go on and on. But all these people without money lived in a society where they had access to other people's money, as a result of a legal system where property rights facilitated the transfer of money from those who had it to those who had entrepreneurial talents but no money.

The Third World is full of peddlers who remain peddlers all their lives. But, in the United States, it was peddlers who began such enterprises as Macy's, Bloomingdale's, and Levi Strauss. For businesses in general, whether large or small, the availability of other people's money is often crucial. Without property rights, lenders are reluctant to lend to people who do not have the cash to pay them back— *and whose homes or other assets are not recognized as theirs by the legal system*, and therefore cannot be used as collateral that can be foreclosed and transferred to the lender in case of default.

Businesses that start small and grow large can seldom get off the ground by issuing their own stocks and bonds before they have established a track record of success. And they have little chance of establishing such a track record without money. Many Third World peddlers and other small-scale entrepreneurs cannot draw on other people's money beyond the narrow circle of their own family and friends, but developing a large corporation requires drawing on money from thousands of strangers, beginning with getting their money indirectly from banks or other financial intermediaries. An absence of property rights cuts off that process early on.

The problem is not simply that particular individuals in the Third World who might become corporate leaders in a society with property rights lack that opportunity. The more fundamental and more important fact is that the whole society could benefit from having numerous major corporate enterprises to provide more goods to consumers, jobs for workers, and tax revenues to governments.

The formal legal system is not the only aspect of law and order. The levels of honesty, cooperation, and civic virtue among the people is not only of social but of economic consequence. For example:

> Malagasy grain traders carry out inspections of each lot of grain in person because they don't trust employees. One third of the traders say they don't hire more workers because of fear of theft by them. This limits the grain traders' firm size, cutting short a trader's potential success. In many countries, companies tend to be family enterprises because family members are the only ones felt trustworthy. So the size of the company is then limited by the size of the family.[19]

What economist William Easterly has called "the radius of trust" varies greatly from group to group and from country to country. Within groups like the Marwaris of India, the Chinese in Southeast Asia, or Hasidic Jews in New York's diamond industry, transactions involving substantial sums of money can take place without written agreements or recourse to the legal system, giving these groups competitive advantage over other members of their respective societies who cannot safely engage in similar low-cost ways of doing business. Whole nations likewise differ in the levels of honesty. Bicycles can be left parked without locks in Tokyo but doing so in many other countries would be a virtual guarantee that they would be stolen.

Population

For more than two centuries, one of the most persistent explanations for poverty, whether in the Third World or elsewhere, has been "overpopulation." But the term has seldom been defined in any meaningful way— that is, in any way that is not tautological. If the term is used to refer to the ratio of people to land, then even a cursory examination of data demonstrates that it is false.

Argentina has fewer people per square mile than the United States but has a per capita real income that is only a fraction of that of Americans. India has a population per square mile that is several times that of either Argentina or the United States— but not quite as many people per square mile as Japan, which has a far higher real income per capita than India. Poverty-stricken sub-Saharan Africa has a population density that is only a fraction of that of Japan.[20] It is also possible to find some poverty-stricken countries with greater population densities than some prosperous countries. But there is no consistent relationship between population density and real income. Looking at what happens over time likewise gives no support to the theory that "overpopulation" causes poverty. As one of the leading development economists of the twentieth century put it:

> Between the 1890s and 1930s the sparsely populated area of Malaysia, with hamlets and fishing villages, was transformed into a country with large cities, extensive agricultural and mining operations and extensive commerce. The population rose from about one and a half to about six million; the number of Malays increased from about one to about two and a half million. The much larger population had much higher material standards and lived longer than the small population of the 1890s. Since the 1950s rapid population increase in densely-populated Hong Kong and Singapore has been accompanied by large increases in real income and wages. The population of the Western world has more than quadrupled since the middle of the eighteenth century. Real income per head is estimated to have increased by a factor of five or more.[21]

Although advocates of the "overpopulation" theory argue that rising population threatens to create more poverty, virtually no one can provide examples of countries that had a higher standard of living when their population was half of what it is today. Various desperate expediencies have been used to try to salvage the "overpopulation" thesis, beginning in Malthus' time and continuing to today.

Some argue that it is not land, but arable land, that matters. However, changing the calculation to arable land merely adds more complication without changing the result. Nor will changing the criterion from land to natural resources in general yield much different results. As already noted, the value of natural resources per capita in Uruguay and Venezuela is some multiple of their value in Switzerland or Japan, while the real income per capita in Switzerland or Japan is some multiple of what it is in Uruguay or Venezuela. Some argue that population should not be compared to raw natural resources but to *developed* resources, in order to determine whether there is overpopulation. However, developed resources are simply another name for wealth, so it is simply a tautology to say that more population relative to developed resources means lower wealth per capita. The real danger in tautologies is that, because they are irrefutable definitions, the irrefutability of what they are saying about the real world— which is nothing— gives a spurious credibility to what they insinuate.

As noted in Chapter 2, thinly populated areas mean much higher costs per person to supply water, electricity, sewage lines, telephone lines, hospitals, and numerous other costly things. Sub-Saharan Africa's thin population per square mile is one of its many major economic handicaps.

Whatever the intellectual deficiencies of the overpopulation explanation of poverty, it has been politically viable for centuries, and Third World governments have imposed birth control policies, with the most draconian being those in China, where there have been severe penalties for exceeding the number of children prescribed by government authorities, usually one child per couple.

Culture

While external factors like property rights and geographical factors can influence the economic development of nations, such internal factors as cultural values can often be of equal or even greater importance. It has not been at all uncommon for people from outside a given culture to come into a society and, beginning at an economic level below that of the existing population, rise over time well above those around them, despite the fact that all of the people in the society live within the same external conditions. Italian immigrants to Argentina, Lebanese immigrants to West Africa, immigrants from India to Fiji, Jewish immigrants to the United States, German immigrants to czarist Russia, and Chinese immigrants to a number of countries in Southeast Asia are just some of the examples of this phenomenon. Many, if not most, of these immigrants arrived destitute financially and often with little or no education.[22] What they had was a culture that was different from that of those whom they overtook and left behind.

Whole industries and sectors of an economy have been created by people from different cultures. Argentina became one of the world's great exporters of wheat after German immigrants settled there, even though the Argentines had *imported* wheat before. The land and its ability to grow wheat had not changed. What had changed were the people who settled on the land. Sometimes new industries were introduced not by immigrants but by sojourners from other countries, as the British built railroads in countries around the world, from India to Africa to Australia and Argentina. Worldwide migrations in recent centuries have led to racially and culturally different peoples interacting in societies far from those in which their forebears originated and developed their different cultures and different economic skills. Often they reproduced in their new destinations the same patterns found in their lands of origin. The mining that was so much a part of the economic history of Wales was also a major part of the history of Welsh immigrants to the United States and Australia. The prominence or predominance of Jews in clothing production in medieval Spain also reappeared later in the Ottoman Empire, in the United States and in South America.

Areas blessed with an abundance of natural resources have been unable to sustain prosperity, even after it has been achieved, when the surrounding institutions and culture do not sustain a dependable framework of law and order. Argentina has been a classic example, though similar patterns have appeared in some other Latin American countries.

Argentina has been described as "among the world's most richly endowed countries," with "some of the world's richest soil" and "substantial oil and natural gas deposits."[23] Early in the twentieth century, it was one of the ten richest nations in the world. Much of its modern development, however, was not internally generated but was due to foreign, mostly British, initiative. The rise of nationalistic and ideological politics, especially under the charismatic leadership of dictator Juan Perón, led to a decline of foreign investment in Argentina from a high of 48 percent of all investment in 1913 to just 5 percent by the 1950s.[24]

Counterproductive domestic political and economic policies marked Argentina's fall from the ranks of the most prosperous nations. As one study put it: "The countries with which Argentina was grouped in terms of economic progress early in this [twentieth] century have attained per-capita GNPs generally four or five times Argentina's, and virtually all of them are viable democracies."[25] By the end of the twentieth century, Argentina's economy and monetary system had collapsed, leading to widespread use of barter. Despite some recovery from that low point, Argentina's gross domestic product per capita in the early twenty-first century was one-tenth that of the United States.[26]

Since the countries which have achieved the kind of prosperity common in Western Europe, North America or Japan remain a minority among the nations of the world, it is the coming together of numerous factors favorable to economic development which requires explanation, rather than the fact that the majority of nations have not been equally fortunate. The fact that most of these prosperous nations took centuries for all these factors to come together underscores the rarity of these achievements. Transplanted European societies such as the United States, Canada, and Australia began their lives in new lands with a legacy of already developed cultures favorable to economic development, rather than having to spend centuries developing such cultures on their own. The fact that earlier leaders in economic and other development, such as China and the Ottoman Empire, lost their leadership and fell far behind the new leaders likewise indicates what a combination of favorable circumstances is required— and how economic prosperity can be lost if vital parts of that combination are lost.

Resistance to the idea of internal reasons for differences among individuals, groups, or nations has been as widespread and desperate as it has been fallacious. One academic, for example, said that Jews were fortunate to arrive in America just as the garment industry was about to take off[27]— ignoring the possibility that it was precisely the arrival of Jews that led to an upsurge in the garment industry, as their arrival in other countries had done.

This widespread refusal to countenance the very possibility that factors internal to particular peoples have had an influence on their economic condition has been expressed in claims that such beliefs are just "stereotypes" which are "blaming the victim" in the case of poorer individuals or nations. So strongly have such views been held that those who have them have not hesitated to dismiss first-hand observations in favor of general presumptions by others like themselves, even when they have neither seen nor studied the people concerned. Such views have affected not only how the past has been seen but also what policies have been advocated for the future— especially the advocacy of foreign aid programs for Third World countries. Because foreign aid in the form of the Marshall Plan was so successful in Western Europe after the Second World War, many have argued that it would have similar benefits in the Third World.

The failure of massive amounts of foreign aid to create any comparable economic development in most of the Third World has not dimmed the luster of foreign aid in the eyes of those who refuse to re-examine the assumptions on which it was based. Yet there is nothing mysterious in those failures when the different cultures are taken into account. Postwar Western Europe had suffered devastations as a result of the war but what had not been destroyed was the knowledge and culture which had in the past industrialized Europe and led the world into the industrial age. Foreign aid saved the people from starvation and helped rebuild the physical surroundings but the crucial knowledge and culture were already there. In much of the Third World, the physical surroundings are intact but that same base of knowledge and culture has yet to be built.

Exploitation

Perhaps the most famous and most influential explanation of economic differences between rich and poor nations was V.I. Lenin's *Imperialism*. It was a masterpiece in the art of persuasion, for it convinced many highly educated people around the world, not only in the absence of compelling empirical evidence, but in defiance of a large body of hard evidence to the contrary.

The thesis of *Imperialism* was that industrial capitalist nations had surplus capital, which would drive down the rate of profit over time in accordance with Marxist theory, unless it were exported to the non-industrial poorer nations of the world, where it could find a wider field for exploitation. What Lenin called the "super profits" to be earned in these poorer nations would save capitalism in the industrial nations and even allow them to share some of the fruits of their exploitation with their own working classes, so as to keep them quiescent and forestall the proletarian revolution which Marx had predicted, but which by Lenin's time showed no signs of materializing. This theory thus neatly explained away the failure of Marx's predictions and at the same time provided a politically satisfying explanation of income differences between rich and poor nations.

A table of statistics in *Imperialism* provided a crucial summary of evidence for Lenin's theory.

Billions of Marks, Circa 1910

	GREAT BRITAIN	FRANCE	GERMANY	TOTAL
Europe	4	23	18	45
America	37	4	10	51
Asia, Africa and Australia	29	8	7	44
TOTAL	70	35	35	140

The countries listed in capital letters across the top of the table are the industrial capitalist nations that were investing the various sums of money shown in the places listed in smaller letters along the side of the table— supposedly in the poorer and less industrially developed parts of the world. But the huge and heterogeneous categories— for example, "America," meaning the entire Western Hemisphere— make it impossible to know whether the industrial nations' investments are being made in the less industrial parts of these sweeping categories or in the more industrialized parts. However, data from other sources make it clear that in fact most of the foreign investments of prosperous industrial nations went to other prosperous industrial nations— then and now.

The United States was then, and is today, the largest recipient of foreign investment from Europe. Likewise, the foreign investments of Americans went primarily to other prosperous modern nations, *not* to the Third World. For most of the twentieth century, the United States invested more in Canada than in all of Africa and Asia put together. Only the economic rise of postwar Japan and, later, other Asian industrializing nations, attracted American investments to Asia on a large scale in the latter part of the twentieth century. In short, the actual pattern of international investments went directly opposite to the theories of Lenin, who concealed that fact within his large and heterogeneous categories of investment recipients.

The combination of Lenin's genius for propaganda and an audience receptive to his thesis allowed his theory of imperialism to be widely accepted among intellectuals, activists and people in the Third World. Exploitation is a virtually perfect political explanation of income differences. It validates whatever envy or resentment may be felt by people with lower incomes toward people with higher incomes. It removes whatever stigma may be felt from implications of lower ability or lower performance on the part of those with lower incomes. It locates the need for change in other people, rather than imposing the burden of change on those who wish to rise. Moreover, it replaces any such burdensome task with a morally uplifting sense of entitlement. Whatever the empirical and logical problems with the theory of exploitation, political movements are seldom based on empirical evidence and logic.

Those who blamed the poverty of Third World nations on colonialism continued to blame the legacy of colonialism for decades after most of these Third World colonies became independent nations. The same belief provided a basis for independent Third World nations to confiscate the property of foreign investors who were seen as "exploiters." In the places where there were sizable European settler communities, as in Zimbabwe or South Africa, such beliefs provided rationales for dispossessing the European settlers. However, in doing so, Third World governments inadvertently revealed the fallacy of the belief that physical wealth was crucial.

If it was, such confiscations would improve the economic conditions of the indigenous population. But, if it was the internal knowledge, skills, and cultural patterns which produced prosperity, then the transfer of physical wealth from those who had the necessary knowledge, skills, and cultural patterns to those who did not would have very different consequences. The African nation of Zimbabwe was an all too typical example. Zimbabwe repudiated the last remnants of its colonial past in the early twenty-first century by dispossessing white landowners, with these results, as reported in the *New York Times*:

> For close to seven years, Zimbabwe's economy and quality of life have been in slow, uninterrupted decline. They are still declining this year, people there say, with one notable difference: the pace is no longer so slow. . .
>
> In recent weeks, the national power authority has warned of a collapse of electrical service. A breakdown in water treatment has set off a new outbreak of cholera in the capital, Harare. All public services were cut off in Marondera, a regional capital of 50,000 in eastern Zimbabwe, after the city ran out of money to fix broken equipment. In Chitungwiza, just south of Harare, electricity is supplied only four days a week.[28]

Foreign Aid

By "foreign aid" is meant international transfers of wealth, either directly from governments in more prosperous nations to governments in poorer nations or indirectly by transfers through international agencies like the World Bank or the International Monetary Fund to governments in the Third World. Whether such transfers will in fact turn out to be an aid to the economic advancement of the poorer countries is an empirical question, rather than a foregone conclusion. Both journalistic anecdotes and scholarly studies often show vast amounts of money being transferred to Third World governments without producing any significant economic growth and, in some cases, there are actual declines in real incomes in the wake of grandiose projects financed by foreign aid.

This should not be surprising. There is no more reason to expect automatic benefits from wealth transfers through international agencies than from wealth transfers through internal confiscations, as in Zimbabwe. The incentives facing those disbursing the aid and those receiving it seldom make economic development the criterion of success. The indicator of success for the aid agencies is how much money they transfer, which is readily visible to the media and to political leaders, while the actual results of these transfers are far away in both space and time. When Robert McNamara was head of the World Bank, for example, he announced, "we proposed to double the Bank's operations in the fiscal period 1969–73 compared to the previous 5-year period 1964–68. That objective has been met."[29] As for the recipient governments, their objectives have been met when they receive the money.

The ability of the international aid agencies to monitor, much less control, the spending of the money they transfer is very limited. Nor do they have strong incentives to withhold money from Third World governments that have used that money ineffectively, counterproductively, or even corruptly. They certainly have no incentives to advertise the disasters they have financed, as that would call into question their own institutions and foreign aid in general. Given these incentives, it is not nearly as surprising as it might be otherwise that international aid agencies continued to transfer money to Tanzania during its draconian and disastrous social experiments under Julius Nyerere and even to Rwanda while genocide was going on. As late as the 1970s, foreign aid was still being transferred to the despotic government of oil-rich Saudi Arabia.

Loans from international agencies are often not repaid, except in the cosmetic sense that existing loans are "repaid" from still larger loans made later by the same agency to the same country. Under the imposing but uninformative title of "structural adjustment loans," the World Bank and the International Monetary Fund, between them, gave the Ivory Coast 26 "structural adjustment loans" during the decades of the 1980s and 1990s, while per capita income declined and the country collapsed into civil war.[30] New loans to pay off old loans were not unique to the Ivory Coast. In 2001, more than half the money lent by the International Monetary Fund was to nations that were long-time borrowers.[31]

In short, what are called "loans," whether by international aid agencies or by national governments like those of the United States or Britain, are in fact gifts of taxpayers' money to Third World political leaders. Calls for "forgiveness" of loans to Third World governments are frequently heard and heeded, as if rewarding financial irresponsibility by officials doing the borrowing is going to lift poor countries out of poverty. Implicit in much that is said about foreign aid is the assumption that such gratuitous international transfers to Third World governments are crucial to a country's rise out of poverty. In reality, there is often far more wealth generated internally, including wealth created "off the books," than what is available in the form of foreign aid. There is often also far more money available in international financial markets, but this money is unlikely to take the form of blank checks for grandiose projects or loans that no one expects to be repaid.

Where international aid agencies do attempt to monitor, influence, or control governments receiving grants or loans, the results have by no means always or usually been positive. Given the many economic problems created by central planning in countries like the Soviet Union[32]— problems severe enough to cause even many socialist and communist governments to abandon central planning by the end of the twentieth century— it should hardly be surprising that a method that has not worked when people were planning economic activities within their own country has not been notably successful when trying to plan for other countries around the world with a variety of languages, traditions, and cultures different from those of the aid agency officials. Nevertheless, those officials acquire a visibility and importance, at home and abroad, from the money they transfer, and so have incentives to promote increases in the money available as foreign aid, whether or not it achieves its ostensible purpose of raising living standards in the Third World.

The preference of many Third World governments for foreign aid over such alternatives as using international financial markets to raise money or encouraging domestic entrepreneurs by relieving them of stifling red tape and bureaucratic control is understandable. Letting private markets operate, domestically and/or internationally, would mean relinquishing both power and lucrative opportunities to reward political supporters and for political leaders to take a cut of the money themselves.

Humanitarian aid to Third World countries in the wake of natural disasters like earthquakes, epidemics or tsunamis has often been administered very differently from the way conventional foreign aid is administered. Humanitarian aid is often provided directly by international agencies like the

Red Cross or by various agencies of the American or other foreign governments, rather than being channeled through Third World governments themselves. Moreover, some of the most effective aid does not require huge spending per capita. It has been estimated that medicine which would prevent half of all deaths from malaria costs only twelve cents a dose.[33] Such medicines, vaccinations of children, and other relatively simple and inexpensive measures can create a great amount of benefit in the Third World. But their very ordinariness and inexpensiveness makes them less likely to attract the kind of attention that is valued by politicians and bureaucrats.

Foreign aid survives not only on the self interest of those administering the transfers of money and those receiving it. It survives on the assumptions of many in the Western world that the fundamental problems of poor countries are external and can be cured by transfers of external wealth. But many poor countries already have ample internal wealth in the form of natural resources that enable some of them to lead the world in the production of things like gold, copper, or rubber. Often poor countries also have many entrepreneurial people, including minorities like the overseas Chinese in Southeast Asia or the Lebanese in West Africa. India, for all its poverty, has for more than a century been exporting people who have risen from poverty to prosperity virtually everywhere they settled around the world.[34] There have even been poor countries, such as Argentina, that were once among the most prosperous in the world.

What then is lacking? Some who have studied less developed countries have pointed out that it is hard to find a well-governed poor nation. What is far more common is to find poverty-stricken countries that are among the most corrupt in the world— for example, Nigeria, Haiti, Bangladesh, and many others. It is not just that the political leaders are corrupt. The level of mutual trust among the people at large has been found to be far lower in such countries than in more affluent nations.[35] Where poor countries contain entrepreneurial minorities who are capable of creating wealth, those minorities are often resented and restricted by discriminatory laws and policies. In some cases, such wealth-producing minorities have been forced out of the country by hostility and outright violence, or even officially expelled, as Indians and Pakistanis were expelled from Uganda in the 1970s— after which the Ugandan economy collapsed.

In other cases, where much of the wealth in a country has been created by foreign investors and foreign entrepreneurs, the resentments against those foreigners has led to the theft of their businesses by the government, or "nationalization" as it is phrased politically. Here too the transfer of wealth from those who created it has often produced no lasting benefits to the indigenous population and has often marked the decline of those businesses and of the local economies. In much of sub-Saharan Africa, standards of living were lower, decades after the departure of the colonial rulers, than these standards were in the era of colonialism despite both "nationalizations" and foreign aid. In short, many of the problems of very poor countries are internal, however politically unpalatable that may be to the inhabitants of those countries or to those in the Western world who prefer other explanations.

This conclusion is reinforced by the history of very poor countries that rose rapidly to higher economic levels, such as Scotland in the eighteenth century, Japan in the nineteenth century and China in the late twentieth century. In all these cases, they raised themselves economically through *internal* changes, brought on by a recognition that such internal changes were necessary. In the case of Scotland, it was the rapid spread of education and the English language. In the case of Japan, it was a national obsession, which included sending many Japanese young people to study in the more industrialized Western nations and bringing Westerners with industrial skills to Japan. In China, it was the successive lifting of government restrictions on their economy and the opening of it to international businesses and investors. In none of these cases were there massive government-to-government transfers of wealth. Other examples of dramatic rises out of poverty, such as Singapore and South Korea, were likewise based on internal changes deliberately undertaken.

The consequences of what has happened in Third World countries with the mere transfer of money or capital were typified by the experience of foreign aid to Tanzania:

In Tanzania, the World Bank financed the Morogoro shoe factory. It was built with modern equipment and shoemaking technology to satisfy all Tanzania's demand for shoes and have capacity for exports to Europe. The Morogoro shoe factory was not a success. Its equipment regularly failed because of lack of maintenance and shortages of spare parts. Workers and managers stole from the plant. The Morogoro plant was designed like a modern Western shoe factory, with aluminum walls and no ventilation system, inappropriate for the Tanzanian climate. The Morogoro shoe factory never operated at more than 5% of capacity and never exported a single shoe.[36]

SUMMARY AND IMPLICATIONS

Although we have, for the sake of convenience, used such terms as "Third World" and "foreign aid," the late Professor Peter Bauer, a distinguished development economist at the London School of Economics, has pointed out how misleading such terms can be. The term "Third World" suggests that there is some special group of nations that are worlds apart from the rest of humanity. In reality, their populations are a majority of humanity, and in the world at large there is a continuum of incomes from the highest to the lowest, with no special break separating some nations' incomes from the incomes of others. Nor is there a racial divide. As Professor Bauer pointed out, "in the Third World as a whole the whites outnumber the blacks."[37]

"Foreign aid" is another misleading term, in that it presupposes that transfers will aid in economic development, despite all too many examples where continued massive transfers of wealth have accomplished nothing, except to solidify the existing regime and make the necessary changes less likely. Foreign aid also gives officials of aid agencies leverage to prescribe whatever economic policies happen to be in vogue at the moment— deflation, "shock treatment," or whatever— without being accountable for the consequences.

Perhaps the biggest fallacy in discussions of Third World countries is the implicit assumption that there is something intellectually baffling or morally wrong about the fact that different nations have different per capita incomes. Given large differences in geography, demography, history and culture, it is hard to imagine how it could be otherwise. Humanitarian aid to enable countries to meet natural disasters beyond their capacity to foresee or avoid need not be based on any assumptions about the reasons for their incomes being what they are. But attempts to remake other countries show no track record comparable to the dramatic improvements that countries have achieved when they have decided to remake themselves.

Chapter 8

PARTING THOUGHTS

Many individual fallacies are part of a larger pattern. These larger patterns include not only the fallacies mentioned in Chapter 1— the zero-sum fallacy, the fallacy of composition, the *post hoc* fallacy, the chess pieces fallacy, and the open-ended fallacy— but also many forms of the fallacy of implicitly assuming sameness when there is no reason to expect sameness.

Differences in geography, demography, history and culture are just some of the differences among individuals, groups and nations. There is no reason to expect women and men to work the same number of hours, nor any reason why they should. There is no reason to assume that the goals, priorities, or abilities of high-school dropouts are the same as those of college graduates, so that differences in their incomes can be attributed to college. There is no reason to expect Third World economies to respond to foreign aid the way that Europe responded to the Marshall Plan, when these economies and societies have been vastly different from those in Europe for centuries.

Throughout history, the world has abounded with differences that are today called "disparities" or "inequities," even in situations where they cannot be explained by discrimination. At one time, in czarist Russia, nearly all of the members of the St. Petersburg Academy of Sciences were of German ancestry,[1] even though people of German ancestry were only about one percent of the population of Russia. Today, more than 40 percent of all the billionaires in the world are in one country— the United States.[2] The list could go on and on, until it filled a book.[3] But, however common such statistical disparities have been around the world and throughout history, many continue to reason as if any statistical differences between any groups are strange and suspicious, if not sinister.

Another fallacy, already noted in Chapters 5 and 7, is what might be called the fallacy of *changing* composition. When statistical categories are compared over time, the changing relationships among these categories can be completely misleading as to what is happening to the people or the nations within those categories, when the composition of these categories is changing over time. There may be growing inequalities between those categories during the very same span of years when there is a *lessening* of inequality between the people or nations who constitute those categories. Moreover, important conclusions and decisions can be based on this fallacy.

As noted in Chapter 7, the growth of international free trade has been said to increase inequality among nations because the 23-to-one ratio between the incomes of the twenty richest and twenty poorest nations in 1960 rose to a 36-to-one ratio in 2000. But the nations constituting the 20 richest and 20 poorest were different in 1960 and 2000. Comparing the *same* twenty richest and twenty poorest nations of 1960 over those decades shows that the ratio between the richest and poorest *declined* to less than ten-to-one.[4] This leads to the directly opposite conclusion, suggesting that freer international trade may have helped reduce inequalities among nations, allowing some of the initially poorest to rise out of the category of the bottom twenty.

Whatever the reason for the declining inequality, the fallacy of believing that international inequality had increased, when in fact it had decreased, is similar to that in an old joke about automobile accidents in Manhattan. In this joke, one friend says to another that statistics show that a man is hit by a car in Manhattan once every 20 minutes. To which the other replies, "He must get awfully tired of that." The fallacy here is that it is obviously not the same man each time. The very same fallacy underlies much more serious conclusions about both personal and international inequalities over time, when it is not the same individuals or the same nations that are being compared, since each moves from one category to another over time. The changing composition of the categories makes conclusions based on comparisons between the categories fallacious.

Statistics are no better than the methods and definitions used in collecting them. Without scrutinizing those methods and definitions, we cannot assume that comparable people are being compared, whether comparing the incomes of high school dropouts with college graduates, the incomes of members of different ethnic groups who have the "same" education, or the incomes of single women with married women, when "single" women includes women who were married for years before getting divorced. Nor can statistics about the amount of air pollution in populated areas versus open space tell us anything about whether letting people move into unpopulated areas will increase the total pollution over all, since it is people— not their locations— that generate pollution.

Perhaps most dangerous of all is the practice of not subjecting fashionable beliefs to the test of facts, but instead accepting or rejecting beliefs according to how well they fit some pre-existing vision of the world. The idea that government intervention is needed to create "affordable housing" is an idea that makes sense only in the context of a preconceived notion, while mountains of hard evidence point in the exact opposite direction. The belief that ghetto riots such as those of the 1960s are a reaction against poverty, discrimination, unemployment, and blighted communities simply will not stand up in the face of hard evidence of when and where those riots took place, which were not in the places or times where these factors were worse.

The entire educational and employment history of women in the first half of the twentieth century is almost invariably ignored, even in scholarly studies, to concentrate attention on what has happened since 1960, which can be made to fit a preconceived vision of the reasons for women's rise. Similarly with blacks, whose rises out of poverty and into middle class occupations are likewise traced almost invariably from some point after 1960, and attributed to the civil rights movement and government actions of that decade, even though the most dramatic rises of blacks out of poverty occurred in the two decades *before* 1960. Nothing is more fallacious than to ignore a trend that began years before some policy or action that is credited with whatever happened as a continuation of a pre-existing trend. Similar fallacies have appeared in discussions of things ranging from automobile fatality rates to market shares of companies after an antitrust lawsuit.[5]

Among the many preconceptions that cannot be subjected to any empirical tests, because they are so subjective, is the notion that third-party observers know better what is good for people than those people know themselves. This implicit assumption pervades discussions of urban and suburban housing,[6] mass transit versus automobiles, and the imposition of international aid agencies' pet theories on Third World countries. The most that can be done in these cases is to (1) make that implicit assumption explicit, (2) demand proof of that superior knowledge, and (3) point out how many disasters in countries around the world have followed in the wake of programs and policies based on that assumption.

A special variant of the implicit assumption of vastly superior knowledge is the sweeping dismissal of the first-hand observations of other people as "stereotypes," such dismissals often being based on little or no first-hand observation by those who dismiss, but based instead on assumptions widely shared by similarly inexperienced and presumptuous people, often insulated against criticisms— or facts— by academic degrees.

Tautologies are another source of fallacies and a major source of their defense. "Overpopulation," for example, can be defined in such a way that a high ratio of people to wealth is said to explain poverty, when all that it does in reality is demonstrate the rules of arithmetic, rather than any fact about the real world. But until people realize that they are talking in a circle, however large that circle may be, they may continue to believe insinuations that give tautologies their power, as if they were conclusions about the external world instead of arbitrary definitions inside their own heads. Tautologies about population are just one of a much larger number of notions whose lack of clarity and concreteness is their greatest asset in convincing people without either evidence or logic. As philosopher Charles Sanders Peirce said, back in the nineteenth century: "Many a man has cherished for years as his hobby some vague shadow of an idea, too meaningless to be positively false."[7]

The particular fallacies discussed in this book are only a small sample of a vastly larger number on a vastly wider variety of subjects. If seeing how these often plausible-sounding fallacies can collapse under the weight of evidence and analysis causes you to examine other beliefs more closely and more analytically, then this book will have achieved its larger purpose.

Notes

CHAPTER 1: THE POWER OF FALLACIES

1. Henry Rosovsky, *The University: An Owner's Manual* (New York: W.W. Norton, 1990), p. 259.
2. Nonie Darwish, *Now They Call Me Infidel* (New York: Sentinel, 2006), p. 43.
3. Harold L. Cole and Lee E. Ohanian, "New Deal Policies and the Persistence of the Great Depression: A General Equilibrium Analysis," *Journal of Political Economy*, Vol. 112, No. 4 (August 2004), pp. 779–816.
4. Adam Smith, *The Theory of Moral Sentiments* (Indianapolis: Liberty Classics, 1976), pp. 380–381.
5. See, for example, Jim Powell, *FDR's Folly* (New York: Crown Forum, 2003), p. 105.
6. Leon Aron, *Yeltsin* (New York: St. Martin's Press, 2000), p. 329.

CHAPTER 2: URBAN FACTS AND FALLACIES

1. Eric Hoffer, *First Things, Last Things* (New York: Harper & Row, 1971), p. 36.
2. Robert Bruegmann, *Sprawl: A Compact History* (Chicago: University of Chicago, 2005), p. 22.
3. Clifton Hood, *722 Miles: The Building of the Subways and How They Transformed New York* (New York: Simon & Schuster, 1993), p. 39.
4. Robert Bruegmann, *Sprawl*, p. 132.
5. Ibid., p. 143; Ted Balaker and Sam Staley, *The Road More Traveled: Why the Congestion Crisis Matters More Than You Think, and What We Can Do About It* (Lanham: Rowman and Littlefield, 2006), pp. 56–57.
6. Edmund Morris, *The Rise of Theodore Roosevelt* (New York: Modern Library, 2001), p. 48.

7. Clifton Hood, *722 Miles*, p. 52.

8. Jeffry A. Frieden, *Global Capitalism: Its Fall and Rise in the Twentieth Century* (New York: W.W. Norton: 2006), p. 62.

9. "A Global Love Affair," *The Economist*, November 15, 2008, special section, p. 4.

10. Randal O'Toole, *The Best-Laid Plans: How Government Planning Harms Your Quality of Life, Your Pocketbook, and Your Future* (Washington: The Cato Institute, 2007), pp. 206, 208.

11. Ibid., p. 164.

12. Ted Balaker and Sam Staley, *The Road More Traveled*, p. 5.

13. Ibid., p. 19.

14. Ibid., pp. 6, 110–111, 119–120, 145.

15. John D. McKinnon, "Bush Plays Traffic Cop in Budget Request," *Wall Street Journal*, February 5, 2007, p. A6.

16. Gopinath Menon, "Congestion Pricing: The Singapore Experience," *Street Smart: Competition, Entrepreneurship, and the Future of Roads*, edited by Gabriel Roth (New Brunswick, N.J.: Transaction Publishers, 2006), p. 123.

17. Leila Abboud and Jenny Clevstrom, "Stockholm's Syndrome," *Wall Street Journal*, August 29, 2006, pp. B1 ff.

18. Ted Balaker and Sam Staley, *The Road More Traveled*, p. 90.

19. Ibid., p. 127.

20. Randal O'Toole, "Do You Know the Way to L.A.? San Jose Shows How to Turn an Urban Area into Los Angeles in Three Stressful Decades," *Policy Analysis*, No. 602, Cato Institute, October 17, 2007, pp. 17–18.

21. Ted Balaker and Sam Staley, *The Road More Traveled*, pp. 45, 46.

22. Ibid., p. 47.

23. Ibid., p. 46.

24. Randal O'Toole, *The Best-Laid Plans*, p. 249.

25. Randal O'Toole, "Do You Know the Way to L.A.? San Jose Shows How to Turn an Urban Area into Los Angeles in Three Stressful Decades," *Policy Analysis*, No. 602, Cato Institute, October 17, 2007, p. 3.

26. Edwin G. Burrows and Mike Wallace, *Gotham: A History of New York City to 1898* (New York: Oxford University Press, 1999), p. 948.

27. Paul Johnson, *Enemies of Society* (New York: Atheneum, 1977), p. 92.

28. Randal O'Toole, "Do You Know the Way to L.A.? San Jose Shows How to Turn an Urban Area into Los Angeles in Three Stressful Decades," *Policy Analysis*, No. 602, Cato Institute, October 17, 2007, p. 6.

29. See, for example, William Julius Wilson, *When Work Disappears: The World of the New Urban Poor* (New York: Alfred A. Knopf, 1996).

30. Ibid., pp. 34–35.

31. John McWhorter, *Winning the Race: Beyond the Crisis in Black America* (New York: Gotham Books, 2005), pp. 37, 49–72.

32. Reynolds Farley, et al., *Detroit Divided* (New York: Russell Sage Foundation, 2000), p. 31.

33. Patrick McGeehan, "After Century, Room and Board in City Still Sting," *New York Times*, May 20, 2006, p. A1.

34. Randal O'Toole, "The High Price of Land-Use Planning," *San Francisco Chronicle*, May 22, 2006, p. B7.

35. Miriam Jordan, "In Tony Monterey County, Slums and a Land War," *Wall Street Journal*, August 26–27, 2006, p. A6.

36. Randal O'Toole, *The Planning Penalty: How Smart Growth Makes Housing Unaffordable* (Oakland: The Independent Institute, 2006), p. 35.

37. Ibid., p. 38.

38. Ibid., pp. 3, 27.

39. Ibid., p. 29.

40. Tim Simmers, "Median Home Cost Over $1M," *San Mateo County Times*, August 16, 2007, p. 1.

41. Foster City Historical Society, *Images of America: Foster City* (San Francisco: Arcadia Publishing, 2005), p. 7.

42. Edward L. Glaeser, Joseph Gyourko and Raven Saks, "Why is Manhattan so Expensive? Regulation and the Rise in Housing Prices," *Journal of Law and Economics*, October 2005, p. 332.

43. Stephen Coyle, "Palo Alto: A Far Cry from *Euclid*," *Land Use and Housing on the San Francisco Peninsula*, edited by Thomas M. Hagler (Stanford: Stanford Environmental Law Society, 1983), pp. 84, 85.

44. Edward L. Glaeser, et al., "Why is Manhattan so Expensive?" *Journal of Law and Economics*, October 2005, p. 332.
45. Ibid., p. 333.
46. Ibid., pp. 337–338.
47. William A. Fischel, *Regulatory Takings: Law, Economics, and Politics* (Cambridge, Massachusetts: Harvard University Press, 1995), p. 238.
48. Randal O'Toole, *The Planning Penalty*, p. 32.
49. Ibid., pp. 32–33.
50. Edward L. Glaeser, et al., "Why is Manhattan so Expensive?" *Journal of Law and Economics*, October 2005, pp. 335, 367.
51. Tracie Rozhon, "Housing Market Heats Up in City," *New York Times*, February 19, 2007, p. B6. A later correction said that the woman identified as "Shavely" was instead named Staveley. See "Corrections: For the Record," *New York Times*, February 22, 2007, p. A2.
52. "Relative Values," *Wall Street Journal*, September 10, 2010, p. W8.
53. Edward L. Glaeser, et al., "Why is Manhattan so Expensive?" *Journal of Law and Economics*, October 2005, p. 337.
54. *Construction Industry Association of Sonoma County v. The City of Petaluma*, 522 F.2d 897 (1975).
55. Miriam Jordan, "In Tony Monterey County, Slums and a Land War," *Wall Street Journal*, August 26–27, 2006, p. A6.
56. Ibid., pp. A1, A6.
57. James Temple, "Exodus of S.F.'s Middle Class," *San Francisco Chronicle*, June 22, 2008, p. A1.
58. Stephen Coyle, "Palo Alto: A Far Cry from *Euclid*," *Land Use and Housing on the San Francisco Peninsula*, edited by Thomas M. Hagler, p. 90.
59. Kimberly A. Strassel, "Rambo's View," *Wall Street Journal*, September 7, 2007, p. A14.
60. Leslie Fulbright, "S.F. Moves to Stem African American Exodus," *San Francisco Chronicle*, April 9, 2007, p. A1.
61. Conor Dougherty, "The End of White Flight," *Wall Street Journal*, July 19–20, 2008, p. A10.

62. Leslie Fulbright, "Social, Economic Factors at Root of Black Exodus," *San Francisco Chronicle*, August 10, 2008, p. B1.
63. William Julius Wilson, *When Work Disappears*, p. 35.
64. Jane Jacobs, *The Death and Life of Great American Cities* (New York: Vintage Books, 1992), p. 10.
65. James Q. Wilson and Richard J. Herrnstein, *Crime and Human Nature: The Definitive Study of the Causes of Crime* (New York: Simon & Schuster, 1985), p. 473.
66. Jane Jacobs, *The Death and Life of Great American Cities*, p. 310. Incidentally, the idea that Franklin D. Roosevelt's New Deal administration was on "an opposite political pole" from the administration of Herbert Hoover has been discredited in recent years by scholars who have pointed out how many of FDR's programs took Hoover's ideas and carried them farther than Hoover was prepared to go. Tugwell himself later wrote: "I once made a list of New Deal ventures begun during Hoover's years as secretary of commerce and then as president. . . . The New Deal owed much to what he had begun." Quoted in Amity Shlaes, *The Forgotten Man: A New History of the Great Depression* (New York: HarperCollins, 2007), p. 149.
67. Herbert Gans, *The Urban Villagers: Group and Class in the Life of Italian-Americans*, updated and expanded edition (New York: The Free Press, 1982), p. 363n.
68. Ibid., p. 380.
69. Ibid., pp. 380–381.
70. Randal O'Toole, *The Best-Laid Plans*, p. 181.
71. Howard Husock, "Let's End Housing Vouchers," *City Journal*, Autumn 2000, p. 84.
72. Ibid., pp. 84, 87.
73. Solomon Moore, "As Housing Program Moves Poor to the Suburbs, Tensions Follow," *New York Times*, August 9, 2008, p. A15.
74. Nicole Gelinas, "Houston's Noble Experiment," *City Journal*, Spring 2006.
75. Robert Bruegmann, *Sprawl*, p. 119.
76. Ibid., p. 118.

77. Ibid., p. 135.
78. Ibid., p. 183.
79. Chuck Squatriglia, "A Million Acres," *San Francisco Chronicle*, July 16, 2006, p. A4.
80. "An Age of Transformation," *The Economist*, May 31, 2008, p. 29.
81. Robert Bruegmann, *Sprawl*, pp. 35–36.

CHAPTER 3: MALE-FEMALE FACTS AND FALLACIES

1. "A Guide to Womenomics," *The Economist*, April 15, 2006, p. 74.
2. Tamar Lewin, "At Colleges, Women are Leaving Men in the Dust," *New York Times*, July 9, 2006, p. 1.
3. Charles Murray, "The Inequality Taboo," *Commentary*, September 2005, p. 16.
4. John B. Parrish, "Professional Womanpower as a National Resource," *Quarterly Review of Economics & Business*, February 1961, p. 58.
5. Jessie Bernard, *Academic Women* (University Park: Pennsylvania State University Press, 1964), pp. 35, 61.
6. John B. Parrish, "Professional Womanpower as a National Resource," *Quarterly Review of Economics & Business*, February 1961, pp. 55–57.
7. Ibid., p. 58.
8. Jessie Bernard, *Academic Women*, p. 55.
9. U.S. Bureau of the Census, *Historical Statistics of the United States: Colonial Times to 1970* (Washington: U.S. Government Printing Office, 1975), p. 19.
10. Jessie Bernard, *Academic Women*, p. 206.
11. John K. Folger and Charles B. Nam, *Education of the American Population* (Washington: U.S. Government Printing Office, 1967), p. 81.
12. U.S. Bureau of the Census, *Historical Statistics of the United States: Colonial Times to 1970*, pp. 19, 49.
13. Diana Furchtgott-Roth and Christine Stolba, *Women's Figures: An Illustrated Guide to the Economic Progress of Women in America* (Washington: American Enterprise Institute, 1999), p. 86.

14. Theodore Caplow, et al., *The First Measured Century: An Illustrated Guide to Trends in America, 1900–2000* (Washington: The AEI Press, 2001), p. 69. See also U.S. Bureau of the Census, "Households, Families, and Children: A 30-Year Perspective," *Current Population Reports*, P23–181, p. 6.
15. *Historical Statistics of the United States: Earliest Times to the Present*, Millennial Edition (New York: Cambridge University Press, 2006), Vol. I, pp. 399–400.
16. Diana Furchtgott-Roth and Christine Stolba, *Women's Figures*, 1999 edition, pp. 23–27.
17. Paula England, "Gender Inequality in Labor Markets: The Role of Motherhood and Segregation," *Social Politics: International Studies in Gender, State, and Society*, Vol. 12, No. 2, Summer 2005, p. 266.
18. Ibid., p. 267.
19. Ibid., p. 273.
20. U.S. Bureau of the Census, *Evidence from Census 2000 About Earnings by Detailed Occupation for Men and Women*, Census 2000 Special Reports, May 2004, p. 10; U.S. Bureau of Census, *We the People: Women and Men in the United States*, Census 2000 Special Reports, January 2005, p. 11.
21. U.S. Bureau of the Census, *Evidence from Census 2000 About Earnings by Detailed Occupation for Men and Women*, Census 2000 Special Reports, May 2004, pp. 6, 26.
22. Diana Furchtgott-Roth and Christine Stolba, *Women's Figures*, 1999 edition, p. 33.
23. John M. McDowell, "Obsolescence of Knowledge and Career Publication Profiles: Some Evidence of Differences Among Fields in Costs of Interrupted Careers," *American Economic Review*, Vol. 72, No. 4 (September 1982), p. 761.
24. Thomas B. Hoffer, et al., *Doctorate Recipients from United States Universities: Summary Report 2005* (Chicago: National Opinion Research Center, University of Chicago, 2006), p. 13.

25. Sylvia Ann Hewlett and Carolyn Buck Luce, "Extreme Jobs: The Dangerous Allure of the 70-Hour Workweek," *Harvard Business Review*, December 2006, pp. 50, 51, 56, 57.
26. Quoted in David Lubinski and Camilla Persson Benbow, "Study of Mathematically Precocious Youth After 35 Years," *Perspectives on Psychological Science*, December 2006, p. 332.
27. Ibid., pp. 333–334.
28. Ibid., p. 332.
29. "A Guide to Womenomics," *The Economist*, April 15, 2006, p. 74.
30. Warren Farrell, *Why Men Earn More: The Startling Truth Behind the Pay Gap and What Women Can Do About It* (New York: Amacom, 2005), pp. 16–17.
31. Ibid., p. xxiii.
32. Louise Story, "Many Women at Elite Colleges Set Career Path to Motherhood," *New York Times*, September 20, 2005, p. A18.
33. Ibid.
34. Jeffrey Wenger, "The Continuing Problems with Part-Time Jobs," *EPI Issue Brief*, Economic Policy Institute, April 24, 2001, p. 1.
35. Ibid., p. 2.
36. "A Guide to Womenomics," *The Economist*, April 15, 2006, pp. 73–74.
37. U.S. Bureau of Labor Statistics, *100 Years of U.S. Consumer Spending* (Washington: U.S. Department of Labor, 2006), p. 58.
38. "The Hand that Rocks the Cradle," *The Economist*, March 4, 2006, p. 51.
39. Francine D. Blau and Lawrence M. Kahn, "Gender Differences in Pay," *Journal of Economic Perspectives*, Autumn 2000, p. 83.
40. Anita U. Hattiangadi and Amy M. Habib, *A Closer Look at Comparable Worth*, second edition (Washington: Employment Policy Foundation, 2000), p. 43.
41. Thomas Sowell, *Education: Assumptions versus History* (Stanford: Hoover Institution Press, 1986), pp. 95, 97.
42. "The Economic Role of Women," *The Economic Report of the President, 1973* (Washington, D.C.: U.S. Government Printing Office, 1973), p. 105.

43. Andrew Hacker, *Money: Who Has How Much and Why* (New York: Scribner, 1997), p. 199.

44. Jessie Bernard, *Academic Women*, p. 241.

45. U.S. Bureau of the Census, "Income, Poverty, and Health Insurance Coverage in the United States: 2004," *Current Population Reports*, P60–229 (Washington: U.S. Government Printing Office, 2005), p. 7.

46. Mickey Meece, "What Do Women Want? Just Ask," *New York Times*, October 29, 2006, Section 3, p. 7.

47. Jeffrey Wenger, "The Continuing Problems with Part-Time Jobs," *EPI Issue Brief*, Economic Policy Institute, April 24, 2001, pp. 1–2.

48. Donald R. Williams, "Women's Part-Time Employment: A Gross Flows Analysis," *Monthly Labor Review*, April 1995, p. 37.

49. Laurence C. Baker, "Differences in Earnings Between Male and Female Physicians," *The New England Journal of Medicine*, April 11, 1996, p. 960.

50. See Ibid., p. 962.

51. Howard J. Wall, "The Gender Wage Gap and Wage Discrimination: Illusion or Reality?" *The Regional Economist*, October 2000, Federal Reserve Bank of St. Louis, pp. 10–11.

52. Francine D. Blau and Lawrence M. Kahn, "Swimming Upstream: Trends in the Gender Wage Differential in the 1980s," *Journal of Labor Economics*, January 1997, pp. 1–42. See also U.S. Bureau of the Census, *Evidence From Census 2000 About Earnings by Detailed Occupation for Men and Women*, Census 2000 Special Reports, May 2004.

53. Francine D. Blau and Lawrence M. Kahn, "Gender Differences in Pay," *Journal of Economic Perspectives*, Autumn 2000, p. 79.

54. June O'Neill, "The Gender Gap in Wages, circa 2000," *American Economic Review*, May 2003, p. 310.

55. Marianne Bertrand and Kevin Hallock, "The Gender Gap in Top Corporate Jobs," *Industrial and Labor Relations Review*, October 2001, p. 17.

56. Steven Greenhouse and Michael Barbaro, "Costco Bias Suit Is Given Class-Action Status," *New York Times*, January 12, 2007, p. C9.

57. *Equal Employment Opportunity Commission v. Sears, Roebuck &
    Company*, 839 F.2d 302 at 311, 360.

58. Clarence Thomas, chairman of the EEOC at the time the case ended,
    later wrote in his memoirs: "I explored the possibility of settling the
    case, but was told that Sears's chairman and CEO felt so strongly that
    the case was unjust that he intended not only to defend it to the bitter
    end but to push for his legal fees. He prevailed, but the company was
    awarded only a portion of the legal fees, which reportedly totaled more
    than $20 million. EEOC had also spent millions prosecuting the case.
    I was right: nobody won." Even a corporation as large as General
    Motors decided to settle out of court. Clarence Thomas, *My
    Grandfather's Son: A Memoir* (New York: HarperCollins, 2007), p. 159.

59. Jessie Bernard, *Academic Women*, pp. xx, 77–78, 84; Alan E. Bayer,
    College and University Faculty: A Statistical Description (Washington:
    American Council on Education, June 1970), p. 12; Helen S. Astin,
    The Woman Doctorate in America (New York: Russell Sage Foundation,
    1969), pp. 23, 25.

60. Compare Jessie Bernard, *Academic Women*, p. 39; Diana Furchtgott-
    Roth and Christine Stolba, *Women's Figures*, 1999 edition, p. 35.

61. James M. McPherson, "White Liberals and Black Power in Negro
    Education, 1865–1915," *American Historical Review*, Vol. 75, No. 5
    (June 1970), p. 1362.

62. Lenore J. Weitzman, "Affirmative Action Plans for Eliminating Sex
    Discrimination in Academe," *Academic Women on the Move*, edited by
    Alice S. Rossi and Ann Calderwood (New York: Russell Sage
    Foundation, 1973), p. 479.

63. Helen S. Astin, "Career Profiles of Women Doctorates," ibid., p. 160.
    See also Jessie Bernard, *Academic Women*, p. 87.

64. Randy E. Ilg, "Change in Employment by Occupation, Industry, and
    Earnings Quartile, 2000–05," *Monthly Labor Review*, December 2006,
    p. 28.

65. U.S. Bureau of the Census, *Special Studies: Earnings in 1981 of
    Married-Couple Families, by Selected Characteristics of Husbands and
    Wives*, Series P–23, No. 133, p. 28.

66. "A Guide to Womenomics," *The Economist*, April 15, 2006, pp. 73–74.
67. David Leonhardt, "Scant Progress on Closing Gap In Women's Pay," *New York Times*, December 24, 2006, p. 16.
68. Quoted in Carol Hymowitz, "A Different Track," *Wall Street Journal*, April 16, 2007, p. R8.

CHAPTER 4: ACADEMIC FACTS AND FALLACIES

1. David Glenn, et al., "The Quality Question," *Chronicle of Higher Education*, September 3, 2010, p. A8.
2. U.S. Department of Education, *Digest of Education Statistics 2006*, National Center for Education Statistics, July 2007, pp. 267, 491, 494, 496.
3. Kelly Field and Goldie Blumenstyk, "For-Profits Spend Heavily to Fend Off New Rule," *Chronicle of Higher Education*, September 10, 2010, p. A1.
4. Martin Ince, "How the Land of the Free Charged Right to the Top," *The Times Higher Education Supplement*, October 6, 2006, p. 11.
5. "Mendicant Scholars," *The Economist*, November 11, 2006, pp. 63, 64.
6. Adam Smith, *The Wealth of Nations* (New York: Modern Library, 1937), p. 717.
7. Jeffrey Selingo, "Trustees: More Willing Than Ready," *Chronicle of Higher Education*, May 11, 2007, pp. A11, A13, A19, A20.
8. Harry R. Lewis, *Excellence Without a Soul: How a Great University Forgot Education* (New York: Public Affairs, 2006), p. 15.
9. Henry M. Wriston, *Academic Procession: Reflections of a College President* (New York: Columbia University Press, 1959), p. 63.
10. Arthur M. Sussman, "University Governance through a Rose-Colored Lens: NLRB v. Yeshiva," *The Supreme Court Review*, Volume 1980, p. 27.
11. "Faculty Senate Report," *Stanford Report*, April 25, 2007, p. 13.
12. Anthony N. DeMaria, "Your Soul for a Pen?" *Journal of the American College of Cardiology*, March 20, 2007, pp. 1220–1222.
13. Derek Bok, *Our Underachieving Colleges* (Princeton: Princeton University Press, 2006), p. 55.

14. Harry R. Lewis, *Excellence Without a Soul*, pp. 253, 256.
15. Richard Vedder, *Going Broke by Degree* (Washington: The AEI Press, 2004), p. 172.
16. Michael E. Gordon, "When B's Are Better," *Chronicle of Higher Education*, August 11, 2006, p. B10.
17. See, for example, Elizabeth F. Farrell and Martin Van der Werf, "Playing the Rankings Game," *Chronicle of Higher Education*, May 25, 2007, pp. A11 ff; Martin Van der Werf, "Rankings Methodology Hurts Public Institutions," ibid., pp. A13 ff; Jeffrey Selingo, "What the Rankings Do for 'U.S. News'," ibid., p. A15.
18. "Measuring Mortarboards," *The Economist*, November 17, 2007, p. 69.
19. Ibid.
20. Richard Vedder, "How to Choose a College," *Forbes*, May 19, 2008, p. 30.
21. "Data: Big," *New York Times*, July 29, 2007, Education Life, pp. 8–9.
22. Dave Curtin, "CU Law Tuition Could Rise by $6,000," *Denver Post*, September 8, 2003, p. B4.
23. Dave Curtin, "CU Law School's Accreditation in Peril: ABA Concerned over New Building," *Denver Post*, May 25, 2003, p. B5.
24. Andrew Gillen, Daniel L. Bennett and Richard Vedder, *The Inmates Running the Asylum?: An Analysis of Higher Education Accreditation* (Washington: Center for College Affordability and Productivity, 2010), p. 9.
25. Ibid., p. 23.
26. Ibid., p. 9.
27. Ibid., p. 8.
28. Ibid., p. 25.
29. George J. Stigler, "The Intellectual and the Marketplace," *The Essence of Stigler*, edited by Kurt R. Leube and Thomas Gale Moore (Stanford: Hoover Institution Press, 1986), p. 83.
30. Henry Rosovsky, *The University: An Owner's Manual* (New York: W.W. Norton & Co., 1990), p. 177.
31. "Faculty Salaries at More Than 1,200 Institutions," *Chronicle of Higher Education*, April 17, 2009, pp. A13–A15.

32. Charles T. Clotfelter, *Buying the Best* (Princeton: Princeton University Press, 1996), p. 186.

33. "College Enrollment by Age of Students, Fall 2007," *Chronicle of Higher Education*, August 28, 2009, p. 10.

34. Sam Whiting, "It's Never Too Late to Educate," *San Francisco Chronicle Magazine*, August 3, 2008, p. 13.

35. Thomas Sowell, *Inside American Education: The Decline, the Deception, the Dogmas* (New York: The Free Press, 1993), p. 107.

36. Scott Baumler, "Undergraduate Origins of Doctorate Recipients," Office of Institutional Research, Grinnell College, October 20, 2006.

37. Carol Hymowitz, "Any College Will Do," *Wall Street Journal*, September 18, 2006, p. B1.

38. Mark Schneider, "How Much Is That Bachelor's Degree Really Worth? The Million Dollar Misunderstanding," The American Enterprise Institute, May 2009, pp. 4, 5, 6.

39. Alan Finder, "Elite Colleges Reporting Record Lows in Admission," *New York Times*, April 1, 2008, p. A16.

40. Paul Marthers, "Admissions Messages vs. Admissions Realities," *Colleges Unranked: Ending the College Admissions Frenzy*, edited by Lloyd Thacker (Cambridge, Massachusetts: Harvard University Press, 2005), p. 73.

41. Eric Hoover, "For Admissions Deans, Waiting-List Roulette Gets Trickier," *Chronicle of Higher Education*, May 30, 2008, p. A1.

42. Ibid., p. A21.

43. "A Note from the Dean on the Class of 2011," *Sixty-First Annual Report to Secondary Schools*, Amherst.

44. Brown Admission, *Facts and Figures*, p. 2.

45. Paul Marthers, "Admissions Messages vs. Admissions Realities," *Colleges Unranked*, edited by Lloyd Thacker, pp. 73–74.

46. Eric Hoover, "On the Road, Measuring the Miles per Applicant," *Chronicle of Higher Education*, December 12, 2008, p. A19.

47. Elizabeth A. Duffy and Idana Goldberg, *Crafting A Class: College Admissions and Financial Aid, 1955–1994* (Princeton: Princeton University Press, 1998), p. 31.

48. Daniel Golden, "Is Admissions Bar Higher for Asians At Elite Schools?" *Wall Street Journal*, November 11, 2006, pp. A1, A5.

49. E. J. Kahn, *Harvard: Through Change and Through Storm* (New York: W.W. Norton & Co., Inc. 1969), p. 33.

50. Dave Bianco, "Number of Applicants Drops Again," *Stanford Daily*, February 9, 1990, p. 1.

51. "Students: College Costs and Financial Aid," *Chronicle of Higher Education*, August 28, 2009, p. 12.

52. Robin Wilson, "A Lifetime of Student Debt? Not Likely," *Chronicle of Higher Education*, May 22, 2009, pp. A1, A18.

53. Harry R. Lewis, *Excellence Without a Soul*, p. 13.

54. Libby Sander, "Student Aid Is Up, but College Costs Have Risen Faster, Surveys Find," *Chronicle of Higher Education*, November 2, 2007, pp. A26–A34.

55. Anthony, Bianco, "The Dangerous Wealth of the Ivy League," *BusinessWeek*, December 10, 2007, pp. 39, 40.

56. "Just Add Cash," *The Economist*, December 1, 2007, p. 44.

57. Beckie Supiano, "Swanky Suites, More Students?" *Chronicle of Higher Education*, April 11, 2008, p. A1.

58. Eric Hoover, "Campuses See Rising Demand for Housing," *Chronicle of Higher Education*, August 1, 2008, p. A1.

59. "Just Add Cash," *The Economist*, December 1, 2007, p. 44.

60. Richard Vedder, *Going Broke by Degree*, p. 160.

61. Ibid.

62. "Faculty Senate Report," *Stanford Report*, March 14, 2007, p. 10.

63. Goldie Blumenstyk, "The $375-Billion Question: Why Does College Cost So Much?" *Chronicle of Higher Education*, October 3, 2008, p. A14.

64. Robin Wilson, "As Competition for Students Increases, Admissions Officers Face Dismissal If They Don't 'Win and Keep on Winning'," *Chronicle of Higher Education*, October 31, 1990, p. A1.

65. Michael S. McPherson and Morton Owen Schapiro, *The Student Aid Game: Meeting Need and Rewarding Talent in American Higher Education* (Princeton: Princeton University Press, 1998), p. 16.

66. Ibid., p. 114.
67. John Gravois, "Tracking the Invisible Faculty," *Chronicle of Higher Education*, December 15, 2006, p. A8.
68. Samantha Stainburn, "The Case of the Vanishing Full-Time Professor," *New York Times*, January 3, 2010, Education Life, p. 6.
69. David J. Powell, "LSA's Road to Insanity," *Michigan Review* (University of Michigan), December 1990, p. 1.
70. John M. De Figueiredo and Brian S. Silverman, "Academic Earmarks and the Returns to Lobbying," *Journal of Law and Economics*, October 2006, p. 608.
71. Robin Wilson, "Wisconsin's Flagship is Raided for Scholars," *Chronicle of Higher Education*, April 18, 2008, pp. A19, A25.
72. U.S. Department of Education, *Digest of Education Statistics 2006*, National Center for Education Statistics, July 2007, pp. 267, 491, 494, 496.
73. Michael S. McPherson and Morton Owen Schapiro, *The Student Aid Game*, p. 84.
74. John M. De Figueiredo and Brian S. Silverman, "Academic Earmarks and the Returns to Lobbying," *Journal of Law and Economics*, October 2006, p. 604.
75. Ibid., p. 601.
76. Daniel S. Greenberg, "A New Source of Research Money," *Chronicle of Higher Education*, March 2, 2007, p. B16.
77. Michael Smith, "Ohio State Lands $110M Deal," *SportsBusiness Journal*, March 30–April 5, 2009, pp. 1 ff.
78. "Of Steroids and Scholarships: Eli Commish Talks to Spec," *Columbia Daily Spectator*, February 8, 1989, p. 5.
79. Mark Yost, "Has Serious Academic Reform of College Athletics Arrived?" *Wall Street Journal*, March 19, 2008, p. D10.
80. Steve Wieberg and Kelly Whiteside, "Football-crazy Ohio State Does All Sports in Big Way," *USA Today*, January 5–7, 2007, pp. 1, 2.
81. Paul Fain, "Oregon Debates Role of Big Sports Donors," *Chronicle of Higher Education*, October 26, 2007, p. A39.

82. Andrew Zimbalist, "Looks Like a Business; Should Be Taxed Like One," *New York Times*, January 7, 2007, Section 8, p. 9.

83. Brad Wolverton, "As Cutbacks Hit College Sports, Baseball Falls Behind in the Count," *Chronicle of Higher Education*, May 15, 2009, p. A1.

84. Harry R. Lewis, *Excellence Without a Soul*, p. 237.

85. Andrew Zimbalist, "Looks Like a Business; Should Be Taxed Like One," *New York Times*, January 7, 2007, Section 8, p. 9.

86. Russell Adams, "The New Big Shots of the Gridiron," *Wall Street Journal*, January 6, 2007, p. P4.

87. Libby Sander, "Have Money, Will Travel: The Quest for Top Athletes," *Chronicle of Higher Education*, August 1, 2008, pp. A1, A10.

88. Audrey Williams June, "After Costly Foray Into Big-Time Sports, a College Returns to Its Roots," *Chronicle of Higher Education*, May 18, 2007, pp. A33–A34.

89. "Too Much Sports?" *Chronicle of Higher Education*, January 25, 2008, p. A4.

90. Brad Wolverton, et al., "Spending Plenty So Athletes Can Make the Grade," *Chronicle of Higher Education*, September 5, 2008, pp. A1 ff.

91. Ibid., pp. A19, A22.

92. Allen Barra, "Pro Football's College Tuition Bill," *Wall Street Journal*, April 30, 2009, p. D6.

93. Craig Karmin, "Big Moan on Campus: Bond Downgrades," *Wall Street Journal*, May 29, 2009, p. C1.

94. R.M. Douglas, "Survival of the Fittest? Postgraduate Education and the Professoriate at the Fin de Siècle," *Daedalus*, Fall 1997, p. 138.

95. Richard Monastersky, "The Real Science Crisis: Bleak Prospects for Young Researchers," *Chronicle of Higher Education*, September 21, 2007, p. A1.

96. Arthur Levine, "How the Academic Profession is Changing," *Daedalus*, Fall 1997, pp. 4–5.

CHAPTER 5: INCOME FACTS AND FALLACIES

1. Alan Reynolds, *Income and Wealth* (Westport: Greenwood Press, 2006), p. 22.

2. "Income Mobility in the U.S. From 1996 to 2005," Report of the Department of the Treasury, November 13, 2007.

3. U.S. Bureau of the Census, "Changes in Median Household Income: 1969 to 1996," *Current Population Reports*, P23–196, p. 1.

4. Theodore Caplow, Louis Hicks and Ben J. Wattenberg, *The First Measured Century: An Illustrated Guide to Trends in America, 1900–2000* (Washington: The AEI Press, 2001), p. 93.

5. Carmen DeNavas-Walt, et al., "Income, Poverty, and Health Insurance Coverage in the United States: 2007," *Current Population Reports*, P60–235 (Washington: U.S. Bureau of the Census, 2008), pp. 7, 8.

6. Alan Reynolds, *Income and Wealth*, p. 64.

7. "The Rich Get Richer, and So Do the Old," *Washington Post* (National Weekly Edition), September 7, 1998, p. 34.

8. Louis Uchitelle, "Stagnant Pay: A Delayed Impact," *New York Times*, June 18, 1991, p. D2.

9. Amy Kaslow, "Growing American Economy Leaves Middle Class Behind," *Christian Science Monitor*, November 1, 1994, p. 2.

10. Benjamin M. Friedman, "The Economic System," *Understanding America: The Anatomy of an Exceptional Nation*, edited by Peter H. Schuck and James Q. Wilson (New York: Public Affairs, 2008) p. 91.

11. Compare Tom Wicker, "LBJ's Great Society," *New York Times*, May 7, 1990, p. A15; Tom Wicker, "Let 'Em Eat Swiss Cheese," *New York Times*, September 2, 1988, p. A27.

12. See, for example, U.S. Bureau of the Census, "The Social and Economic Status of the Black Population in the United States: An Historical View, 1790–1978," *Current Population Reports*, Series P–23, No. 80 (Washington: U.S. Government Printing Office, no date), p. 102.

13. Herman P. Miller, *Income Distribution in the United States*, a 1960 Census Monograph (Washington: U.S. Government Printing Office, 1966), p. 7.

14. Robert Rector and Rea S. Hederman, *Income Inequality: How Census Data Misrepresent Income Distribution* (Washington: The Heritage Foundation, 1999), p. 11.

15. Alan Reynolds, *Income and Wealth*, p. 25.

16. Data on numbers of heads of household working in high-income and low-income households in 2000 are from Table HINC–06 from the Current Population Survey, downloaded from the Bureau of the Census web site.

17. Alan Reynolds, *Income and Wealth*, pp. 26–27.

18. Robert Heilbroner and Lester Thurow, *Economics Explained*, revised and updated edition (New York: Touchstone, 1994), p. 48.

19. Alan Reynolds, *Income and Wealth*, p. 27.

20. W. Michael Cox and Richard Alm, *Myths of Rich & Poor: Why We're Better Off Than We Think* (New York: Basic Books, 1999), p. 85.

21. Alan Reynolds, *Income and Wealth*, p. 28.

22. Robert Rector, "The Myth of Widespread American Poverty," *The Heritage Foundation Backgrounder*, No. 1221, September 18, 1998, p. 4.

23. Alan Reynolds, *Income and Wealth*, p. 67.

24. Carmen DeNavas-Walt, et al., "Income, Poverty, and Health Insurance Coverage in the United States: 2007," *Current Population Reports*, P60–235 (Washington: U.S. Bureau of the Census, 2008), p. 14.

25. Bob Herbert, "The Millions Left Out," *New York Times*, May 12, 2007, p. A15.

26. Carmen DeNavas-Walt, et al., "Income, Poverty, and Health Insurance Coverage in the United States: 2007," *Current Population Reports*, P60–235 (Washington: U.S. Bureau of the Census, 2008), p. 15.

27. Alan Reynolds, *Income and Wealth*, pp. 57–59.

28. W. Michael Cox and Richard Alm, *Myths of Rich & Poor*, p. 18.

29. Theodore Caplow, Louis Hicks and Ben J. Wattenberg, *The First Measured Century*, p. 161.

30. Alan Reynolds, *Income and Wealth*, p. 63.

31. Ibid., p. 64.

32. W. Michael Cox and Richard Alm, *Myths of Rich & Poor*, p. 21.

33. Ibid., p. 132.

34. Alan Reynolds, *Income and Wealth*, p. 64.
35. These more technical problems with the statistics are among those discussed in Chapter 4 of *Income and Wealth* by Alan Reynolds.
36. Ibid., pp. 69–70.
37. Ibid., pp. 70–71, 83–84.
38. Federal Reserve Bank of Dallas, *Annual Report: 1995*, p. 8.
39. Peter Saunders, *Poor Statistics: Getting the Facts Right About Poverty in Australia* (St. Leonards, Australia: Centre for Independent Studies, 2002), p. 5; David Green, *Poverty and Benefit Dependency* (Wellington: New Zealand Business Roundtable, 2001), pp. 32, 33; Jason Clemens and Joel Emes, "Time Reveals the Truth about Low Income," *Fraser Forum*, September 2001, The Fraser Institute in Vancouver, Canada, pp. 24–26.
40. "Movin' On Up," *Wall Street Journal*, November 13, 2007, p. A24. The original data are available in greater detail in "Income Mobility in the U.S. from 1996 to 2005," Report of the Department of the Treasury, November 13, 2007, p. 10.
41. "Income Mobility in the U.S. from 1996 to 2005," Report of the Department of the Treasury, November 13, 2007, p. 15.
42. Ibid., pp. 2, 4.
43. W. Michael Cox and Richard Alm, *Myths of Rich & Poor*, p. 16.
44. Ibid.
45. U.S. Bureau of the Census, "Money Income in the United States: 2000," *Current Population Reports*, P60–213 (Washington: U.S. Government Printing Office, 2001), p. 2; U.S. Bureau of the Census, "65+ in the United States: 2005," *Current Population Reports*, P23–209 (Washington: U.S. Government Printing Office, 2005), p. 109.
46. Ibid., p. 95.
47. Carmen DeNavas-Walt, et al., "Income, Poverty, and Health Insurance Coverage in the United States: 2007," *Current Population Reports*, P60–235 (Washington: U.S. Bureau of the Census, 2008), pp. 13, 22.
48. U.S. Bureau of the Census, "65+ in the United States: 2005," *Current Population Reports*, P23–209 (Washington: U.S. Government Printing Office, 2005), pp. 111, 114.

49. David Leonhardt, "Defining the Rich in the World's Wealthiest Nation," *New York Times*, January 12, 2003, Section 4, p. 16.

50. Ari Fleischer, "The Taxpaying Minority," *Wall Street Journal*, April 16, 2007, p. A15.

51. See Alan Reynolds, *Income and Wealth*, Chapter 8.

52. "Money Income in the United States: 2001," *Current Population Reports*, P60–218 (Washington: U.S. Bureau of the Census, 2002), p. 20.

53. "Spare a Dime? A Special Report on the Rich," *The Economist*, April 4, 2009, special section, pp. 3, 4.

54. Paul Krugman, *Peddling Prosperity: Economic Sense and Nonsense in the Age of Diminished Expectations* (New York: W.W. Norton & Company, 1994), p. 58.

55. Alan Reynolds, *Income and Wealth*, p. 48.

56. Carmen DeNavas-Walt, et al., "Income, Poverty, and Health Insurance Coverage in the United States: 2007," *Current Population Reports*, P60–235 (Washington: U.S. Bureau of the Census, 2008), p. 31.

57. "Where the Money Is," *Forbes*, June 30, 2008, p. 114.

58. Ellen Simon, "Yahoo May Not Be No. 1, But CEO's Pay Package Is," *San Francisco Chronicle*, June 12, 2007, p. C5.

59. Andrew Ross Sorkin and Eric Dash, "Private Firms Lure C.E.O.'s With Top Pay," *New York Times*, January 8, 2007, pp. A1 ff.

60. Ellen Simon, "Yahoo May Not Be No. 1, But CEO's Pay Package Is," *San Francisco Chronicle*, June 12, 2007, p. C5.

61. Donald E. Graham, "The Gray Lady's Virtue," *Wall Street Journal*, April 23, 2007, p. A17.

62. "Merrill Board's 2nd Chance," *Wall Street Journal*, October 31, 2007, p. C14.

63. Some of these changes in the retail sector are discussed in Chapter 5 of my *Basic Economics*, 4th edition (New York: Basic Books, 2011).

64. Federal Reserve Bank of Dallas, *Annual Report: 1995*, p. 8.

65. Ibid., p. 14.

66. Janny Scott and David Leonhardt, "Class in America: Shadowy Lines That Still Divide," *New York Times*, May 15, 2005, pp. A1, A26.

67. Ibid., p. A26.
68. David Wessel, "As Rich-Poor Gap Widens in the U.S., Class Mobility Stalls," *Wall Street Journal*, May 13, 2005, pp. A1 ff.
69. Bernard Shaw, *The Intelligent Woman's Guide to Socialism and Capitalism* (New York: Brentano's Publishers, 1928), p. 22.
70. Steve DiMeglio, "With Golf Needing a Boost, Its Leading Man Returns," *USA Today*, February 25, 2009, pp. A1 ff.
71. Thomas J. Stanley and William D. Danko, *The Millionaire Next Door: The Surprising Secrets of America's Wealthy* (Atlanta: Longstreet Press, 1996), p. 3.

CHAPTER 6: RACIAL FACTS AND FALLACIES

1. Paul Johnson, *Enemies of Society* (New York: Atheneum, 1977), p. 106.
2. Stephan Thernstrom and Abigail Thernstrom, *America in Black and White: One Nation, Indivisible* (New York: Simon & Schuster, 1997), p. 526.
3. Sharon M. Lee and Marilyn Fernandez, "Trends in Asian American Racial/Ethnic Intermarriage: A Comparison of 1980 and 1990 Census Data," *Sociological Perspectives*, Vol. 41, No. 2 (1998), p. 328.
4. Stephan Thernstrom and Abigail Thernstrom, *America in Black and White*, p. 526.
5. U.S. Bureau of the Census, *We the People: Asians in the United States*, Census 2000 Special Reports, December 2004, p. 6.
6. Ibid., p. 9.
7. Jessica W. Davis and Kurt J. Bauman, "School Enrollment in the United States: 2006," *Current Population Reports*, P20–559 (Washington: U.S. Bureau of the Census, 2008), p. 5.
8. Thomas B. Hoffer, et al., *Doctorate Recipients from United States Universities: Summary Report 2005* (Chicago: National Opinion Research Center, University of Chicago, 2006), p. 15.
9. See Thomas Sowell, *Affirmative Action Around the World: An Empirical Study* (New Haven: Yale University Press, 2004), p. 67.

10. Some of these many and wide-ranging differences have been elaborated in my trilogy, *Migrations and Cultures* (New York: Basic Books, 1996), *Conquests and Cultures* (New York: Basic Books, 1998), and *Race and Culture* (New York: Basic Books, 1994).

11. The Economist, *Pocket World in Figures, 2007* (London: Profile Books Ltd., 2006), p. 20.

12. Bernard Lewis, *The Jews of Islam* (Princeton: Princeton University Press, 1984), pp. 129, 214.

13. Ibid., pp. 134–135; Jane S. Gerber, *The Jews of Spain* (New York: The Free Press, 1992), pp. 163–164.

14. Bernard Lewis, *The Jews of Islam*, p. 133.

15. Aryeh Shmuelevitz, *The Jews of the Ottoman Empire in the Late Fifteenth and the Sixteenth Centuries: Administrative, Economic, Legal and Social Relations as Reflected in the Responsa* (Leiden, The Netherlands: E.J. Brill, 1984), pp. 128–129, 135, 136.

16. Stephan Thernstrom and Abigail Thernstrom, *America in Black and White*, p. 233.

17. U.S. Bureau of the Census, "The Social and Economic Status of the Black Population in the United States: An Historical View, 1790–1978," *Current Population Reports*, Series P–23, No. 80 (Washington: Bureau of the Census, no date), p. 74.

18. *Historical Statistics of the United States: Earliest Times to the Present*, Millennial Edition (New York: Cambridge University Press, 2006), Vol. 2, p. 660.

19. Daniel J. Boorstin, *The Americans*, Vol. II: *The National Experience* (New York: Random House, 1965), p. 203.

20. Compare Robert C. Davis, *Christian Slaves, Muslim Masters: White Slavery in the Mediterranean, the Barbary Coast, and Italy, 1500–1800* (New York: Palgrave Macmillan, 2003), p. 23; Philip D. Curtin, *The Atlantic Slave Trade: A Census* (Madison: University of Wisconsin Press, 1969), pp. 72, 87, 91.

21. See, for example, R. W. Beachey, *The Slave Trade of Eastern Africa* (New York: Harper & Row, 1976), p. 137; Ehud R. Toledano, *The*

Ottoman Slave Trade and Its Suppression: 1840–1890 (Princeton: Princeton University Press, 1982), pp. 66–67.

22. Robert C. Davis, *Christian Slaves, Muslim Masters*, pp. 7, 15.

23. Thomas Jefferson, *The Papers of Thomas Jefferson*, Volume I, edited by Julian P. Boyd (Princeton: Princeton University Press, 1950), p. 426.

24. Herbert G. Gutman, *The Black Family in Slavery and Freedom, 1750–1925* (New York: Vintage Press, 1977), pp. 231, 236, 238.

25. Orlando Patterson, *Slavery and Social Death* (Cambridge, Massachusetts: Harvard University Press, 1982), pp. 55, 189.

26. John K. Fairbank, Edwin O. Reischauer, and Albert M. Craig, *East Asia: Tradition and Transformation* (Boston: Houghton Mifflin Company, 1989), p. 509.

27. "Names," *The New Encyclopedia Britannica* (Chicago: Encyclopedia Britannica, Inc., 1991), Vol. 24, p. 731.

28. Herbert G. Gutman, *The Black Family in Slavery and Freedom*, pp. 230, 236–237.

29. Most estimates of the number of Africans enslaved by Europeans are below 12 million, while the number of Africans enslaved by Arabs is usually placed at 14 million. See, for examples, Philip D. Curtin, *The Atlantic Slave Trade: A Census*, p. 87; Hugh Thomas, *The Slave Trade: The Story of the Atlantic Slave Trade, 1440–1870* (New York: Simon & Schuster, 1997), p. 862 and appendix three; Ralph A. Austen, "The Trans-Saharan Slave Trade: A Tentative Census," *The Uncommon Market*, edited by Henry A. Gemery and Jan S. Hogendorn (New York: Academic Press, 1979), pp. 66, 68, 69; Ronald Segal, *Islam's Black Slaves* (New York: Farrar, Straus and Giroux, 2001), p. 57.

30. Herbert G. Gutman, *The Black Family in Slavery and Freedom*, pp. 32, 45; Leon F. Litwack, *Been in the Storm So Long* (New York: Alfred A. Knopf, 1979), p. 238.

31. Henry A. Walker, "Black-White Differences in Marriage and Family Patterns," *Feminism, Children and the New Families*, edited by Sanford M. Dornbusch and Myra H. Strober (New York: The Guilford Press, 1988), p. 92.

32. U.S. Bureau of the Census, *Historical Statistics of the United States: Colonial Times to 1957* (Washington, D.C.: U.S. Government Printing Office, 1960), p. 72.
33. U.S. Bureau of the Census, *Trends in Premarital Childbearing: 1930 to 1994*, Special Studies, P23–197, p. 2.
34. U.S. Bureau of the Census, "The Black Population in the United States: March 1994 and 1993," *Current Population Reports*, P20–480, p. 16.
35. Stephan Thernstrom and Abigail Thernstrom, *America in Black and White*, p. 238.
36. U.S. Bureau of the Census, "Households, Families, and Children: A 30-Year Perspective," *Current Population Reports*, P23–181, p. 32.
37. "Historical Poverty Tables: Table 4," U.S. Bureau of the Census, Current Population Survey, Annual Social and Economic Supplements. Downloaded June 29, 2007 from: http://www.census.gov/hhes/www/poverty/histpov/hstpov4.html.
38. See, for example, "The Frayed Knot," *The Economist*, May 26, 2007, pp. 23–25.
39. See, for examples, my *Black Rednecks and White Liberals* (San Francisco: Encounter Books, 2005), pp. 1–27.
40. Davidson M. Douglas, *Jim Crow Moves North: The Battle over Northern School Segregation, 1865–1954* (New York: Cambridge University Press, 2005), p. 16.
41. Alexis de Tocqueville, *Democracy in America* (New York: Alfred A. Knopf, 1966), Vol. I, p. 365; Frederick Law Olmsted, *The Cotton Kingdom: A Traveller's Observations on Cotton and Slavery in the American Slave States*, edited by Arthur M. Schlesinger (New York: Modern Library, 1969), pp. 476n, 614–622; Hinton Rowan Helper, *The Impending Crisis of the South: How to Meet It*, enlarged edition (New York: A. B. Burdick, 1860), p. 34.
42. See my *Black Rednecks and White Liberals*, pp. 3–6.
43. Ulrich Bonnell Phillips, *The Slave Economy of the Old South: Selected Essays in Economic and Social History*, edited by Eugene D. Genovese (Baton Rouge: Louisiana State University Press, 1968), p. 269.

44. H.J. Butcher, *Human Intelligence: Its Nature and Assessment* (New York: Harper, 1968), p. 252.

45. Stephan Thernstrom and Abigail Thernstrom, *America in Black and White*, pp. 354–355.

46. Ibid., p. 159.

47. Ibid., p. 162.

48. U.S. Bureau of the Census, *We the People: Blacks in the United States*, Census 2000 Special Reports, August 2005, pp. 13, 14.

49. U.S. Bureau of the Census, *We the People: Asians in the United States*, Census 2000 Special Reports, December 2004, pp. 15, 16.

50. Ibid., p. 7.

51. D. John Grove, "Restructuring the Cultural Division of Labor in Malaysia and Sri Lanka," *Comparative Political Studies*, July 1986, pp. 190–193.

52. Merle Lipton, *Capitalism and Apartheid: South Africa, 1910–1984* (Totowa, N.J.: Rowman and Allanheld, 1985), p. 209.

53. Harry J. Holzer, Steven Raphael and Michael A. Stoll, "Perceived Criminality, Criminal Background Checks, and the Racial Hiring Practices of Employers," *Journal of Law and Economics*, October 2006, pp. 452, 473.

54. Stephan Thernstrom and Abigail Thernstrom, *America in Black and White*, p. 37.

55. Ibid., pp. 354–355.

56. U.S. Bureau of the Census, "Household and Family Characteristics: March 1980," *Current Population Reports*, Series P–20, No. 366 (Washington, D.C.: U.S. Government Printing Office, 1981), pp. 182, 184.

57. Richard B. Freeman, *Black Elite* (New York: McGraw-Hill, 1976), Chapter 4.

58. Ibid., p. 88.

59. Richard J. Herrnstein and Charles Murray, *The Bell Curve: Intelligence and Class Structure in American Life* (New York: The Free Press, 1994), p. 323.

60. Stephan Thernstrom and Abigail Thernstrom, *America in Black and White*, p. 446.

61. An early example was David Caplovitz, *The Poor Pay More* (New York: Free Press of Glencoe, 1967). But see a critique of their conclusions by Walter Williams, "Why the Poor Pay More: An Alternative Explanation," *Social Science Quarterly*, September 1973, pp. 375–379.

62. Walter E. Williams, *The State Against Blacks* (New York: McGraw-Hill, 1982), p. 31.

63. Glenn B. Canner, et al., "Home Mortgage Disclosure Act: Expanded Data on Residential Lending," *Federal Reserve Bulletin*, November 1991, p. 870.

64. Ibid., pp. 859, 867, 868, 875.

65. Jesse Jackson, "Racism is the Bottom Line in Home Loans," *Los Angeles Times*, October 28, 1991, p. B5.

66. Joël Glenn Brenner, "Mortgage Loan Bias Persists, Fed Finds," *Washington Post*, October 28, 1992, pp. A1 ff.

67. Glenn B. Canner, et al., "Home Mortgage Disclosure Act: Expanded Data on Residential Lending," *Federal Reserve Bulletin*, November 1991, p. 870; Glenn B. Canner and Dolores S. Smith, "Expanded HMDA Data on Residential Lending: One Year Later," *Federal Reserve Bulletin*, November 1992, pp. 807, 808.

68. U.S. Commission on Civil Rights, *Civil Rights and the Mortgage Crisis* (Washington: U.S. Commission on Civil Rights, 2009), p. 53.

69. Board of Governors of the Federal Reserve System, *Report to the Congress on Credit Scoring and Its Effects on the Availability and Affordability of Credit*, submitted to the Congress pursuant to Section 215 of the Fair and Accurate Credit Transactions Act of 2003, August 2007, p. 80.

70. Edmund L. Andrews, "Blacks Hit Hardest by Costlier Mortgages," *New York Times*, September 14, 2005, pp. C1, C17.

71. Glenn B. Canner, et al., "Home Mortgage Disclosure Act: Expanded Data on Residential Lending," *Federal Reserve Bulletin*, November 1991, p. 865.

72. Ibid., p. 865n.

73. Alicia H. Munnell, et al., "Mortgage Lending in Boston: Interpreting HMDA Data," Federal Reserve Bank of Boston, Working Paper No. 92–7, October 1992, p. 25.

74. Glenn B. Canner, et al., "Home Mortgage Disclosure Act: Expanded Data on Residential Lending," *Federal Reserve Bulletin*, November 1991, p. 869.

75. Loc. cit.

76. See, for example, my *Civil Rights: Rhetoric or Reality?* (New York: William Morrow, 1984), pp. 130–131.

77. Alicia H. Munnell, et al., "Mortgage Lending in Boston: Interpreting HMDA Data," Federal Reserve Bank of Boston, Working Paper No. 92–7, October 1992, p. 44.

78. Bob Zelnick, *Backfire: A Reporter's Look at Affirmative Action* (Washington: Regnery Publishing, Inc., 1996), p. 330.

79. Peter Brimelow, and Leslie Spencer, "The Hidden Clue," *Forbes*, January 4, 1993, p. 48.

80. Ibid.

81. Ibid.

82. See the *Wall Street Journal* of August 16, 2001 in a front-page story titled "As Economy Slows, 'Subprime' Lending Looks Even Riskier."

83. Rochelle Sharpe, "Losing Ground: In Latest Recession, Only Blacks Suffered Net Employment Loss," *Wall Street Journal*, September 14, 1993, p. A12.

84. W.E.B. DuBois, *The Philadelphia Negro: A Social Study* (New York: Schocken Books, 1967), p. 395.

85. Senator Edward W. Brooke, *Bridging the Divide: My Life* (New Brunswick: Rutgers University Press, 2007), p. 4.

86. See Theodore Dalrymple, *Life at the Bottom: The Worldview That Makes the Underclass* (Chicago: Ivan R. Dee, 2001).

87. Joyce Lee Malcolm, *Guns and Violence: The English Experience* (Cambridge, Massachusetts: Harvard University Press, 2002), pp. 164–166.

CHAPTER 7: THIRD WORLD FACTS AND FALLACIES

1. Fernand Braudel, *The Mediterranean and the Mediterranean World in the Age of Philip II*, Vol. I (Berkeley: University of California Press, 1995), p. 35.
2. Fernard Braudel, *A History of Civilizations*, translated by Richard Mayne (New York: The Penguin Group, 1994), p. 124.
3. See, for examples, Thomas Sowell, *Conquests and Cultures: An International History* (New York: Basic Books, 1998), pp. 101–109.
4. *Ethnologue: Languages of the World*, Vol. I, fourteenth edition, edited by Barbara F. Grimes (Dallas: SIL International, 2000), p. 846; Thomas M. McDevitt, *World Population Profile: 1998* (Washington: U.S. Agency for International Development and U.S. Department of Commerce, 1999), p. A–5.
5. See my *Conquests and Cultures*, pp. 101–109, 175–177.
6. The Economist, *Pocket World in Figures*, 2007 edition (London: Profile Books Ltd, 2006), pp. 29, 55.
7. Ibid., pp. 29, 52–55.
8. John Kay, *Culture and Prosperity: The Truth About Markets— Why Some Nations Are Rich but Most Remain Poor* (New York: HarperBusiness, 2004), p. 27; *The World Almanac, 2005* (New York: World Almanac Books, 2005), pp. 790–791, 834, 843, 845.
9. William Easterly, *The White Man's Burden: Why the West's Efforts to Aid the Rest Have Done So Much Ill and So Little Good* (New York: The Penguin Press, 2006), p. 41.
10. Deepak Lal, *Reviving the Invisible Hand* (Princeton: Princeton University Press, 2006), p. 136.
11. Winston S. Churchill, *A History of the English-Speaking Peoples* (New York: Dorset Press, 1956), Vol. I, p. 39.
12. Quoted in Bernard Lewis, *The Muslim Discovery of Europe* (New York: W.W. Norton, 1982), p. 139.
13. The Economist, *Pocket World in Figures*, 2007 edition, pp. 29, 176.
14. Ibid., p. 72.
15. William W. Finan, Jr., "The Indian Way," *Current History*, April 2007, p. 189.

16. The Economist, *Pocket World in Figures*, 2007 edition, p. 20.
17. John Kay, *Culture and Prosperity*, pp. 283–284.
18. "No Title," *The Economist*, March 31, 2001, pp. 20–22; Hernando de Soto, *The Mystery of Capital* (New York: Basic Books, 2000), pp. 20, 33–34.
19. William Easterly, *The White Man's Burden*, p. 81.
20. The Economist, *Pocket World in Figures*, 2007 edition, pp. 110, 156, 168, 234.
21. P.T. Bauer, *Equality, the Third World, and Economic Delusion* (Cambridge, Massachusetts: Harvard University Press, 1981), p. 43.
22. See, for example, my *Migrations and Cultures* (New York: Basic Books, 1996), *Conquests and Cultures*, and the essay, "Are Jews Generic?" in *Black Rednecks and White Liberals* (San Francisco: Encounter Books, 2005).
23. Lawrence E. Harrison, *Underdevelopment Is a State of Mind* (Lanham, Maryland: University Press of America, 1985), p. 103.
24. Ibid., p. 114.
25. Ibid., p. 103.
26. The Economist, *Pocket World in Figures*, 2007 edition, pp. 110, 234.
27. See Stephen Steinberg, *The Ethnic Myth: Race, Ethnicity, and Class in America* (New York: Atheneum, 1981), pp. 99–103.
28. Michael Wines, "As Inflation Soars, Zimbabwe Economy Plunges," *New York Times*, February 7, 2007, p. A1.
29. Quoted in William Easterly, *The White Man's Burden*, p. 182.
30. Ibid., p. 67.
31. Ibid., p. 228.
32. See, for example, a study by two Soviet economists, Nikolai Shmelev and Vladimir Popov, *The Turning Point: Revitalizing the Soviet Economy* (New York: Doubleday, 1989).
33. William Easterly, *The White Man's Burden*, p. 3.
34. See, for example, my *Migrations and Cultures*, Chapter 7.
35. William Easterly, *The White Man's Burden*, pp. 79–80.
36. John Kay, *Culture and Prosperity*, p. 280.
37. P.T. Bauer, *Equality, the Third World, and Economic Delusion*, p. 88.

CHAPTER 8: PARTING THOUGHTS

1. Fred C. Koch, *The Volga Germans: In Russia and the Americas, from 1763 to the Present* (University Park: Pennsylvania State University Press, 1977), p. 195.
2. "Billionaire Bacchanalia," *Forbes*, March 27, 2006, p. 116; "Wild Wealth," *Forbes*, March 26, 2007, pp. 104, 114.
3. A sample of such disparities can be found in various books of mine: *The Vision of the Anointed* (New York: Basic Books, 1995), pp. 35–37; *Conquests and Cultures* (New York: Basic Books, 1998), p. 330; *Civil Rights: Rhetoric or Reality?* (New York: William Morrow & Co., 1984), pp. 18–19.
4. Deepak Lal, *Reviving the Invisible Hand* (Princeton: Princeton University Press, 2006), p. 136.
5. Automobile fatality rates fell in the years after federal safety legislation— but they fell even more in the years *preceding* federal safety legislation. See Chapter 5 of my *Applied Economics* (New York: Basic Books, 2004). Standard Oil's market share declined after a landmark antitrust lawsuit. But it declined for years before that suit. See Richard Epstein, *Antitrust Consent Decrees in Theory and Practice: Why Less is More* (Washington: The AEI Press, 2007), p. 19.
6. This implicit assumption is often transparent in the snide condescension of "experts" toward the decisions that people have chosen to make for themselves, as in Paul Knox, "Schlock and Awe," *The American Interest*, March/April 2007, pp. 58–67.
7. Charles Sanders Peirce, *Essays in the Philosophy of Science* (New York: Liberal Arts Press, 1957), p. 35.

INDEX